T0356871

Get a Hobby

Get a Hobby

365 Things to Do for Fun (Not Work!)

JASMINE CHO

UNION
SQUARE
& CO.

NEW YORK

UNION
SQUARE
& CO.

NEW YORK

ISBN 978-1-4549-5427-9
ISBN 978-1-4549-5428-6 (e-book)

Library of Congress Control Number: 2024935999

For information about custom editions, special
sales, and premium purchases, please contact
specialsales@unionsquareandco.com.

Printed in India

2 4 6 8 10 9 7 5 3 1

unionsquareandco.com

Interior design by Lucy Giller
Cover and interior illustrations by Lucy Giller

To Jacob

From skateboarding to hiking to root beer floats made with chocolate chip ice cream—thank you for being the coolest brother who introduced me to every good thing that makes life rich beyond measurable value. William is so lucky to have you as his dad.

Introduction

The term "hobby" in the English language originated in the fourteenth century, referring to a small horse often called a *hobi* or *hobyn*. The hobbyhorse toy that rose in popularity during the sixteenth to eighteenth centuries—usually a stick with a stuffed horse's head on one end, but sometimes a small rocking horse that children rode back and forth—indicated the nature of hobbies being either for pleasure or intended to go nowhere. In India during the same period, wooden horse toys were used during celebrations of the folk deity Ramdev Pir* who came to symbolize ideas of equality and social justice. The Chinese word for hobby is 爱好 (ài hào), which is a combination of the characters for "love" and "good." Considering these vast historical and cultural origins, hobbies can encompass activities that expand our joy, provide us with respite or escape, or even help us cultivate a deeper sense of purpose, meaning, and a connection to the sacred.

With a background in art therapy and a very nontraditional career path of becoming known as a cookie activist, I've turned to hobbies for various reasons, understanding their positive impact on my mental health and wellness. Baking was pure love and fun for me but also turned into a way of empowering myself and tangibly giving back to multiple communities. Putting together puzzles and LEGO sets allow me to zone out while completing a task with a clear beginning and end, helping me gain a sense of control within contained

---

* *Known to Hindu communities as Baba Ramdev and as Ramsha Pir to Muslim communities.*

parameters of chaos. I turned to Argentine tango to heal after a long string of unsuccessful relationships, while heels dancing helped me reconnect with and reignite parts of my identity that I had lost.

This book intends to serve as a starting point to briefly introduce you to a realm of wild and wonderful hobby possibilities. Though I certainly hope you end up trying some activities, I also want you to have fun learning about all the ways in which people around the world cope and enrich their lives every day.

Included on each page is a general guideline of the costs for starting each hobby. Separated into three categories, from low to high, the tiers are defined this way: low is free to $39, medium is $40 to $79, and high is $80 or more. You should keep in mind that these tiers only reflect the initial monetary investment of getting started on a hobby and do not account for other costs like your time and energy expended.

While it was initially challenging to identify 365 distinct hobbies, I not only managed to find them but also learned of several more along the way that may need to wait for another book. If you notice any that I've left out, I would love to hear from you! Send me an e-mail at hello@jasminemcho.com, and I'll find a way to make sure the world knows about your unique hobby. Happy hobbying!

3D Printing

"I love fabricating solutions to unique problems. With 3D printing, I can design and create objects that are practical, custom, and functional. I love that the real-world applications are endless."

—JOE KENNEDY,
Real Estate Contractor

TECH   **COST: $$$**

Initially developed in the 1980s to increase efficiency in industrial manufacturing and prototyping, 3D printing became accessible to everyday hobbyists in the early 2010s. It works by constructing objects one layer at a time with heat, laser, or liquid resin to fuse the layers together. Using spools of filament like PLA or PETG, 3D printers are based on a digital model created with CAD (computer-aided design) and slicing software. From figurines to household gadgets, 3D printing allows hobbyists to create items for play and for purpose.

GET STARTED

1. **Determine what you want to print.** 3D printers vary in the size and volume they print. If you want to print cosplay parts, the best printer may be different than for someone who mostly wants to print cookie cutters.

2. **Consider a workspace.** Some 3D printers emit heat and fumes that will require a well-ventilated area. They also work best when on firm and level ground, so you'll want to consider a place with minimal environmental disturbance.

3. **Familiarize yourself before investing.** Check with makerspaces or libraries in your area that carry 3D printers so you can experiment with them before investing in your own. You will also need to learn CAD and slicing software. There are many online resources and communities that offer free tutorials and support.

Acrylic Painting

"There's something about the smell of the paints that soothes me, and time becomes nonexistent while painting and surrounding myself with colors."

—EMILY SALERNO,
Content Production Specialist

ART   COST: $$

Acrylic paints are made of pigment suspended in acrylic polymer emulsion. They are water-soluble but become water-resistant when dry. This medium offers a variety of vibrant colors and textures and is typically distinguished by a matte finish. The development of acrylic paint during the 1940s and '50s is attributed to Leonard Bocour and Sam Golden, founders of Bocour Artist Colors. The versatility and durability of acrylics were quickly embraced by artists, notably by the pop art movement in the 1960s. Acrylics dry quickly and can be painted over if the artist desires to make changes. This makes acrylics a popular choice for both beginners and experienced artists who enjoy layering and blending colors. Additionally, acrylic paint can be applied on a wide range of surfaces, including canvas, paper, wood, and fabric.

GET STARTED

1. **Gather the supplies.** Acquire the painting essentials, such as a variety of acrylic paints, brushes of various sizes, a palette for mixing colors, and a sturdy surface like canvas or acrylic paper.

2. **Learn the basics.** Experiment with techniques such as blending, dry brushing, or stippling. There are countless online tutorials and local classes available for beginners.

Acrylic Pouring

"For years I've been enchanted with all the amazing acrylic paint pours I see on social media. Come to find out, even a left-brained nerd like myself can create beautiful artwork with fluid acrylic pouring." *

—DAVID VOORHIES,
Computer Technologist

ART   COST: $$

Acrylic pouring is a type of fluid art made by mixing acrylic paints with different additives or mediums. The result is a piece of organic art that can be described as intricate marbling.

Some point to the 1930s Mexican social realist painter David Alfaro Siqueiros as the originator of acrylic pouring. His "accidental painting" technique is very similar but more of a drip-and-splatter method. Pouring acrylics surged in popularity as a modern-day technique due to creators sharing the process via captivating videos online.

Acrylic pouring is an ideal painting technique for beginners due to its relatively simple and straightforward process.

GET STARTED

1. **Gather the supplies.** You'll need a variety of acrylic paints, a pouring medium like Liquitex, canvas or thick paper to pour on, and sticks to mix your paints.

2. **Prep your workspace.** Prepare a large, protected space in which to work. You'll want to elevate the canvas or paper you're pouring on so that excess paint can drip off the sides.

3. **Mix your paints.** The consistency you're aiming to create with your pour is like honey or heavy cream. You'll also want to avoid creating bubbles to ensure a smooth pour.

* *https://leftbrainedartist.com/*

Antiquing

"I went to an estate sale with a friend and immediately fell in love with the surprise and wonder I felt as part of the exploration and discovery process."

—RACHEL CHUNG,
Professor

COLLECTING   COST: $$$

Antiquing includes the buying, collecting, and selling of antique items. Antiques are typically at least a century old and their value is determined by their historical, cultural, or artistic significance. Antiquing originated as a movement against the mass production of uniform goods during the Industrial Revolution. As people took solace in the preservation of unique craftsmanship from earlier generations, antiquing became a widespread hobby based in a shared appreciation of the past. Some antiquers are drawn to the historical research involved, while others simply enjoy the aesthetics of older wares. Antiquing as a hobby doesn't need to be expensive. You might discover an invaluable family heirloom sitting right in your home.

GET STARTED

1. **Choose what you collect.** Antiques range from paintings to books and even barber chairs. Selecting an object or time period you're most interested in will help focus your antiquing journey.

2. **Avoid being duped.** Take time to learn antique valuing, which considers factors like rarity, condition, age, and quality. Reference antique pricing guides like Kovels to educate yourself.

3. **Know what not to collect.** Be aware of legal and ethical ramifications for certain antiques, such as ivory and other parts of endangered wildlife. Certain cultural artifacts like funerary items are also protected by international law.

Aquascaping

"I started aquascaping because I am really into plants. It also allows me to create worlds that I can escape into."

—STACI OFFUTT,
Director in Higher Education

NATURE/OUTDOOR   COST: $$$

Aquariums are no longer just a place to show off your fish but your gardening skills too! Aquascaping is the practice of arranging different aquatic elements like plants, stones, and driftwood within an aquarium to create a serene and mesmerizing underwater landscape. The growth of contemporary aquascaping is largely credited to the Japanese cyclist and photographer Takashi Amano, who produced books on the subject in the 1990s as well as aquarium supplies to encourage other aquarists. Rooted in traditional Japanese gardening concepts like *wabi-sabi*—which revolves around simplicity, asymmetry, transience, and imperfection—aquascaping requires some initial effort to begin but can become an exercise in tranquil creativity.

GET STARTED

1. **Research the care and maintenance required.** Make the initial effort to learn the ins and outs of aquatic plant care and tank maintenance to avoid costly and preventable mistakes.

2. **Acquire your equipment.** Along with the aquarium tank, you'll need to consider equipment for lighting, filtration, hardscaping like rocks and other decorative elements, and a substrate in which your plants will best thrive.

3. **Contemplate your style.** The most common style in aquascaping is Nature Aquarium, which focuses on replicating nature as closely as possible. Iwagumi style is distinguished by the presence of large rocks. Consider your aesthetic preferences and be sure to design your layout before you begin planting.

Arborsculpting

"It's a medium that embraces time, that forces you to think about what the tree was like when it was younger, and what will it be like when it gets older. People realize the value in an art project that requires years to take its ultimate shape."*

—RICHARD REAMES,
Artist (coined the term "arborsculpture")

NATURE/OUTDOOR   **COST: $$$**

Arborsculpting is the shaping of living trees into abstract forms or functional structures. Imagine a tree trunk shaped like a chair or diamond fence; this is likely the work of a dedicated arborsculptor who spent years, if not decades, manipulating the tree's growth into an intentional design. Arborsculpting is achieved by grafting and bending a tree's trunk and stems. Though a relatively newer hobby enjoyed by horticulturalists and artists, arborsculpting originates from centuries-old Indigenous communities around the world like the Khasi of northeast India, who weaved fig tree roots together to create intricate bridges for safe crossing over bodies of water during monsoon seasons. Arborsculpting is a long-term hobby ideal for those with patience, creativity, and a love of nature.

GET STARTED

1. **Select the right tree species.** The tree species that are most flexible and able to withstand shaping include willow, oak, and sycamore, but you'll also want to consider the climate and amount of space you have.

2. **Design your vision and train your tree.** Sketch out your idea so you know how to guide your branches toward your design. Training includes shaping, pruning, using stakes or wires for support, and maintenance.

---

* *Joshua Foer, "How to Grow a Chair: An Interview with Richard Reames,"* Cabinet, *Winter 2005–2006, https://www.cabinetmagazine.org/issues/20/foer_reames.php.*

Archery

*"Archery is not about how well you see, but how well you execute your shot. Form is what brings legitimacy to the sport and that legitimacy is important to me."**

—JANICE WALTH,
Independent Service Provider

PHYSICAL FITNESS   **COST: $$$**

Archery is the use of a bow to shoot arrows at stationary or moving targets. It debuted as an Olympic sport in 1900, but surged in modern appeal after it was reintroduced as a regular part of the Summer Games in 1972. Successfully hitting a target requires focus and patience, offering both a sense of thrill and quiet meditation while developing archery skills. Visually impaired archery has been growing in popularity since the 1980s and involves a sighted spotter and adaptive equipment like audible target locators, foot markers, and tripod mounts. Archery is a versatile hobby that can be practiced indoors or outdoors and is suitable for different ages and abilities.

GET STARTED

1. **Find a range.** Search for an archery range or club in your area that provides equipment rentals and introductory lessons. If there are no spaces near you, start in your backyard or in an open field with a backdrop like a wall, fence, or hillside to catch your misfired arrows.

2. **Master the basics.** There are three main types of bows to consider: recurve, compound, and traditional. Each varies in design and resistance. Begin with shorter target distances and master your stance, grip, and aim.

---

* *Jasmine Shahbandi, "Janice Walth, Blind Archer," Sacramento News & Review, March 15, 2015, https://www.newsreview.com/sacramento/content/janice-walth-blind-archer/16527591/.*

Argentine Tango

"Tango takes me out of my head and into my body. I become a vessel for the music and for wordless communication to flow between me and my partner in an endless loop."

—JENNIFER KOROSKENYI,
Marketing Consultant

DANCE   COST: $

Argentine tango emerged in the late nineteenth century from the working-class neighborhoods of Buenos Aires. Mostly populated by immigrants from Europe and Africa who blended their music and dance traditions, Argentine tango was a spontaneous expression of their joys and struggles, especially regarding love and heartbreak. The dance was a way to socialize and often took place in the streets and other informal settings like bars and cafés. Characterized by a chest-to-chest connection with a partner, the dance requires a leader and a follower who nonverbally communicate through subtle shifts in weight, tension, and body movement.

GET STARTED

1. **Take a class.** Though a partner dance, you can show up to classes alone. You will likely be partnered up with the instructor or other solo practitioners to develop your skills.

2. **Listen to the music.** Argentine tango is as much about connecting to the music as it is about connecting with your dance partner. Tango music typically features a 4/4 time signature, but other styles include *milonga, vals,* and *tango nuevo,* each varying in tempo.

3. **Connect to a community.** Argentine tango communities span the world. There is even a Facebook group for people waiting on a connection at an airport who want to partner up for a quick *tanda*—a set of three to four songs people dance to before switching partners.

ASMR Recording

"I love creating ASMR content because it allows me to help others while still allowing myself to be creative."

—MARIA,
Content Creator

TECH   **COST: $**

Autonomous Sensory Meridian Response, or ASMR, recording started in the early 2000s as a niche hobby but exploded into a global phenomenon with the rise of related content shared on various online and social media platforms. An enthusiast, Jennifer Allen, coined the term in 2010 to provide scientific legitimacy to what most were labeling as tingling sensations or a "brain orgasm" to describe pleasurable responses to certain auditory, visual, or tactile stimuli.* Common ASMR triggers include nature sounds, whispering, tapping, and eating or cooking sounds. People pursue ASMR recordings to increase relaxation and reduce stress and anxiety.

GET STARTED

1. **Understand your ASMR triggers.** People's responses to different sensations vary widely; immerse yourself in the ASMR community to find what works for you. ASMR is an enjoyable and calming experience, so let these feelings guide you to your positive triggers.

2. **Choose your recording equipment.** Select a microphone, headphones, and recording software that effectively emphasizes the auditory or visual trigger. Pop filters help reduce popping sounds and improve sound clarity.

3. **Share your content.** You can enjoy feedback and response from larger communities by sharing your recordings online.

---

* *Jamie L. Keiles, "How A.S.M.R. Became a Sensation," The New York Times Magazine, April 4, 2019, https://www.nytimes.com/2019/04/04/magazine/how-asmr-videos-became-a-sensation-youtube.html.*

Astrology

"Astrology is a language of animation, participation, and co-creation. When we speak it, we bring the worlds within us and the worlds around us more fully alive."

—BESS MATASSA,
Author

EDUCATIONAL   COST: $

Astrology is both a belief system and field of study that revolves around the positions and movements of celestial bodies and their corresponding influence on human affairs, personality, and the natural world. Looking to the stars for guidance happened across different ancient civilizations from India to Rome. Babylonians are credited with the most popular form of Western astrology, which divides the sky into twelve sections based on the position of the Sun in relation to the vernal equinox—when the Earth experiences an equal amount of daylight and darkness. Each section represents a zodiac sign and an astrological house that represents a different area of a person's life. Chinese astrology, on the other hand, is based off the lunar calendar and twelve-year cycles with zodiac signs represented by animals, the five natural elements (Water, Fire, Wood, Earth, and Metal), and the concept of Yin and Yang.

GET STARTED

1. **Learn the basics.** Choose which form of astrology most interests you and begin studying their core concepts.

2. **Explore your astrology.** Start researching your own zodiac signs, charts, and elements. There are many books, online resources, and apps where you can glean information for free.

3. **Consult an astrologer.** Consider connecting with a professional astrologer who can provide more information and guidance into any aspect of your sign or chart with a reading.

Astronomy

"My father-in-law gifted us a telescope for Christmas. I love it because it reminds me how truly immense the universe is and that just being here is truly a miracle."

—BECKY FLAHERTY,
Nonprofit CEO

NATURE/OUTDOOR   **COST: $**

Astronomy shares ancient origins with astrology but became a distinct discipline over time with influences from thinkers like Claudius Ptolemy of ancient Greece and Nicolaus Copernicus of the European Renaissance who focused on empirical and mathematical data. While astrology studies the sky as a means of interpreting human affairs, astronomy uses math, physics, and chemistry to understand the physical properties of objects and phenomena beyond Earth's atmosphere. Astronomy practiced as a hobby is often synonymous with stargazing, where the primary enjoyment comes from chasing comets and observing the night sky to identify different constellations and planets. Many hobbyists also choose to collect data to contribute to different citizen science projects.

GET STARTED

1. **Elevate your stargazing.** You can start stargazing with your naked eye by simply taking an evening stroll out to an area with minimal light pollution. When you are ready to enhance your stargazing capabilities, invest in a stargazing app, binoculars, or a telescope.

2. **Join a club.** Search locally for an astronomy group who can provide safety in numbers on your night out but also guide you to the best stargazing spots.

3. **Document and learn.** Consider keeping a stargazing journal to record your observations and delve into books and online resources to learn more.

Axe Throwing

"This hobby teaches that if you can handle competing against yourself, you will always win against your actual opponent."

—SETH BRODY,
Chemist

PHYSICAL FITNESS   COST: $$

Axe throwing began to surge as a modern hobby in the 2010s with the establishment of recreational ranges and bars throughout North America. The National Axe Throwing Federation (NATF) of Canada is additionally credited for its rise in popularity after standardizing gameplay for axe throwing as a sport. The objective of recreational axe throwing is to land a small, handheld axe into a wooden bullseye target that is typically set 12 to 15 feet (3.7 to 4.6 meters) away in a contained lane. Basic throwing techniques include a one-handed or two-handed overthrow. Similar to darts but on a full-body scale with the use of a weapon, axe throwing offers an extra layer of thrill and can be a fun and unconventional way to unwind, build a skill, and bond with others.

GET STARTED

1. **Find a local venue.** Axe-throwing venues where you can pay an hourly rate or sign up for a membership are growing in popularity. These venues typically provide an introductory lesson for newbies to review the basics and fundamental safety protocols. If there are no venues near you, start by researching local laws and regulations around the safe use of axes on private and public properties to verify what is allowed in your area.

2. **Join a community.** Participating in leagues and competitions can provide opportunities to hone your skills and link up with other axe-throwing enthusiasts.

Backpacking

"I got started after I ruptured my ACL. My time in recovery led me to YouTube videos about backpacking. It led me to such huge life changes both physically and mentally."

—CHELSIE FRIS,
Teacher

NATURE/OUTDOOR   COST: $$$

Backpacking is an ideal hobby for adventurers who enjoy the opportunity to connect with nature, build self-reliance, and break from the routine of everyday life. A form of travel and recreation that often entails hiking and setting up camp in various areas of wilderness, backpacking involves carrying one's essentials and setting out on a minimalistic journey. Backpacking trips can span from a day's hike to a months-long trip. It can be a physically demanding activity with backpacks weighing anywhere from 10 to 50 pounds (4.5 to 23 kilograms). Whether you choose to go solo or with others, backpacking can offer the benefits of environmental exploration and awareness, improvement in physical and mental health, and survival skills.

GET STARTED

1. **Join a club.** Backpacking clubs provide a variety of activities for different skill levels. If none are near you, consider exploring similar outdoor activity clubs, guided tours, or online forums.

2. **Select a backpack and shoes.** Ultralight backpacks are great for beginners to keep things minimal. Choose one that provides stability and has multiple compartments and straps to host various gear. Look for shoes with features like breathability, ankle support, and waterproof fabric.

3. **Plan your adventure.** Check the weather, research permits and regulations, and map out rest stops and water sources. Be sure to share your plans with others to ensure your safety as well.

Ballet

*"I was really struggling with my mental health and it was getting to the point that I needed a healthy outlet for my energy. [Ballet] felt very ritualistic for me."**

—KARLISTA MARONEY,
Marketing

DANCE   COST: $$

Distinguished by elegant leaps, delicate toe steps, and pirouettes—rotating on one leg with the other leg drawn into the knee or outward—ballet requires a remarkable sense of balance and strength to express body movements that appear weightless. Ballet is also recognized by its unique attire: leotards or unitards, tights, ballet slippers, and tutus (skirts made of layers of tuille). With more studios opening classes to hobbyists, many adults have turned to ballet as a modern activity for fitness, stress relief, and a segue into the performance arts.

GET STARTED

1. **Join a studio.** Ballet is challenging to learn without the direct guidance of a qualified instructor, but if you don't have access to a local studio, there are online tutorials and communities available. Having ample space with a full-length mirror for you to check your form and posture will be instrumental to developing your skills.

2. **Purchase your attire.** You can start with tights or leggings; tutus serve an aesthetic purpose more than a functional one. Full-soled slippers are best for beginners.

---

* *Emily Lefroy, "That's On Pointe! Adult Ballet Classes Are the Hot New Fitness Trend," New York Post, February 13, 2023, https://nypost.com/2023/02/13/adult-ballet-classes-are-the-new-fitness-trend/.*

Ballroom Dance

"Ballroom dance itself is almost like going to learn poetry or sitting down to meditate. I would use the word 'harmony.'" *

—EDWARD WAN,
Retired

DANCE   COST: $

Ballroom is a set of diverse dance styles that involve a partner. The most popular types of ballroom dance include waltz, foxtrot, cha-cha, rumba, and tango. The overarching goal of all ballroom dance styles is to develop strong lead-and-follow skills, making it an ideal social activity that enhances connection and communication. Ballroom dance is also popular in the competition circuit, leading to a focus on form, precision, and performance. The structured nature of ballroom dance offers a solid foundation to build upon, making it especially attractive and amenable to novices.

GET STARTED

1. **Find ballroom dance classes.** Check out recreation centers or community colleges in addition to dance studios. Don't feel obligated to bring a partner; ballroom dance classes are usually designed to encourage partner rotation.

2. **Listen to ballroom dance music.** Listening to the different styles of music used in ballroom dance can help familiarize you with the mood and rhythms of each dance. Waltz is distinguished by a 3/4 time signature that creates a graceful and elegant atmosphere, while the cha-cha is known for its quick-quick-slow syncopated 4/4 rhythm.

---

* *Kimmy Yam, "How Ballroom Dance Became a Refuge for Asian Immigrants," NBC News, January 27, 2023, https://www.nbcnews.com/news/asian-america/ballroom-dance-become-refuge-asian-immigrants-rcna67446.*

Barbecuing

*"Instead of a pacifier, my mom used a spare rib."**

—COLE PEPPER,
Former Sports Anchor

FOOD   COST: $$$

Barbecuing is a slow method of cooking that exposes foods, usually meat-based proteins, to a direct or indirect heat source. The most common heat source for barbecuing is an open flame, but other heat sources include charcoal, wood, gas, and electricity contained within a pit, grill, or smoker. The heat sources and slow cooking time—sometimes up to twenty-four hours or more—result in uniquely smoky flavors, succulence, and tenderness in meats that distinguish it from other cooking methods. Preparation for barbecuing also includes creating rubs (a dry mixture of spices and herbs), marinades, and sauces. Mastering temperature and flavors are some of the biggest draws for hobbyists, especially those interested in the culinary arts.

GET STARTED

1. **Create a space to grill.** Barbecuing can pose several safety hazards from involving high temperatures and smoke, so you will need a well-ventilated outdoor space to start. If you don't have access to an outdoor space, start with recipes that can provide similar results by using a small indoor grill.

2. **Select your equipment.** The most economical way to start barbecuing is by investing in a small charcoal grill. A few basic tools you will need include tongs, a long-handled spatula, and a grill brush for maintenance.

---

* *Charlie Patton, "'Barbecue Snob' Using Hobby to Raise Money," The Florida Times-Union, May 14, 2009, https://www.jacksonville.com/story/lifestyle/food/2009/05/14/barbecue-snob-using-hobby-to-raise-money/15985880007/.*

Basket Weaving

"I use this hobby to maintain a connection to nature that helps me balance time spent at my computer. I love creating a physical space that can beautifully contain and protect its contents."

—COURTNEY FRANCIS,
Project Manager

ART   COST: $

Basket weaving is accomplished by interlacing flexible materials like reed, straw, or paper to construct containers for aesthetic or utilitarian purposes. One of the oldest woven baskets discovered near Grenada, Spain, was recently carbon-dated back 9,500 years to the Mesolithic era when hunting and gathering was the predominant way of life. With its rhythmic nature, basket weaving promotes stress relief and relaxation as well as focus and concentration. Popular modern iterations of basket weaving include sculptural basketry that emphasizes visual impact over functionality and eco-friendly basketry, which promotes sustainability by using renewable materials like bamboo.

GET STARTED

1. **Gather the supplies.** Materials that are best for beginning basket weavers are ones that are forgiving and readily available like reed, paper cord or twine, and raffia.

2. **Practice fundamental techniques.** Some of the basic techniques of basket weaving include plaiting, twining, coiling, and waling. Different techniques result in differences in structure, strength, and style.

3. **Follow tutorials.** You can find step-by-step tutorials in books and online. Start with small-scale projects to focus on honing your weaving skills.

Basketball

"Basketball enables me to channel my competitive spirit, perfects my skills both on an individual level and within the construct of a team, and ultimately helps keep me in shape in middle age."

—CHUCK K.,
Lender

PHYSICAL FITNESS   COST: $

Did you know that the first basketball game was actually played with a soccer ball? Invented in 1891 by Canadian physical education teacher Dr. James Naismith, the objective of basketball was simple enough: throw a ball into the opposing team's basket to score. As it evolved into a professional sport, rules that better defined scoring, team players, and game duration were established. The typical requirement is five players per team, but many find it just as enjoyable to shoot hoops solo. Street basketball culture that rose to fame during the late 1990s and early 2000s via clothing brands like AND1 were pivotal in popularizing another side of basketball that focused on pickup games, one-on-one competitions, and unconventional antics and tricks.

GET STARTED

1. **Get a basketball and an air pump.** Starter basketballs are typically made of rubber. As you progress in skill, you may want to invest in higher-end basketballs made with leather and designed for better grip and durability. Don't forget to invest in a pump to ensure your ball is inflated adequately.

2. **Find a court or game.** Gyms and community centers usually have basketball courts that you can reserve if you are a member; however, many public courts exist throughout neighborhoods that can be used for free. If you're ready for team play, sign up for recreational leagues or find a pickup game.

Baton Twirling

"I love achieving new tricks, competing against other great twirlers, making friends with teammates, and traveling to perform!"

—MAKAYLA YEE,
Student

PHYSICAL FITNESS   **COST: $**

Baton twirling is a visually captivating performance art that involves elements of dance, gymnastics, and the skillful manipulation of one or more rods made of plastic or metal. Twirling objects has historically been part of many religious and ceremonial practices in ancient cultures around the world. However, the modern art of baton twirling originated in the United States during the late nineteenth century as part of parade and circus performances. By the mid-twentieth century, it grew into a standardized international sport where key skills like spinning, tossing, and catching are evaluated alongside choreography, timing, and showmanship. Baton twirling usually involves a single baton, but many baton twirlers enjoy the challenge of including more as their skill level advances. Hobbyists can expect gains in physical fitness, mental focus, eye-hand coordination, and artistic expression in addition to performance opportunities.

GET STARTED

1. **Choose a baton.** The size of your baton should be close to the length of your arm from armpit to fingertips. Batons are available in a variety of materials, like steel, aluminum, and fiberglass. Each material varies in weight and flexibility, so consider your personal preference when choosing your baton.

2. **Find a coach or class.** Many dance studios offer baton twirling classes, but you can also check with recreational community centers. Baton twirling classes are often geared toward youth, so you may want to work privately with a coach or start with online tutorials.

Beading

"I was told to do my bucket list items, as I am chronically ill. Concerts are my happy place. I wanted to make something to share with the crowd. The reaction people have when they get my beaded bracelets makes my heart full."

—AMY ROSS,
Nanny

ART   COST: $

Beading has a long history across cultures, and is used for storytelling, art, and religious items. By threading together beads of different colors, shapes, and sizes, you can create attractive objects from jewelry to home decor. Popular methods of beading include stringing, knotting, weaving, and embroidery; the latter two methods require a needle, while the former can be accomplished with just string, thread, or wire. The affordability, variety, and accessibility of beading make it an especially welcoming hobby for people of all ages and backgrounds. Additionally, its effectiveness as a therapeutic distraction and its ability to carry meaningful symbology have made beading a particularly impactful activity within pediatric hospital settings for both patients and community members.

GET STARTED

1. **Gather the supplies.** Materials include a needle, a variety of beads, thread or wire, clasps (used to secure jewelry pieces), pliers, and scissors. There are many affordable jewelry-making kits available that include these supplies within a conveniently portable case.

2. **Start stringing or follow a template.** Stringing is the easiest method to get started, where you can practice by choosing beads as you go. If you prefer more direction and enjoy being able to visualize the end product, there are many templates you can follow instead.

Beekeeping

"I love how honeybees will act in a way that benefits the colony as a whole. There is so much order and organization in the hive that we, humans, are still trying to understand."

—AMANDA SOURBEER,
Civil Engineer

NATURE/OUTDOOR   COST: $$$

Beekeeping, also known as apiculture, is a rewarding hobby for those who are passionate about nature, sustainability, and continuous learning. The earliest recorded origins of beekeeping trace back to ancient Egypt, but its modern resurgence in popularity is largely due to increased access and environmental awareness. Though rural areas or large backyards are traditionally ideal for beekeeping, urban beekeeping in spaces like rooftops, community gardens, and vacant lots has opened doors to even more hobbyists. Hobby beekeepers get to enjoy the intrinsic rewards of conserving a vital part of our ecosystem while producing products like honey, beeswax, and pollen.

GET STARTED

1. **Select a location.** Ideal spaces for beehives include adequate sun exposure, protection from strong winds, and access to water. Depending on where you live, you may need to apply for a permit or register your hives.

2. **Buy your equipment.** Beekeeping equipment includes your hives, protective gear, a feeder, and tools for hive inspection and management like a smoker and a bee brush. You will also want equipment for collecting your honey, like an extractor, strainers, and storage containers.

3. **Obtain bees.** Check with local beekeepers or bee supply companies to purchase a nucleus colony, an established colony contained within frames that are great for beginners.

Beer Brewing

"I was visiting a local brewer with my wife and found a poster on a cork board about a class on home brewing at the local library. I took it and never looked back!"

—RAFIQ PAYNE,
Bank Employee

FOOD   COST: $$$

One of the earliest records of beer production is linked to the *Hymn to Ninkasi**, a song of praise to the Sumerian goddess of beer with lyrics denoting a recipe for brewing. Brewing beer has evolved significantly throughout history. Prohibition-era home brewing happened under secretive circumstances with low-quality ingredients and limited resources. However, when the craft beer movement emerged in the late twentieth century, the emphasis on independent and small batch production encouraged greater access to quality resources for hobby home brewers.

GET STARTED

1. **Research first.** Read books, watch tutorials, and consider joining online or in-person brewing communities for tips and help with troubleshooting.

2. **Gather equipment.** Starter kits for home brewing typically include a fermenter, airlock, siphon, and bottles. Some basic ingredients you will need are malt, hops, yeast, and water. Sanitation is critical in the brewing process, so ensure that you have the proper space and cleaning supplies before you begin.

3. **Practice and patience are key.** You can expect to taste your first brew in about one to two weeks, but you can explore different fermentation and aging periods and how they affect flavor. Experimentation is an integral part of home brewing!

* *A written record was dated 1800 BCE, but it was likely an oral tradition dating back to at least 3400 BCE.*

Being a Conversation Partner

"[Being a conversation partner] is a real opportunity to meet people—and get rid of some of those biases and stereotypes." *

—KUNIKO NIELSEN,
Professor

VOLUNTEERING   COST: $

Being a conversation partner typically revolves around helping students, immigrants, or refugees learn the majority language in whatever region they currently reside (for example, a native English speaker paired with a non-native English speaker). However, you can also volunteer as a conversation partner for older adults in memory care to help counter declines in their communication processes. Conversation activities can be virtual or in-person. Signing up to be a conversation partner usually requires a brief orientation to familiarize you with the organization and population you are serving.

GET STARTED

1. **Choose an organization or population.** Language centers, universities, community centers, and public libraries are great places to start when looking for a conversation program to join.

2. **Learn more about your population.** Once you choose a population to engage with, take time outside of the required orientation to learn cultural differences to enhance a respectful atmosphere when connecting with your conversation partners.

3. **Volunteer consistently.** Determine your availability before you commit and then stay consistent in your service for the greatest impact—both for yourself and your partners.

---

* *"Community Outreach Program Pairs OU Students with Non-Native Speakers of English,"* Oakland University Magazine, *March 18, 2020, https://oakland.edu/oumagazine/news /cas/2020/community-outreach-program-pairs-ou-students-with-non-native-speakers-of-english.*

Being a Foodie

"I was pretty picky about my food as a kid, but after years of watching my family eat everything with gusto, I realized that there are so many delicious dishes and cuisines out there."

—MARLEEN PAN,
Proofreader and copy editor

FOOD   COST: $$

The term "foodie" was coined around the 1980s to describe people who exhibit an intense passion and pursuit of diverse culinary experiences. With the advent of social media, foodies gained popularity as a type of culinary ambassador who documented and shared their gastronomic adventures with the greater public. According to food writer Katie Horst: "A foodie will dedicate a vacation to tasting the best food in the region."* If food is a source of pleasure that you will make great sacrifices to experience, embrace your foodie nature and consider encouraging others to expand their tastebuds as well.

GET STARTED

1. **Seek and explore.** Research local news for restaurants, farmer's markets, or food festivals and start planning your adventures to taste each venue and event.

2. **Document and share.** Consider guidelines around etiquette to remain a positive culinary voice in your community. Be respectful of restaurant staff and other patrons, ask for permission to take photos, and practice cultural sensitivity.

3. **Expand your culinary skills and education.** You can enhance your foodie hobby by studying cookbooks, taking classes, or recreating some of your favorite dining experiences in your own kitchen.

* Katie Horst, "'Foodie' Had a Different Connotation when Gael Greene Coined the Term," Tasting Table, November 1, 2022, https://www.tastingtable.com/1081164/foodie-had-a-different-connotation-when-gael-greene-coined-the-term/

Being an Extra

"I love being a part of a production and seeing the process of how things are made. The celebrity sightings and craft services make it fun!"

—LEIGH-ANNE WEISS,
Small Business Owner

GAMES/SOCIAL   COST: $

One of the earliest examples of extras in film can be traced to *The Kingdom of the Fairies* (*Le Roytaume des Fées*) by French filmmaker Georges Méliès in 1903. Extras play a pivotal role in heightening realistic or emotional elements of a story. Working as an extra can often be time-consuming but serves as a fascinating hobby for those interested in the entertainment industry. Hobbyists can witness what happens behind the scenes and even catch a glimpse of their favorite celebrities. For those with acting aspirations, being an extra can sometimes lead to more spotlighted opportunities. Marilyn Monroe's first on-screen role was as an extra in the 1948 movie *Scudda Hoo! Scudda Hay!* International martial arts movie star Jackie Chan also began his film career as an extra and stunt double in Bruce Lee's movies.

GET STARTED

1. **Research opportunities.** Start with local casting agencies and production companies who usually post casting calls regularly. There are also large national websites like Backstage or Actors Access that you can use to find opportunities.

2. **Create a profile.** Oftentimes casting calls look for specific types of background actors that match a certain demographic in age or ethnicity. Setting up a profile or account with a casting agency or website can help filter opportunities specifically for you.

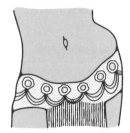

Belly Dancing

"I don't feel 100!" *

—CATHERINE FURST,
Retired Hairdresser

DANCE   COST: $

Belly dancing is characterized by both fluid and isolated movements of the torso, hips, and arms. Heralding a complex heritage that has evolved over thousands of years, earliest forms of the dance can be traced back to various regions in the Middle East, North Africa, and the Mediterranean. Belly dancing music is distinguished by rhythmic percussive beats and melodic instruments like the *oud* (a fretless lute) and the *qanun* (a type of stringed instrument). Belly dancing attire is designed to enhance the sensory experience for the performer and audience. Attire usually includes a midriff blouse, a skirt or harem pants, a hip scarf or coin belt, and additional jewelry or props like a veil and cane. Belly dancing is renowned as a mesmerizing dance that celebrates femininity and sensuality but is inclusive to all genders, ages, and backgrounds.

GET STARTED

1. **Find an instructor.** Whether at a local dance studio or online, consider your primary goals when choosing a method of instruction. Are you most interested in it for fitness, cultural appreciation, or performance?

2. **Choose a style.** Egyptian belly dance is known for its serpentine movements and graceful arm gestures, while Turkish belly dance emphasizes quick hip and chest movements with dynamic footwork. American Tribal Style (ATS) is a fusion belly dance known for improvised movements and the use of props like finger cymbals.

* *Erin Guy, "Catherine Furst: 100-Year-Old Belly Dancer Still Has Moves," ABC WPBF News, November 18, 2014, https://www.wpbf.com/article/catherine-furst-100-year-old-belly-dancer -still-has-moves/1323915.*

Bento Art

*"I thought it was a beautiful message and that's really what inspired me to make them every morning for my daughter."**

—LAUREN MCINTYRE,
Professor

FOOD   COST: $$

Bento is the Japanese word for a well-balanced meal presented in a compact container. The main components of a typical bento are rice, proteins, vegetables, and side dishes. Bento art, also known as *charaben* (pronounced "kya-ra-ben"), infuses artistic expression into the traditional bento by transforming each of its components into whimsical representations of characters, animals, objects, or scenes. Some common bento art pieces include mini sausages cut to resemble octopuses or rice balls decorated with seaweed to look like panda bears. As a unique culinary challenge and versatile outlet for creativity, bento art has become an attractive hobby for people around the world.

GET STARTED

1. **Gather bento equipment.** Common equipment for bento art include bento boxes, rice molds and shapers, tweezers, mini cookie cutters, seaweed punchers, and food-safe accessories like decorative toothpicks.

2. **Follow templates and tutorials.** Refer to bento box templates and watch online tutorials to learn basic techniques like shaping rice and cutting seaweed.

---

* *Elizabeth Hamilton, "Putting Together These Japanese Boxes Turns a Meal into a Work of Art—and a Show of Love," The Gainesville Sun, October 1, 2015, https://www.gainesville.com/story/lifestyle/magazine/2015/10/01/putting-together-these-japanese-boxes-turns-a-meal-into-a-work-of-art-and-a-show-of-love/31388190007/.*

Billiards

"It is a game that is just as enjoyable alone as it is with others. The table is its own world, simple rules and angles that take a lifetime to master."

—HANSEN BRENKUS,
Electrical Engineer

GAMES/SOCIAL   COST: $

Billiards is a recreational sport that encompasses several different games played on a rectangular table with long sticks, called cues, and a designated number of phenolic resin or acrylic balls. The game originated as a pastime for aristocrats in fifteenth-century Europe but has evolved into a popular hobby for people around the world who enjoy both its competitive and relaxing aspects.

Eight-ball is played on a table with six pockets. Players aim to pocket all seven of their balls, distinguished by stripes or solid colors. Carom billiards, on the other hand, is played on a table without pockets. The objective is to use a cue ball to hit two object balls while accomplishing three or more rebounds off the side cushions of the table. Whether or not pockets are involved, billiards games require strategizing skills, an understanding of angles, and the ability to control the speed and power of a shot.

GET STARTED

1. **Find a billiards table.** Billiards tables can be costly, so find places to practice the game before deciding to purchase your own table and equipment. You can find tables at bowling alleys, recreational centers, arcades, bars, or coffee shops.

2. **Choose your cue.** Heavier cues are preferred for power and control, whereas lighter cues are used for quicker strokes. One tip is to roll a cue on the table to ensure it's not warped.

Bingo

*"What else can you do for $20 for a couple of hours and have a chance to win money?"** *

—JUDY BROWN,
Retired

GAMES/SOCIAL   COST: $

Originally called "beano" and played with dried beans, an accidental yell of "Bingo!" is credited with cementing the game's new identity in 1929. Bingo evolved from a sixteenth century Italian lottery into a game of chance. Players each hold a 5-x-5 gridded card with the letters B-I-N-G-O across the top and numbers ranging from one to ninety placed randomly within the squares of the grid. A designated "caller" will call out a letter-number combination (for example, B-5) and players mark off the corresponding spaces. The objective of the game is to mark off a consecutive row on the card, after which a player can yell out "Bingo!" to announce their win.

GET STARTED

1. **Understand the rules.** Different variations exist depending on the setting and number of players. Some games will base a win off a specific pattern, like the top row or a full card.

2. **Link with a game or venue.** Although bingo is typically an in-person, multiplayer game, online apps enable solo play. You can also search for online bingo games that connect you to other live players. Many organizations use bingo as a fundraising activity, so you can play while supporting a worthy cause.

---

* *Robert McCune. "Bingo More than a Hobby for Local Regulars." The Independent, January 6, 2015. https://www.indeonline.com/story/lifestyle/2015/01/06/bingo-more-than-hobby -for/35591353007/.*

Birding

"Every birder has a spark bird that ignites a passion that often becomes lifelong. My spark bird ignited a curiosity and appreciation for their history, geography, and beauty"

—TRINIDAD REGASPI,
Stockroom Supervisor

NATURE/OUTDOOR   COST: $$

The hobby of watching and listening to birds in their natural habitat originated in Great Britain during the late 1800s when conservationists began to voice increasing concern over the hunting of birds for sport and fashion. The availability of field guides and household binoculars began to grow, leading to birding becoming a popular pastime and sport for folks throughout Europe and the United States.

For some, the passion for learning about and spotting as many different species as possible leads to travels around the world to participate in bird-watching excursions, festivals, and competitions. There are around two hundred birding festivals hosted every year throughout the United States and Canada alone. Birding provides an opportunity to connect with nature, while studying a specific part of its ecosystem.

GET STARTED

1. **Get a field guide.** Field guides, or bird guides, contain lists of different bird species in a particular area along with maps to help you locate them. Search your local library for guides, purchase one, or download a bird identifying app on your smartphone.

2. **Buy binoculars.** Binoculars are distinguished by a specification like "12 x 25," where the first number indicates the level of magnification and the second number indicates the size of the objective lens. The larger the objective lens, the clearer the image will appear.

Blacksmithing

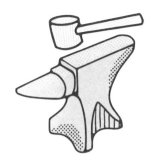

*"It is the requirement of focused and physically coordinated movement, so inversely related to the dynamic of my schoolwork, that allows the hobby to be especially relaxing for me."**

—DANISH BAJWA,
Student

ART   COST: $$$

Blacksmithing is the art of shaping metal by fire. The term originates from Old English, with "*blaec*" referring to the black appearance of soot and metals when forged by a worker known as a smith. Iron and steel are the most common metals used in blacksmithing because of their malleability when heated. The full process of blacksmithing involves cycling through heating, hammering, and cooling. It is a versatile craft that can produce a variety of functional and decorative objects like knives and cutlery or weapons and jewelry.

GET STARTED

1. **Participate in workshops.** Attending a workshop or ongoing classes would be the most economical way to explore blacksmithing. Some places to look for classes are makerspaces, art schools, or historical and cultural centers.

2. **Prepare your workspace and equipment.** You will need a safe and well-ventilated space like an outdoor shed. Required equipment includes a forge (a hearth for heating your metals), an anvil, shaping tools, a cooling station, and safety gear. Compact propane forges, which can measure as small as 12 inches (30 centimeters) in length, width, and height, are best for a novice.

---

* Danish Bajwa, "Forging Ahead with a New Craft: Blacksmithing," Youth Journalism International, October 19, 2022, https://youthjournalism.org/forging-ahead-with-a-new-craft-blacksmithing/.

Blogging

"Writing about things in your own words is a great way to solidify them in your mind and keep your communicative skills sharp, and in my case became a useful way to feel more connected to my communities."

—BRIAN DEUTSCH,
Administrative Assistant

TECH　　COST: $

A blog is a regularly updated website that serves as a personal journal, magazine, or public platform for sharing expertise. The term "blog" derived from the term "weblog," which was coined in 1997 by Jorn Barger to refer to the process of logging the web. Blogging played a catalytic role in defining the digital landscape during the early 1990s and for democratizing information by empowering individuals with an easy way to publish and freely express ideas and information. Blogging is an ideal hobby for people who enjoy writing to communicate their knowledge and passions and are attracted to the idea of building an online presence to connect with like-minded individuals.

GET STARTED

1. **Choose a platform.** There are several free blogging platforms to help you get started, including WordPress, Blogger, and Medium.

2. **Decide on a theme.** Focusing on a theme becomes important when you're hoping to build an audience or community. Blogging can span any theme imaginable: health and wellness, financial literacy, travel, spirituality, pets, and so on. Choose what compels you to write!

3. **Stay consistent.** Share your posts and articles regularly on social media platforms and keep readers engaged through comments and facilitating discussions.

Board Games

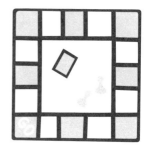

"I am so fascinated by the genius-ness of the game creation and by how there is so much variability in how they are played by different people. Board games are so much fun, and I love how they bring people together."

—VATSAL BHATT,
Physician

GAMES/SOCIAL   **COST: $**

The oldest known board game is believed to be a 5,000-year-old Egyptian game called *Senet*. Involving two players who use dice and pawns to play on a board of thirty squares, the game involves elements of both strategy and luck. With their variety and physical engagement, board games have continued to carry a timeless and universal appeal by encouraging social·bonding and interaction, intellectual stimulation, competition, and imagination. Board games range in styles from card play and strategy to partnerships and party games. Though they are traditionally played with two or more players, solo board games often focus on thematic or narrative experiences involving decision-making, resource management, and problem-solving.

GET STARTED

1. **Join or create a community.** Although you can choose to focus on a specific game, board game hobbyists often enjoy the opportunity to learn and engage in a variety of games. Look for local clubs or meetups to find other players or consider hosting regular board game dates with friends and family.

2. **Build a collection.** Consider gathering a few different styles of board games over time to increase the number of play options you have available for different situations.

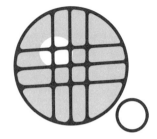

Bocce

*"We feel relaxed when we play.
That's why we play."** *

—GIUSEPPE CHIRUMBOLO,
Retired

GAMES/SOCIAL   COST: $

Pronounced "bot-chi," bocce is an ancient Italian sport where the objective is to get your team's balls (designated by color) as close as possible to a smaller white target ball called a *pallino*. Teams take turns rolling their bocce balls, with the team farthest from the pallino continuing to throw until they gain the advantage. The game continues until a set number of points are scored. Traditionally played outdoors in teams of four, bocce is a flexible game that can also be played one-on-one. Bocce is a low-impact, leisurely sport that is great for relaxing while socializing with friends.

GET STARTED

1. **Gather the equipment.** Traditional bocce sets come as a carrying case with eight large balls (divided into two sets of colors) and the pallino. Invest in higher quality balls that will roll more accurately to ensure enjoyable game play.

2. **Find a place to play.** Check to see if bocce courts are available near you. Parks or a backyard serve as equally suitable areas. The area for bocce play is usually 60 feet (18 meters), but you can still play within shorter distances.

3. **Join a team.** Joining a bocce league or team can be a fun way to meet new people and play the game more regularly. Check with local parks, clubs, or community centers.

* Abby Mackey, "Discovering the Secrets to Longevity—on a Mt. Lebanon Bocce Court," Pittsburgh Post-Gazette, *October 29, 2023, https://www.post-gazette.com/news/health /2023/10/29/blue-zones-bocce-okinawa-buettner-longevity/stories/202310220002.*

Book Club

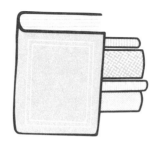

"Reading is a hobby that transports us to curious new worlds, which makes book clubs a way to take along our friends on that journey."

—JESSICA FRIEDRICHS,
Social Work Professor

GAMES/SOCIAL   COST: $

Book clubs are social events where readers gather regularly to discuss and explore chosen material together. Participating in book clubs is great for both avid readers and those who seek a sense of accountability to commit to reading a book. Gathering to discuss literature can date back to the salons of ancient Greece and Rome, but the modern idea of a book club began to take shape in the nineteenth century when women's reading groups, often called "literary societies," were established to promote reading and discussion. If you're looking to rekindle your passion for books, joining a book club could be the perfect hobby for you.

GET STARTED

1. **Find or create a book club.** Your local library or bookstore is a great place to start your search for a book club. There are also virtual book clubs you can join through online platforms like Goodreads or Reddit.

2. **Determine what to expect.** Book clubs vary in culture and level of engagement. Some may host a brief weekly check-in, while others dive deep into character analyses and coordinate viewings of film adaptations.

3. **Set and commit to a schedule.** Book clubs usually meet once a month or biweekly. Set aside time to read to ensure that you're meeting your group's pace.

Bookbinding

"Bookbinding is something that I knew existed for a while. I've been learning little tricks, how I can take a simple pattern and make it a little bit more elaborate." *

—MARTY GETRAER,
Retired Salesperson

ART   COST: $

Bookbinding is the art of creating and binding books by hand. There are a wide variety of bookbinding methods and techniques like sewn bindings, adhesive bindings, stapling, and spiral bindings. Bookbinding is an excellent hobby for those who enjoy working with their hands and want to exercise artistic creativity to craft something both functional and beautiful. Common bookbinding projects include journals, sketchbooks, family heirlooms, and personalized gifts for others.

GET STARTED

1. **Gather the materials.** Some basic supplies to start are paper, cardboard (or other heavyweight paper for covers), thread or glue, and tools like bone folders, awls, and cutting implements.

2. **Create your cover and pages.** Cut sheets according to size (if needed) and fold to form individual pages. You can decorate your cover with illustrations or use unique materials like leather or fabric.

3. **Bind your book.** The basic method for binding a book is stitching the paper sections together down the middle and gluing to the spine of your cover. Unconventional forms of bookbinding include accordion binding, Japanese stab binding (decorative stitching), and *dos-à-dos* binding, which links two books together with each book opening in an opposite direction.

---

* Phyllis Braun, *"When He's Not Repairing Books, Local Retiree Turns Them into Works of Art,"* AZ Jewish Post, *November 8, 2019, https://azjewishpost.com/2019/when-hes-not -repairing-books-local-retiree-turns-them-into-works-of-art/.* .

Bottled Sand Art

"Old people in the nursing homes can't go to the beach, so I wanted to share it with them." *

—TAYLOR ZEINSTRA,
Student

ART   COST: $

Bottled sand art is created by layering colored sand in glass bottles or containers to create picturesque landscapes, patterns, and images. The origins of sand art are diverse and span various cultures across the globe, from Native American sand paintings to Tibetan sand mandalas, which feature complex, symmetrical designs often contained within a circle. More specifically, layered sand in bottles and jars became a popular maritime souvenir created by sailors in the United Kingdom during the nineteenth century. Ideal for individuals who appreciate delicate and time-intensive crafts, each bottle allows hobbyists to tell a story, capture a mood, or portray a scene that is frozen in time yet alive with color and texture.

GET STARTED

1. **Gather the materials.** You can purchase colored sands or color your own fine grain sand by using food coloring or artist pigments. Find glass or plastic bottles of varying shapes and sizes as well as funnels or spoons to use for pouring.

2. **Master the basics.** The fundamental technique of creating sand art is pouring, but more advanced methods might involve using tools like straws or toothpicks to carefully position the sand for finer detail. Precision is key, so take your time with each layer.

---

*   Erin Albanese, *"Students Create Art to Bring to Local Nursing Homes,"* School News Network, *March 17, 2021, https://www.schoolnewsnetwork.org/2021/03/17/students-create-art-to-bring-to-local-nursing-homes/.*

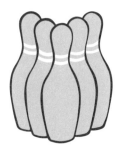

Bowling

"I started bowling at six up in Erie, PA. Erie is frozen four to six months a year, so bowling is a popular sport for families to do together."

—JOE KOLENDA,
Freelance Musician and Promoter

GAMES/SOCIAL   COST: $

Bowling is a recreational sport where the objective is to roll a heavy, spherical ball down a long, narrow lane to knock down a set of arranged pins. The earliest form of bowling can be traced back to ancient Egypt. As a modern sport, it became known as *kegel*, or nine-pin bowling, throughout Europe during the Middle Ages (originating from Germany). European immigrants introduced the game during the seventeenth century, evolving it into a popular American pastime. Bowling offers various accommodations to support different abilities including lightweight balls, ramps and ball assist devices, and bumper rails.

GET STARTED

1. **Visit a bowling alley.** Admission to a bowling alley typically includes a set number of games, different weighted balls for you to choose from, and rented shoes.

2. **Choose the right equipment.** Most alleys require specially designed bowling shoes for safe sliding and braking on the smooth surface of their floors. Alleys are required to maintain sanitation practices for shoe rentals but consider investing in your own pair if the idea of borrowing shoes bothers you. Bowling balls range in size and weight from 6 to 16 pounds (2.7 to 7.3 kilograms). Choose what feels comfortable for you.

3. **Learn the basics.** In addition to understanding the basic rules, be sure to practice lane etiquette like avoiding to roll at the same time someone next to you is rolling.

Boxing

"Boxing provides a healthy outlet to get extra energy and aggression out while being a monumental workout for all parts of my body."

—JOSHUA HAMAKER,
Video/Film Editor

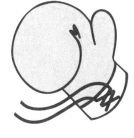

PHYSICAL FITNESS   **COST: $**

Boxing, also known as pugilism, can be traced back to ancient Rome when it was known as *pugilatus* after the Latin word for "fist"—*pugnus*. Boxing involves two competitors paired according to weight class who aim to knock the other out or score higher according to the quality and quantity of punches delivered. A boxing match takes place in a 16-foot (4.9 meter) square ring and consists of ten to twelve rounds, with each lasting up to three minutes. Competitors wear protective equipment such as headgear, padded gloves, and a mouthguard.

Fitness boxing classes have increased in popularity for hobbyists who enjoy the physically intense workout without the sparring. These classes center around bag training instead of partner work.

GET STARTED

1. **Choose a style and studio.** Traditional boxing gyms include a ring for sparring practice and have a more competitive edge in their training. You can expect to work one-on-one with coaches who will hone your posture and footwork. Fitness boxing studios offer group-based aerobic-style classes with music where you train on your own punching bag.

2. **Acquire proper attire.** The minimum attire you will need include hand wraps, a set of gloves, and appropriate footwear. Cotton and gel-padded wraps are the most common for beginners.

3. **Master the fundamentals.** The basic punches of boxing are jabs, crosses, hooks, and uppercuts. You will need to master a balanced stance and keeping up your guard.

Breadmaking

"The geeky part of me is fascinated by the chemistry, that magical alchemy that results from combining the most mundane of ingredients—flour, water, salt, and yeast." *

—DIANE BATCHIK,
National Security Professional

FOOD   COST: $$$

Breadmaking is one of the oldest culinary practices in human history that combines both art and science. Leavened bread emerged around 2000 BCE in Egypt when the process of fermentation was discovered. The emphasis on yeast and fermentation sets breadmaking apart from other forms of baking, although gluten-free breads often rely on chemical leaveners and alternative binders that distinguish its own processes. Breadmaking is a highly sensory experience—from its aromatics to the tactile kneading process it often requires—that can feel therapeutic to many.

GET STARTED

1. **Gather the basics.** Basic equipment typically includes a mixing bowl, measuring cups and spoons, a baking stone or tray, and a kitchen scale. Essential ingredients include flour, water, yeast, and salt.

2. **Start simple.** Introductory recipes for breadmaking include white or whole wheat bread, focaccia, and baguettes. These tend to be more straightforward than advanced breads like sourdough, challah, or bagels.

3. **Take a class or workshop.** Taking an in-person or online class can be extremely helpful in understanding textures and appearances to expect at different stages of your breadmaking process.

---

* *Diane Batchik, "I Baked a New Bread Every Week for a Year. Here's Why," The Washington Post, May 10, 2023, https://www.washingtonpost.com/food/2023/05/10/baking-bread-for-a-year/.*

Breakdancing

*"It's a dance that encourages us to be choreographers of our own styles."** *

—JOHNNY TANG,
Photographer

DANCE   COST: $

Breakdancing, also known as breaking, is a dynamic and high-energy form of street dance that originated in the South Bronx of New York City during the 1970s. Breakdancing emerged as an element of broader hip-hop culture with key figures and groups like DJ Kool Herc, Grandmaster Flash, and the Rock Steady Crew contributing to its evolution and development. Its foundational movements include toprock (standing dance moves), downrock (floor-based moves), power moves (spins and flips), and freezes (poses). Breakdancing is typically danced to a subgenre of hip-hop music known as breakbeats, which is characterized by both syncopated and repetitive beats with musicality influenced by funk, soul, R&B, and jazz.

GET STARTED

1. **Join a community.** Breakdancing is as much about its social culture as it is about learning the movements. A huge part of breaking is competitions known as battles, which are great social events to build your skills, confidence, and connect with other dancers.

2. **Access an ideal space for breakdancing.** A smooth wood, linoleum, or vinyl surface is recommended to minimize injuries, as well as ample space to practice unrestricted footwork and spins. A space with mirrors is also ideal for self-correction and practice.

---

* Deanna Schwartz, "From Rapping to Raising Goats, You've Got Some Wonderful Hobbies," NPR, August 7, 2022, https://www.npr.org/2022/08/07/1112564993/hobby-ideas#johnny-tang.

Breeding Butterflies

"It's just amazing how everything complements each other and elements [of nature] just click. People are so in their minds, they don't realize how much they miss."*

—SHARON MILLER,
Retired

NATURE/OUTDOOR   COST: $$

Breeding butterflies has gained traction as a popular modern hobby since the late twentieth century thanks to increased educational initiatives, environmental awareness, and advancements in breeding techniques and supplies. Breeding butterflies is an educational hobby that promotes conservation and personal relaxation and is especially rewarding for those who appreciate butterflies and enjoy watching their metamorphosis. Some hobbyists also like to join citizen science projects to contribute data from observing, breeding, and tagging butterflies for public research.

GET STARTED

1. **Educate yourself.** Learn which butterfly species are local to your area and the requirements for their care. You can find information through field guides, books, websites, or local clubs.

2. **Create a habitat.** Set up an enclosure that mimics the natural environment of your butterfly species. It needs to have proper ventilation, food sources, and the ability to control humidity.

3. **Collect caterpillars.** Purchase eggs or caterpillars from local reputable sources like butterfly farms, gardens, and other breeders.

4. **Observe and release.** Keep records to document your caterpillars developing into butterflies. You can release adult butterflies into the wild or keep them for ongoing observation and study.

---

* Noha Shaikh, "For Butterfly Enthusiast, a Hobby Fueled by Hope," The Daytona Beach News-Journal, *July 30, 2019, https://www.news-journalonline.com/story/lifestyle/home-garden/2019/07/30/for-butterfly-enthusiast-hobby-fueled-by-hope/4582834007/.*

Bullet Journaling

"There's something special about putting down electronics and using paper and pen instead. And I love that it's so customizable for however life changes, too!"

—MELINDA ANGELES,
Systems Engineer (GIS)

ART   COST: $

Bullet journaling, also known as Bujo, is an organizing methodology that combines the aspects of a journal, planner, to-do list, and sketchbook. It is essentially creating a full planner completely catered to your needs and is especially attractive to people who prefer a hands-on, tangible approach and enjoy exercising creative expression as part of their organizing process. The concept was created by digital product designer Ryder Carroll in 2013 who developed a unique symbol system to denote different entries: a bullet point represents a task, an open circle (O) denotes an event, a dash indicates a note, and an "×" marks a completed task.

GET STARTED

1. **Gather the materials.** Bullet journaling begins with either a blank or dotted notebook, quality pens and markers, and a ruler. Many enjoy adding washi tape and stickers or using stencils to add flair to their journals.

2. **Create your index page.** At the beginning of your bullet journal, create an index page to outline the symbols you will use to organize your entries. You can use Ryder Carroll's system or create your own symbols or color coding.

3. **Design and customize.** Based on your needs and wants, you can choose to add a habit tracker, goal lists, pages for doodling, and any other artistic elements to make your bullet journal a unique representation of you.

Burlesque

"I'm naturally pretty timid and silly, and so trying to be sexy is totally out of my comfort zone and seemed like a fun experiment."*

—ANNEMARIE DOOLING,
Product Manager

DANCE   COST: $

Burlesque is a type of theatrical performance that combines elements of dance, comedy, and sensuality. The modern iteration of burlesque distinguished by its risqué nature emerged during the mid-to-late 1800s as a popular form of cabaret entertainment throughout the United States and United Kingdom. Burlesque performers wear eye-catching, glittery outfits like corsets, feather boas, stockings, and high heels. While burlesque involves elements of striptease, the objective is to tantalize the audience's imagination in a cheeky manner rather than explicit nudity. Burlesque is an ideal hobby for boosting your confidence, sensuality, personal expression, and theatrical flair.

GET STARTED

1. **Find a class.** Burlesque is best learned with others in in-person classes or workshops. You can familiarize yourself with the basics of its culture through online videos and forums.

2. **Choose a persona.** Creating a persona is an essential part of burlesque performance. Choose a stage name that represents an artistic alter ego that will help you embody characteristics you otherwise would not express.

3. **Select or craft your costumes.** The costumes and accessories of burlesque are essential elements that enhance your storytelling. Teasing is key to a burlesque performance, so focus on creating layers of clothing that keeps things exciting and playful.

---

* *Rebecca Jennings, "Birding, Burlesque, Breadmaking: 10 People on How Much They Spend on Their Hobbies," Vox, September 27, 2018, https://www.vox.com/the-goods/2018/9/27/17896992/hobby-ideas-plants-ceramics-birding-crossfit.*

Bushcraft

"You can truly feel the freedom of thriving in the wild, and obtain a sense of accomplishment by building your own shelter and tools with the materials you find in nature." *

—HAN HO-JUN,
Business Owner

NATURE/OUTDOOR   COST: $$

The term "bushcraft" emerged in the nineteenth and twentieth centuries in countries like the United Kingdom and Canada to refer to a set of wilderness and woodcrafting skills focused on surviving and thriving in natural environments. Unlike backpacking, bushcraft focuses on minimalism—surviving in the wild with minimal tools and resources while making minimal impact on the environment. Whether you're an aspiring explorer, seasoned camper, or someone eager to disconnect from technology, bushcraft provides an opportunity to escape into nature and develop invaluable survival skills along the way.

GET STARTED

1. **Research and learn.** Before jumping into the wild, take the time to read books, tap into online communities, or take courses on bushcraft to build fundamental knowledge and practice.

2. **Gather the essential tools.** Bushcraft emphasizes the ability to adapt to whatever is available in the natural environment, but some basic tools to start would include a versatile knife, folding saw, fire starter, and backpack.

3. **Practice with others.** Start by setting aside weekends or outdoor excursions with others to practice your skills like fire-building, identifying edible plants, and creating simple shelters.

---

* *Jo He-rim, "'Bushcraft, the Real Charm of Outdoor Camping.'" The Korea Herald. June 1, 2018. https://www.koreaherald.com/view.php?ud=20180601000544.*

Busking

*"Plenty of people come up to you and tell you really sweet things. It gives you a really nice belief in yourself when people do walk up to you and engage."**

—NATSCI KATYA BUNGAY-HILL,
Student

GAMES/SOCIAL   COST: $

Busking is the art of street performance and can be a rewarding hobby for those who want to share or develop a unique skill or talent in front of a public audience. Busking encompasses a wide variety of acts that include music, magic, acrobatics, and comedy. Some performances are particularly unique to busking like posing as a living statue or creating paintings and caricatures of passersby on the spot. Many hobbyists are driven by a desire to infuse life into public spaces and pursue busking to satisfy a passion for performance, gain exposure, or practice interacting with a diverse audience.

GET STARTED

1. **Research local laws.** Check with your local government for laws and regulations surrounding busking. Most cities have designated busking zones or require permits, while others have rules about noise levels, hours of operation, and safety.

2. **Choose and prepare your act.** Determine what kind of performance you want to showcase. It might be based on an incredible talent you already have or a newer skill you want to hone with the help of an interactive audience (like magic tricks). Consider how to be as captivating as possible in an outdoor setting that will have limitations around space and sound.

* *Emily Lawson-Todd, "Busking in Cambridge: The Good, the Bad and the Ugly," Varsity, October 15, 2023, https://www.varsity.co.uk/music/26198.*

Butter Sculpting

"Teaching is the second-best job in the world. The first is carving butter heads." *

—GERRY KULZER,
Art Teacher

ART   COST: $

The earliest instances of butter sculpting can be traced back centuries to religious ceremonies and festivals held in Tibet. Still practiced by Tibetan monks, intricate sculptures called *torma* are made by mixing barley flour with yak butter and dyeing them with natural pigments to present as offerings that symbolize fragility and impermanence. In Western cultures, particularly in North America and Europe, butter sculptures became popular during the nineteenth century as a way for farmers to showcase their crafting skills and promote dairy products at state fairs and agricultural exhibitions. These butter sculptures can range in size and detail and depict anything from famous people to animals or landscapes.

GET STARTED

1. **Grab your butter and supplies.** Butters with high fat content can withstand warmer conditions better than low-fat butters. Use butter knives, spatulas, toothpicks, and brushes to get started.

2. **Maintain a cool temperature.** Keep your room cool and your tools chilled. Make space in your refrigerator to store your sculpture; you'll likely need to keep placing it back in the fridge as you go. Avoid freezing your butter as it can detrimentally change its texture and structure.

3. **Document and compost.** Take photos and video throughout the entire process and then compost any leftover butter with your melted masterpiece.

* Christina Morales, "His Medium, Salted Butter. His Craft, Sublime." The New York Times, August 23, 2022, https://www.nytimes.com/2022/08/23/dining/minnesota-state-fair-butter-sculpture.html.

Button Making

*"When my dad passed away, we were going through all this stuff, and we opened up this shoebox. There were a bunch of old buttons that I had sent him like 'World's Greatest Dad.' It made me think, 'this is part of my heritage.'"** *

—TOM HOWES,
Tour Guide

ART   COST: $$$

In the late nineteenth century, an American manufacturing company named Whitehead & Hoag patented the design for pin-back buttons and promoted them as a medium for political campaigning and advertising. The use of buttons as symbols of personal affiliation and self-expression particularly surged during the rise of countercultural movements in the 1960s and 1970s, worn by anti-war protesters and punk rock fans alike. As affordable and user-friendly button-making machines became available, making buttons has become a popular craft hobby. Button making is a pastime that can offer a creative outlet for self-expression and relaxation.

GET STARTED

1. **Grab your supplies or join a workshop.** Many makerspaces and recreational or community centers offer button-making workshops if you'd like to try a class out before investing in your own equipment.

2. **Design your buttons.** You can design buttons by hand using drawings and photographs or create them digitally with design software.

3. **Assemble your buttons.** Buttons are assembled by using a machine to compress together a button blank, your design, and a mylar cover.

---

* *Chase McCleary, "Do You Know the Button Man?" Rocky Mountain PBS, January 26, 2024, https://www.rmpbs.org/blogs/rocky-mountain-pbs/button-man-colorado-springs/.*

Cake Making

"Baking is my way of sharing love with others and provides me an opportunity to bring a smile to someone face (through their tastebuds) doing something I truly enjoy."

—JOUENE JONES-WALKER,
Human Resources Manager

FOOD   COST: $$

The modern art of cake making can be traced back to medieval Europe when tiered cakes and the use of marzipan to create intricate decorations became increasingly popular symbols of wealth and social status during feasts and celebrations. As cake making became more accessible through industrialization, it has continued to grow in popularity among hobbyists who enjoy baking and pushing the boundaries of three-dimensional artistry with an edible medium. With the world being more connected online, a variety of cake-making trends continue to develop and evolve rapidly, making cakes a truly limitless platform for artistic expression.

GET STARTED

1. **Gather the equipment.** Basic tools and equipment to get started include cake pans, a hand or stand mixer, bowls, spatulas, and piping bags and tips. Fondant, gum paste, and modeling chocolate are common ingredients used to customize sculptural elements in cakes.

2. **Master recipes and basic techniques.** Familiarize yourself with basic cake, filling, and frosting recipes and focus your practice on cutting, icing, and layering tiers before incorporating additional decorating elements like fondant. There is an abundance of cake-making classes, tutorials, and resources available to help you.

Camping

"Now I see the secret of making the best person: it is to grow in the open air and to eat and sleep with the earth."

—WALT WHITMAN,
Poet

NATURE/OUTDOOR   **COST: $$$**

While camping as a hobby is enjoyed by people worldwide, its historical development as a recreational pursuit has stronger ties to Western societies, particularly in Europe and North America. British author Thomas Hiram Holding wrote *The Camper's Handbook* in 1908, and is credited with helping to popularize camping as a leisure activity, as are youth organizations like the Boy Scouts and Girl Scouts that emphasize camping as part of their educational framework. Camping can be enjoyed in various environments like the forest, beach, or desert. Though traditional camping encourages self-reliance, other forms of camping like glamping (glamour camping) and RV camping offer the comforts of familiar amenities while still giving you a chance to be immersed in nature more than you may be on a day-to-day basis.

GET STARTED

1. **Choose a destination.** Research rules and regulations that pertain to your chosen location. Many campgrounds require fees and reservations as well as quiet hours and rules around trash disposal.

2. **Acquire camping gear and pack essentials.** Traditional camping usually requires a tent, sleeping bag, a first aid kit, and basic cooking equipment. Consider weather conditions for your clothing and pack food supplies according to the length of your camping trip.

3. **Show respect.** Be sure to clean up and properly dispose of your trash. Respect the area by minimizing your impact on the environment.

Candle Making

"Making [candles] was the first time I realized that you don't have to be good at something for it to be a hobby, as long as you enjoy it." *

—SOFIA RIVERA,
Editor

ART   COST: $$

The art of candle making has a rich history that traces back to ancient times. Initially, candles were made from tallow or animal fat by various civilizations across the globe. Advancements in materials led to the use of beeswax, paraffin, soy, and even gel (made of polymer resin and mineral oil), offering a variety of textures and burning properties. Whether you're drawn to the soothing process of melting and molding wax or the joy of selecting and infusing scents to create a mood, candle making is a sophisticated craft with endless possibilities that can appeal to a wide range of hobbyists.

GET STARTED

1. **Choose your wax.** Soy wax is popular for its clean burn and environmental friendliness, while paraffin wax is known for its scent throw (how much scent permeates a space). Beeswax, with its natural honey aroma, offers a toxin-free experience.

2. **Gather the equipment.** You'll need a melting pot, thermometer, pouring jug, wicks, and molds or containers. Customize your candles with fragrance oils and dye blocks.

3. **Melt and pour.** Melt your wax in a double boiler to 170°F (77°C). Add fragrance and dye, then carefully pour the wax in your mold or container. Center your wick and let it set.

---

* *Sofia Rivera, "As It Turns Out, You Don't Actually Need to Be Good at Your Hobbies,"* Apartment Therapy, *April 25, 2022, https://www.apartmenttherapy.com/making-candles-hobbies-37068018.*

Canning

*"Actually seeing, when you open up your cabinets, all these beautiful jars of preserved foods. That in itself, I think, is such a joy to many people."**

—JENNA SMITH,
Nutrition and Wellness Educator

FOOD   COST: $$

The invention of canning is credited to French confectioner Nicolas Appert (1749–1841) who presented his heat-sealed approach to the French government in a contest that sought a way to preserve food for the army and navy. Canning began to gain popularity as a hobby during the 1970s when awareness around health and environmental issues grew alongside a renewed interest in self-sufficiency. Home canning allows you to extend the shelf life of seasonal foods while controlling the amount and type of sugar, salt, and other preservatives used. Popular canned foods include jams, jellies, pickles, relishes, and sauces.

GET STARTED

1. **Gather the equipment.** Tools to start your canning journey include jars with lids, a canning pot, jar lifters, a funnel, and a ladle.

2. **Use fresh ingredients.** Use high-quality, fresh ingredients that will help produce higher quality results in preservation and taste.

3. **Sterilize the canning jars.** Be sure to carefully study and follow food safety protocols for canning to prevent spoilage and food-borne illnesses. Jars need to be sterilized before filled, and time and temperature need to be measured accurately to ensure bacteria, yeasts, or molds are destroyed.

---

* Lilley Halloran, "Canning Is Making a Come-Back in the Midwest," KCUR, December 21, 2023, https://www.kcur.org/2023-12-21/canning-hobby-popular-home-preserves-american-tradition.

Card Collecting and Trading

"Collecting cards is a great way to eradicate boredom, have a great time, and even make a little bit of money!"

—ROB EISENSTEIN,
Web Business Owner

COLLECTING   COST: $

The origins of card collecting can be traced back to the late nineteenth century when tobacco companies began including baseball cards in cigarette packs as a marketing strategy. The type of cards that hobbyists collect have since expanded significantly. Baseball cards continue to remain popular but other cards that are popular among hobbyists include toy and media franchise cards like Garbage Pail Kids and Marvel or game cards like Pokémon and Yu-Gi-Oh! The allure of card collecting lies in the thrill of the chase but can also be an exciting investment for some. The most expensive card to date is a Mickey Mantle baseball card that sold for $12.6 million in August 2022. Card collecting is an appealing hobby if you appreciate history, art, and the reward of building a collection that is both unique and personally meaningful.

GET STARTED

1. **Choose a card subject.** Consider what subjects you are most drawn to, whether it be sports, fantasy, or a specific celebrity or franchise.

2. **Research and learn.** Connect with other hobbyists through online forums, local hobby shops, or collector groups to trade and gather information on how to grow your personal collection.

3. **Organize and protect.** You can store your cards in individual card sleeves or binders. A toploader sleeve is a sturdier type of plastic holder that can protect high-value cards.

Card Games

"I keep in my writing room a Bible, a dictionary, Roget's Thesaurus, a bottle of sherry, cigarettes, an ashtray, and three or four decks of playing cards. I use every object, but I play solitaire more than I actually write."*

—MAYA ANGELOU,
Author

GAMES/SOCIAL   COST: $

Playing card games is a hobby enjoyed across generations that blends strategy, social interaction, and often a touch of luck. From classic 52-card deck games like Poker and Bridge to modern group games like UNO and Cards Against Humanity, card games offer a diverse and endless range of entertainment. The history of playing cards dates to the ninth century in China, with their popularity spreading through Asia and into Europe by the fourteenth century. Card games are beloved for their ability to bring people together, though single-player games are also a popular pastime for individuals.

GET STARTED

1. **Pick a deck.** The traditional deck of 52 cards offers hundreds, if not thousands, of game variations. Some popular ones include matching games like Go Fish and shedding games like Old Maid where the goal is to get rid of all your cards. Popular group card games include Exploding Kittens, Apples to Apples, and The Game of THINGS.

2. **Join or create a group.** Consider gathering with others regularly to play card games. If single-player games appeal to you more, some popular games to learn are versions of Solitaire, including Pyramid and Forty Thieves (which uses two decks).

---

* *"Writers at Work: Solitaire, Time Zones & a Quilt,"* The Washington Post, *October 4, 1984, https://www.washingtonpost.com/archive/lifestyle/1984/10/05/writers-at-work-solitaire-time -zones-38/e0589d56-755e-4fe0-b4c3-68edeb5d7329/*

Card Stacking

*"The moment I wore my headphones and started working on the structure, I was in a different world."**

—ARNAV DAGA,
Student

COMPETITIVE   COST: $

Card stacking is a delicate and intriguing hobby that involves carefully balancing playing cards to create impressive structures. Beyond a simple house of cards, hobbyists enjoy pushing the boundaries of physics and artistry to create intricate towers, castles, and even detailed sculptures. Card stacking gained significant popularity in the late twentieth century with the rise of notable card stackers like American architect Bryan Berg, who set a Guinness World Record with a tower that stood at 25.29 feet (7.7 meters) by using 91,800 cards.

GET STARTED

1. **Select the right cards.** Heavier cards with a rough or matte finish tend to be stiffer and provide more stability. Traditional playing cards are great to start as long as they are reserved just for stacking; the more wear and tear, the less stable they become.

2. **Create a workspace.** Clear a stable surface to build on that is protected from disruptions like wind or vibrations. A large cutting board, wood floor, or nonslip tabletop are ideal.

3. **Master balancing and patience.** Cards are stacked by leaning them together into right angles. Don't panic when cards fall, which is bound to happen. Card stacking can be as much of a meditative practice as it can be an exercise for building mental stamina.

---

* Sanj Atwal, "Teen Stacks 143,000 Playing Cards to Create World's Largest Card Structure," Guinness World Records, October 6, 2023, https://www.guinnessworldrecords.com/news /2023/10/teen-stacks-143-000-playing-cards-to-create-worlds-largest-card-structure-759373.

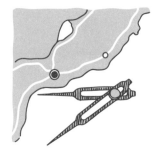

Cartography

*"I call maps a distant mirror. You have these little stories that are taking you on a time travel adventure."**

—MANUEL EISNER,
Criminology Professor

ART   COST: $

Cartography is the art and science of mapmaking that blends a love for geography, creativity, and storytelling. The origins of cartography date back to ancient civilizations, with some of the earliest maps found in Mesopotamia around the fifth century BCE. These early maps were often more symbolic than navigational. Over centuries, cartography has evolved by incorporating advances in knowledge and technology. Cartography allows a way to visually represent the world around us, though many hobbyists also enjoy depicting maps of fantasy worlds. Cartography is a hobby to explore if you are attracted to the challenge of accurately depicting landscapes, cities, and seas, while also having the freedom to bring your own creative vision to life.

GET STARTED

1. **Learn the basics of mapmaking.** Study the fundamentals of geography and how to read maps. Familiarize yourself with scale, symbols, and projection types (how the curved surface of the Earth is represented).

2. **Choose your medium and style.** You can create traditional paper maps with basic art materials or delve into digital cartography with software like Google My Maps or ArcGIS Online. Add as much or as little artistic flair on your maps as you'd like!

---

*   Sofia Quaglia, "How a Medieval Murder Map Helped Solve a 700-Year-Old London Cold Case," Atlas Obscura, *January 25, 2024, https://www.atlasobscura.com/articles/medieval -murder-maps-london.*

Catching Sunrises and Sunsets

"The 'wow' factor associated with these encounters might unlock small but significant bumps in feelings of beauty and awe, which could in turn have positive impacts for mental well-being."*

—DR. ALEX SMALLEY,
Researcher

NATURE/OUTDOOR   COST: $

Catching sunrises and sunsets is not just a visual feast but a continued practice of reverence for the sun. Throughout history, civilizations have recognized the sun as the ultimate life source, critical for growth, warmth, and sustenance. In ancient Egypt, the sun was personified as Ra, the Sun God. Each sunrise was seen as Ra's victory over the night and symbolized rebirth and renewal. In Hindu mythology, the god Surya is celebrated for his journey across the sky, and his return at sunset is seen as a time of transition and preparation for the spiritual world. Catching sunrises and sunsets can still stir a sense of ancient spiritual connection but is often embraced for the sheer joy and tranquility it brings.

GET STARTED

1. **Research and plan.** Look up times for sunrises and sunsets in your area and research best locations that offer a clear view of the horizon. Make sure to check the weather forecast and dress accordingly.

2. **Reflect and be present in the moment.** Consider bringing a sketchbook or journal to jot reflections that come up as you bask in the moment.

---

* Dale John Wong, "Watching the Sunrise/Sunset Is Good for Your Health, Scientists Say," Mashable SE Asia, January 31, 2023, https://sea.mashable.com/science/22433/watching-the-sunrisesunset-is-good-for-your-health-scientists-say.

Chain Mail Weaving

"I started weaving chain mail after searching for a grounding activity to keep my hands busy after a few stressful years. I needed something that wasn't fiber arts—I had thrown many a knitting needle across the room out of frustration."

—TORI HIRSH,
Multimedia Designer

ART   COST: $

Chain mail or maille weaving is an ancient craft of linking small metal rings to create a mesh that's both flexible and strong. This art form is often associated with the medieval knights of Europe, but its origins trace back much further and spans various cultures from the Celts to the Eastern Zhou Dynasty in China. It was used not just for armor but worn as a symbol of affluence and decorated temples. Chain mail weaving is a confluence of history, artistry, and engineering. Its use of metal rings offers a more solid tactile weaving experience that uniquely bears weight and withstands tension compared to other weaving methods, materials, and styles.

GET STARTED

1. **Gather the materials.** You can choose among aluminum, steel, or copper rings which differ in weights and malleability. Each material will affect the appearance and feel of your final piece. Pliers are essential—get two pairs for opening and closing rings with ease. Opt for those with comfortable grips to reduce hand fatigue.

2. **Master the basics.** The European 4-in-1 is the most traditional weave, where each ring passes through four others. It's the foundation upon which you can build more complex designs. Practice the opening and closing of rings to achieve uniformity. Your rings should close with little to no gap to create a smooth, cohesive fabric.

Cheerleading

"The joy I get from cheerleading is sometimes unexplainable. I'm a natural-born performer; the adrenaline rush I get on stage is unmatched." *

—NA'KYA MCCANN,
Reporter and Student

PHYSICAL FITNESS   COST: $

In 1898, a medical student named Johnny Campbell assembled a group and led the crowd in a cheer at a University of Minnesota football game, marking the birth of organized cheerleading. A combination of athleticism, creativity, and teamwork, cheerleading is ideal for those who enjoy physical activity, have a flair for performance, and thrive in a team environment. The scope of cheerleading encompasses a variety of performance venues like festivals, parades, and charity events. An Arizona-based cheerleading group called Sun City Poms is comprised of adults fifty-five years and older who dance and march to inspire both older and younger generations alike with an endless cheer for life.

GET STARTED

1. **Join a team or class.** Search community centers, schools, or specialized cheer gyms. You can follow online tutorials to learn some cheerleading moves on your own, but this activity is intended to be group based.

2. **Incorporate supplemental training.** Regular exercise focusing on core strength, flexibility, and cardiovascular fitness are crucial for cheerleading.

3. **Prepare to invest in attire.** As you progress and become part of a team, you may need to invest in performance uniforms and accessories like pom-poms.

---

* *Kiersten Brown, "A Year After the Buffalo Shooting, These Black Cheerleaders Come Together to Share Their Stories," Black Girl Nerds, https://blackgirlnerds.com/a-year-after-the-buffalo-shooting-these-black-cheerleaders-come-together-to-share-their-stories/.*

Cheese Making

*"I milk my own cow and that helps.
I probably wouldn't be doing it if I wasn't
milking my own cow."*

—PHYLLIS ABELA,
Retired

FOOD   COST: $$

Cheese making is an artisanal craft that transforms milk into cheese through a fascinating process of curdling, draining, and aging. This hobby involves combining milk with cultures and rennet (a complex set of enzymes), then nurturing the product through various stages until it reaches the desired flavor and texture. The origins of cheese making date back over seven thousand years. While no specific individual is credited with the invention of cheese, it's believed to have originated in the Middle East or Europe. Cheese making appeals to those who enjoy culinary experimentation, appreciate the subtleties of flavor, and have a penchant for craftsmanship.

GET STARTED

1. **Gather the equipment and ingredients.** Basic cheese making requires equipment like a large pot, thermometer, cheesecloth, and ingredients like milk, cultures, and rennet.

2. **Start with simple recipes and learn the basics.** Simple cheeses that don't need aging and have a straightforward process include ricotta, paneer, and fresh mozzarella. Start with recipes for these to learn the principles of cheese making. As you gain experience, you can attempt more complex recipes, such as for cheddar, gouda, and blue cheeses, which usually require more time, temperature control, and care.

---

* *Janessa Ekert, "Habana Resident and Hobbyist Cheesemaker Phyllis Abela Holds Cheesemaking Class as Fundraiser for Habana and District Progress Association," The Courier Mail, July 5, 2021, https://www.couriermail.com.au/news/queensland/mackay/community/habana -resident-and-hobbyist-cheesemaker-phyllis-abela-holds-cheesemaking-class-as-fundraiser-for -habana-and-district-progress-association/news-story/a2ca5ef88f9c74c7d111c90b0fc3cfde?amp.*

Chess

"I've found you can go to any major city in the world and there will be people to play chess with. Even if you don't speak the same language, you'll find people who share the same passion for the hobby."

—ZACK THOMPSON,
Research Chemist

GAMES/SOCIAL   COST: $

Chess is a two-player board game with each player starting with sixteen pieces: one King, one Queen, two Rooks, two Knights, two Bishops, and eight Pawns. Each side is distinguished by color, usually black and white, and each piece moves differently across a checkered board. The objective of the game is to place your opponent's King in checkmate—a position where it cannot move without being attacked.

Chess originated in India during the sixth century and was called *chaturanga,* which roughly translates to "four-limbed" and alluded to the four divisions of their ancient military: infantry, elephantry, calvary, and chariots. If you're looking for a cerebral hobby to keep your mind sharp, chess is great to play on your own or with others who share passion for the game.

GET STARTED

1. **Learn the game.** Familiarize yourself with the rules of chess. A great place to start is by playing online chess games or on apps that offer an option to highlight the possible movements of a piece on the board.

2. **Practice different strategies.** Playing chess solo is also known as "solving" chess like a puzzle. Many books and online resources provide puzzles where you can practice different tactics. Search both online communities and local clubs so you can gain more opportunities to play and hone your skills.

Chess Boxing

"The art of mastering chess boxing lies in the switch from boxing to chess. Your mind is constantly trying to gain control over the hormones to be able to outwit your opponent on the chessboard."

—IEPE B. T. RUBINGH,
Creator of Chess Boxing

PHYSICAL FITNESS   **COST: $$**

Chess boxing (or chessboxing) is an unconventional hobby that combines the mental rigor of chess with the physical intensity of boxing. The concept of chess boxing was conceived by French comic book artist Enki Bilal in 1992 and brought to life by Dutch artist Iepe B. T. Rubingh as a performance art in 2003. Rubingh organized the first competitive chess boxing match in Amsterdam while forming the World Chess Boxing Organization (WCBO) to oversee future competitions. The sport has since gained popularity in various countries, particularly in Germany, the United Kingdom, India, and Russia. A chess boxing match consists of eleven alternating rounds—six rounds of chess and five rounds of boxing—with each round lasting three minutes. Chess boxing offers an unusual yet fascinating challenge for those looking to push the boundaries of their mental and physical abilities between two distinct disciplines.

GET STARTED

1. **Learn chess and boxing.** Before engaging in the sport of chess boxing, be sure to master your understanding of both disciplines. Develop physical endurance and mental stamina by exercising and playing chess regularly.

2. **Join or create a club.** Chess boxing is mostly popular in Europe and India, making it easier to find a club or gym if you reside in these areas. If you don't have access to a chess boxing gym, consider linking up with local enthusiasts to practice.

Choir Singing

"You leave feeling lighter. You leave feeling happier, you leave in a better mood than you showed up." *

—SHAWN VOMUND,
Teacher and Musician

MUSIC   COST: $

Choir singing is a communal musical activity where people sing together in harmony. Choirs vary in size and style and cover a diverse repertoire that can include classical, religious, folk, or contemporary music. Choir singing does not necessarily require professional training, making it accessible to people with varying levels of musical experience. The focus on harmonizing to create a rich and layered sound offers a uniquely fulfilling and collaborative creative experience. Whether joining a small ensemble or large chorus, choir singing is a wonderful hobby for those seeking artistic expression, community engagement, and a way to amplify the joy of music.

GET STARTED

1. **Find a choir.** Look for choirs in your community, such as those associated with local churches, community centers, or schools. Many choirs welcome new members without auditions.

2. **Attend rehearsals and stay engaged.** Regular attendance at rehearsals is crucial. This is where you'll learn new pieces, practice harmonies, and blend with other voices. Choir singing is as much about community as it is about music. Engage with fellow choir members and participate in performances and social events.

---

* Chad Plein, "Ozarks Life: The Shanty Choir of Springfield," KY3, August 26, 2022, https://www.ky3.com/2022/08/26/ozarks-life-shanty-choir-springfield/.

Circus and Aerial Arts

"It's a great workout; it stretches my creative and artistic abilities, and it's a mental challenge. Circus arts also tend to attract a diverse, friendly group of people."

—SOPHIA CHEN,
Management Consultant

PHYSICAL FITNESS   COST: $

Circus arts include clowning, acrobatics, aerials, object manipulation like juggling, and equilibristics or the mastery of balancing (for example, tight-rope walking or unicycling). Tracing their origins to both Chinese acrobats of the Han Dynasty and equestrian acts of eighteenth-century England, contemporary circus performances like Cirque du Soleil that focus on feats of the human body led to a rise in the circus arts becoming a unique form of physical fitness and creative expression. If you enjoy physical challenges, performance, and a strong connection with your community, the circus arts might be your next hobby!

GET STARTED

1. **Determine your goal.** What about circus arts most intrigues you? The performance aspect of the arts or the physical?

2. **Choose a discipline.** How you get started will depend on the discipline of circus arts you want to try. Your juggling hobby can start as easily as gathering a few non-bouncy balls and practicing on your own by watching online tutorials. However, to get started in acrobatics or aerials, you'll want to find a training facility or coach.

3. **Wear the right attire.** You'll need to wear form-fitting clothes. Loose clothing, jewelry, and even lotion can run the risk of interfering with your moves that often require gripping, tumbling, and climbing.

Clay Shooting

*"It's really intimidating when you first shoot, but once you get that confidence after you break a few birds, it becomes a pleasure."** *

—NICK SISLEY,
Author

PHYSICAL FITNESS   **COST: $$**

Clay shooting is a sport where participants use shotguns to aim at flying targets often referred to as clay pigeons (hence its alternative name, clay pigeon shooting). These targets, made of clay or a similar material, are catapulted into the air to simulate the flight pattern of birds, providing a dynamic shooting experience. The practice of clay shooting dates to the late nineteenth century in England. It evolved as a nonlethal method of honing bird-hunting skills with the first clay targets introduced as an ethical alternative to live pigeon shooting. This change was partly driven by the increasing controversy surrounding the use of live animals in sport shooting. Clay shooting attracts individuals who enjoy the outdoors and the challenge of a moving target.

GET STARTED

1. **Find a shooting club or range.** Enroll in a course or session at your local shooting range. Some offer multi-session courses so you can master fundamentals, while others provide a brief orientation to have you shoot under supervision relatively quickly.

2. **Learn different disciplines.** Clay shooting includes different disciplines, each with its own set of rules, styles, and challenges. Try different ones as you progress to see which one you enjoy the most.

---

* *Joy Frank-Collins, "The Growing Popularity of Shooting a Clay Pigeon," Pittsburgh Magazine, January 17, 2018, https://www.pittsburghmagazine.com/the-growing-popularity-of-shooting-a-clay-pigeon/.*

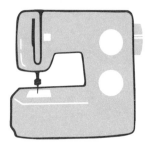

Clothes Making

"The joy of sewing for one's self is that the result is clothing that is unique and exactly what you want."

—BEN S.,
Teacher

FASHION/BEAUTY   COST: $

Making clothes, or garment construction, is an age-old practice of creating wearable attire from various materials. It involves several steps, from designing and pattern making to cutting and sewing fabric. This creative process requires a blend of artistic vision, technical skill, and a keen eye for fashion. The oldest known piece of clothing is a linen garment called the "Tarkhan Dress" discovered in Egypt in 1913 and believed to be about five thousand years old.

Clothes making is a hobby that marries creativity with practicality. It's a hobby well-suited for those who harbor a passion for fashion, love to experiment with designs, and enjoy the tactile experience of working with fabrics.

GET STARTED

1. **Learn the basics.** Start by acquiring fundamental sewing skills. This includes understanding different types of stitches, how to operate a sewing machine, and the properties of various fabrics. You can learn through online tutorials, local sewing classes, or comprehensive sewing books.

2. **Gather the equipment and supplies.** Essential items for a beginner include a basic sewing kit (needles, thread, scissors), fabric, a reliable sewing machine, and sewing patterns.

3. **Start with simple projects.** Great beginner projects to start with are scarves, simple skirts, aprons, or pajama pants.

Cloud Gazing

"Ever-changing clouds are an antidote cheaper than psychoanalysis and beautiful for their own sake." *

—GAVIN PRETOR-PINNEY,
Author

NATURE/OUTDOOR   COST: $

Cloud gazing is the simple act of observing clouds as they drift across the sky. Far from being passive observation, cloud gazing can be a meditative journey into the realms of imagination and relaxation, where each cloud formation tells a story or paints a picture in the mind's eye. Cloud gazing is a universal pastime that transcends cultures and ages. Across civilizations, cloud formations have been interpreted as omens, folklore symbols, and inspirations for art and poetry. The appeal of cloud gazing lies in its profound simplicity and the calm it brings. It's a hobby for anyone and everyone—from those seeking a moment of peace in a busy day to nature enthusiasts and creative minds in search of inspiration.

GET STARTED

1. **Choose a spot.** Research your local parks or other cleared areas that offer an unobstructed view of the sky. Ideally, you find a space where you can lie down or sit back and gaze upward without distractions.

2. **Study clouds.** Familiarizing yourself with different types of clouds like cumulus, nimbus, or stratus can enhance your experience, though it's not necessary. Let your mind drift as you gaze at the clouds and see where you imagination leads.

* Stephen Nett, "'Cloudspotting' Expert Says Best Way to Relax the Mind Is to Look Up," The Press Democrat, April 4, 2018, https://www.pressdemocrat.com/article/lifestyle/cloudspotting -expert-says-best-way-to-relax-the-mind-is-to-look-up/.

Cobbling and Shoemaking

"It started with, 'How hard would it be to replace the heel on my dress shoes?' Then, 'How hard would it be to just make a whole pair of shoes?'"

—RANDAL MILLER,
Performing Arts Curator

FASHION/BEAUTY   COST: $$$

Cobbling focuses on the repair of shoes, while shoemaking is the creation of an entirely new shoe. The skills involved may differ slightly, but cobbling and shoemaking have become interchangeable, with hobbyists often learning to do both. The etymologies of cobblers and cordwainers (shoemakers) link to medieval Europe, but one of the oldest archaeological evidence of shoes found in Armenia dates to 3500 BCE. As a contemporary hobby, cobbling and shoemaking will be especially enjoyable for people with a penchant for fashion, craftsmanship, and practicality.

GET STARTED

1. **Gather old shoes and tools.** Mending and studying old shoes is a great place to start. Basic equipment includes: shoe lasts (foot-shaped mechanical forms), leather or other synthetic shoe material, cutting tools like a utility knife, a sewing machine for cobbling or needles with strong thread, shoemaking pliers, a shoemaking hammer, and an adhesive like contact cement.

2. **Learn pattern making.** Crafting shoes requires precise patterns for each component of the shoe from the heel to the upper. Explore books, online tutorials, or local classes to aide you in creating your first shoe template.

3. **Explore various shoe styles.** Moccasins, flats, or sandals are great to begin with for their straightforward designs. Build your way up gradually to more complex constructions like boots and heeled shoes.

Coding

—ZACH WONG,
Systems Engineer

TECH   COST: $

```
_ript setup>
mport { resolveDirective, wit
} from 'vue';

/ Find the already registered
y name
:onst focusDirective = resolve[
ive('focus');

// Wrap the button with the di
:onst render = () ⇒ withDirect
  h('button', {}, []),
  // An array of directives to i
  [
    [focusDirective]
```

Coding, or computer programming, is the art of crafting instructions for computers to execute. These instructions, written in various programming languages like Python, Java, or C++, enable computers to perform a wide range of tasks from simple calculations to controlling complex systems. Augusta Ada King, known as Ada Lovelace (1815–1852), was an English mathematician and is often celebrated as the first computer programmer. Her contributions to Charles Babbage's early computer, the Analytical Engine, laid the groundwork for the algorithms and programming concepts used today. Learning to code is akin to learning a new language, but instead of conversing with people, you're instructing a machine.

GET STARTED

1. **Begin with an easy language.** Beginner-friendly programming languages include Python, JavaScript, Ruby, and HTML/CSS. These feature simpler syntax making for easier readability than more advanced languages like C/C++ or Scala.

2. **Learn online or join a community.** The nature of coding being computer-based lends itself to a wealth of learning resources online. If you don't have access to a computer or internet, public libraries are great places that usually offer access to both in addition to community coding classes. Learning with others can provide valuable support, motivation, and insights.

---

*   Stephen Nett, "Coding: The Hobby of Opportunities," Scot Scoop, February 10, 2016, https://scotscoop.com/coding-the-hobby-of-opportunities/.

Coffee Roasting

"I started roasting using a popcorn popper [that] I tweaked to control the heat and airflow. I got into it and I got better and better, and I learned from my mistakes." *

—WILFREDO ALONSO,
Engineer and Business Owner

(FOOD)　(COST: $)

Coffee roasting is the process of transforming green, raw coffee beans into the rich, aromatic beans that are ground and brewed for coffee. The history of coffee roasting dates back to the fifteenth century and has roots in the Middle East, particularly in countries like Yemen and Ethiopia. The major appeal of coffee roasting lies in the hands-on experience of crafting a personalized flavor profile. It's a sensory hobby well-suited for those who revel in the nuances of taste and aroma, and for anyone who enjoys the process of creating and experimenting.

GET STARTED

1. **Acquire the equipment.** You can start with a home coffee roasting machine or even a popcorn popper for small batches.

2. **Choose your beans.** The two main types of coffee beans are Arabica and Robusta, the latter having a stronger and more bitter taste and more often used for espresso. Look for beans that are ethically sourced by researching suppliers that are transparent about their farming practices.

3. **Experiment and learn.** Roast your beans at different times and temperatures and take notes along the way.

---

* Katie Hatzfeld, *"Engineer by Day, Roaster by Night: Liam & Ian Coffee Roasters,"* Slug Mag, December 1, 2021, https://www.slugmag.com/community/food/food-features/liam-ian-coffee-roasters/.

Coffee Shops

"I love spending time at coffee shops for so many reasons, but the main one being that there is very little that cannot be accomplished with good company and a good cup of coffee."

—EMILY PAIGE ARMSTRONG,
Artist and Educator

FOOD/SOCIAL   COST: $

From the earliest coffeehouses of the Islamic world during the fifteenth century to the "penny universities"* of seventeenth-century England, coffee shops have historically served as social hubs for peers of diverse backgrounds to exchange ideas and engage in intellectually stimulating debates. Coffee shops equally serve as havens for introverts who can escape into a cozy atmosphere to read, work, or draw on their own. Every coffee shop boasts a unique ambiance influenced by various factors like theme, decor, menu, and soundtrack. Thanks Nature Café in Seoul, Korea, allows you to interact with two fluffy sheep while enjoying your waffles and coffee.

GET STARTED

1. **Research coffee shops.** Some coffee shops are loud and facilitate an environment better for socializing, while others are quieter and promote an ambiance for individuals to get work done.

2. **Practice general etiquette.** Remember that most coffee shops are small businesses that rely on your patronage. Make purchases to compensate for the time you spend, share your table when you can and follow cleanliness policies.

3. **Create a routine or ritual.** Choosing a regular day and time to visit different coffee shops can create a sense of ritual around your hobby. You may want to use the time to journal, meet up with friends, or simply sit in mindful observation.

---

*   *Dubbed as such to refer to the price of a cup of coffee while gaining knowledge from thought-provoking conversations.*

Coin Collecting (Numismatics)

"My mom started collecting quarters with every year she could find starting from 1950, and she had a booklet with little pockets where each quarter would go. I thought it was so calming and satisfying to see all those shiny coins in their spots."

—NANCY BYUN AGUSTIN,
Public High School Teacher

COLLECTING   COST: $

Coin collecting, also known as numismatics, is a hobby that involves the acquisition and study of coins, tokens, and other forms of minted legal tender. It's much more than just accumulating currency; it's an exploration of history, art, and culture through the lens of coinage. The origins of coin collecting date back to ancient times, with evidence of the hobby as early as the Roman Empire. However, it was during the Renaissance that coin collecting gained prominence among European kings and nobles who sought ancient coins for their historical and artistic value. Unlike other collectibles, coins serve as direct links to the economic, political, and societal narratives of different eras and regions.

GET STARTED

1. **Research and learn.** Start with coins you already have and research their histories. Familiarize yourself with the basics of coin collecting, which includes understanding different types of coins, grading systems, historical periods, and preservation techniques.

2. **Store your coins properly.** You should generally avoid cleaning your coins as it can cause more harm than good and reduce their value. Instead, handle coins carefully by their edges and store in acid-free containers. You may want to consider insuring your collection and keeping them in a safety box.

Collaging

"I find collage so therapeutic. I'm in ongoing recovery from anxiety and depression and collage makes me feel joy in a way that I haven't in years. Now I just want to get the whole world collaging!"

—MELANIE LINN GUTOWSKI,
Museum Educator

ART   COST: $

Collage is an art form created by combining and arranging different materials, images, or textures together into a single composition. Traditional collaging is a very tactile activity that involves cutting, tearing, and gluing, but digital collaging is another method that is particularly appealing for anyone with sensory sensitivities. A collage composition can be predesigned and representational or spontaneously created as you go and completely abstract. There are many therapeutic benefits to collaging including stress reduction, mindfulness, and self-expression. The process of gathering, cutting, and arranging also offers a sense of ritual that can feel grounding.

GET STARTED

1. **Gather the supplies.** Start with glue, scissors, and either paper or canvas to serve as your main surface. For your collage pieces, use any kind of materials that you can cut, strip, or tear into pieces. Magazine clippings are popular, but also consider photographs, fabrics, or natural elements like leaves or flowers. If you prefer to go digital, use image editing software. Canva, GIMP, and Pixlr are free and can be easily accessed online. You can gather images from the web or the software's library.

2. **Play before you paste.** Experiment by taking your time to play and arrange the pieces in different ways before pasting them into your final composition. Digital collages are easier to continue editing forever. Consider saving edits on a single digital composition as separate files to see how the collage evolves over time.

Coloring

"Coloring can be a form of escapism where one can shed the stress and worries of the day and just focus on a simple creative task."*

—DEANNA TRATENSEK,
Wife and Mother

ART   COST: $

Coloring, a simple yet profoundly therapeutic activity, involves filling in outlined images with colors of your choice. It's akin to painting, but instead of creating your own lines and shapes, you're presented with a pre-drawn canvas. One of the earliest examples of a coloring book was *The "Little Folks" Painting Book,* published in 1879 by the McLoughlin Brothers in New York. However, the concept of adding color to pre-drawn artwork dates back even further, with historical ties to the practice of coloring maps and religious texts in medieval times. Coloring is particularly suited for those seeking a creative outlet without the pressure of creating art from scratch. It offers a delightful journey back to the simpler joys of childhood through a means as satisfying as it is relaxing.

GET STARTED

1. **Choose your coloring books.** There is a vast array of coloring books available, catering to interests from intricate mandalas and nature scenes to thematic books on literature, fantasy, and more.

2. **Gather coloring supplies.** Choose from a variety of coloring tools, such as colored pencils, markers, or crayons, based on your preference for texture and blending.

3. **Create a ritual.** Amplify the therapeutic effects of coloring by creating space or a ritual around your hobby. You can set aside time and space that is solely dedicated to coloring, even if it is only for ten minutes a day.

* *Jessica Roy, "Meet the Adults Who Love to Color," The Cut, May 7, 2015, https://www.thecut .com/2015/05/meet-the-adults-who-love-to-color.html.*

Comics

"My father would take my brother and me to the newsstand, and we'd get Superman or Spider-Man comics. I loved comics because the stories and characters were larger than life."

—ERIC CADENA,
Middle School Teacher

COLLECTING   COST: $

Pictorial narratives can be traced back to the earliest days of humanity, but the rise of modern comics began in the United States during the late nineteenth century. Comics started as short strips that provided humor and sociopolitical commentary in newspapers. Beginning in the 1930s, comic books and graphic novels gained meteoric success through superhero stories—a genre that remains beloved by many to this day. Iconic character illustrations and common archetypes like heroes and villains contribute to the enduring appeal of comics for all ages. Hobbyists can enjoy activities from reading comics to collecting them and frequenting comic book stores.

GET STARTED

1. **Visit a comic book store.** Comics are a visual medium, and their illustrations and styles are as diverse as their stories. See what you're drawn to; it is totally okay to choose a comic based on its art!

2. **Create a pull list.** A pull list is a system offered by comic book shops for reserving issues of comics as they are released. This is a great way to invest in an ongoing series, especially popular ones where finding new issues might become challenging.

3. **Share in community.** Connect with fellow enthusiasts to discuss, debate, and share theories around the stories. There are ample communities available, from social media groups to online forums and in-person meetups.

Concertgoing

"The energy and community feel at punk rock shows are incredible. Getting knocked down and then being helped back up by the person that knocked you down is an incredible feeling."

—NATHAN L. OLSON,
Group Home House Coordinator

GAMES/SOCIAL   COST: $

Concertgoing is the engaging pursuit of experiencing live music, a tradition that forms an integral part of human culture. The modern concept of a public concert began to evolve in the seventeenth century during the Baroque period, particularly in Europe. This era saw the rise of classical music with composers like Vivaldi, Bach, and Handel. Going to concerts provides a chance to see your favorite artists perform live and to be part of a moment that can never be exactly replicated. Concerts offer a spectrum of experiences from the high-energy ambiance of rock concerts to the intimate, soulful settings of acoustic sessions. Engaging in concertgoing is not just about hearing music but experiencing it in its most vibrant form.

GET STARTED

1. **Discover and explore.** Explore beyond your usual preferences to find new sounds that might resonate with you. There's a thrill to scoring tickets to your favorite popular artists, but don't forget to look up live performances at local coffeehouses, jazz clubs, or outdoor community venues that are often free or affordably priced.

2. **Practice etiquette and safety.** Be mindful of others and prioritize safety to ensure a collectively pleasant concertgoing experience. Limit phone use to stay present in the moment, respect the artists, and remain aware of your surroundings.

Confectionary Art

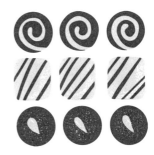

"There's actually a decent amount of chemical engineering involved in chocolate manufacturing, which I hadn't expected."*

—BRENDA BARNICKI,
Former Chemical Engineer and
Business Owner

FOOD   COST: $$

Confections refer to food items that are rich in sugar and carbohydrates and include items like truffles, pralines, and lollipops. Confectionary art encompasses a wide range of techniques and mediums from sculpting chocolate and sugar to crafting edible flowers and petits fours. Distinct from pastries, which are a type of baked good that can be light and savory, confections are not always baked and can be dense in texture. The confectionary art form as many know it today began to take shape in the Middle Ages as status symbols in European courts. The allure of confectionary art lies in its unique blend of precision, creativity, and the joy of creating something both beautiful and delectable.

GET STARTED

1. **Choose a confection.** Start with simpler confections like truffles or fudge and progress your way to making caramels and marshmallows. Making sugar sculptures or tempering chocolate are each advanced confectionary categories that require greater precision, patience, and skill.

2. **Take classes or workshops.** Learning techniques from an instructor can be very helpful to understanding the nuances involved with confectionary art, especially with other class participants who are on the same journey.

---

*   Naveen Kumar, "Making Chocolate for a Cause," Washington Magazine, August 11, 2022, https://source.wustl.edu/2022/08/__trashed-3/.

Cookie Decorating

"I started watching baking shows and decorating sugar cookies and found it to be so relaxing and fun. I love decorating cookies because it's a fun family hobby that I can enjoy alone or with family and friends."

—JACLYN BEATTY,
Business Owner and Sales Consultant

FOOD   COST: $

Cookie decorating transforms the humble cookie into a canvas for creative expression. It involves embellishing baked cookies with icing, sprinkles, and other edible decorations, turning them into edible pieces of art. The origins of cookie decorating can be traced back to around 500 BCE with the pre-Christian Germanic festival of Julfest, also known as Yule, when the craft of baking gingerbread emerged as part of its winter solstice celebrations. Though a time-honored activity, cookie decorating has surged in popularity as a modern hobby thanks to social media with its community of enthusiasts identifying themselves as "cookiers."

GET STARTED

1. **Master basic recipes.** Sugar cookies or gingerbread are best for decorating as they are easy to roll and don't spread. Royal icing is the most common frosting to use because of its smooth texture and the way it hardens with a candy-like finish.

2. **Gather the right tools.** Use a rolling pin with removable rings to evenly roll your dough and use sturdy cookie cutters. Basic decorating supplies include piping bags or bottles, tips and nozzles, food coloring, and assorted sugars and sprinkles. Gel-based colors are typically preferred as they maintain nicely saturated colors without disrupting the texture of your icing.

Cooking

"My passion stems from some of my earliest memories of spending time with my grandmother at her restaurant in Madrid, Spain."

—DIEGO BYRNES DEMICHELI,
Artist and Musician

FOOD   **COST: $$$**

Cooking as a hobby can be a wonderfully creative and stress-relieving outlet. In addition to building practical life skills, consciously choosing your ingredients can offer a sense of empowerment over your health and your budget. Cooking also serves as a gateway into other cultures and flavors.

There are multiple avenues in cooking that can speak to diverse hobbyists. Someone who is interested in creating innovative dishes with a scientific approach may prefer molecular gastronomy, whereas someone passionate about sustainability may choose farm-to-table cooking and focus on creating dishes based on what is locally and seasonally available.

GET STARTED

1. **Equip your kitchen.** Some basic tools to start cooking include a decent chef's knife, a cutting board, pots and pans, and utensils like tongs or a wooden spoon. Remember to also stock up on basic spices like salt, pepper, and garlic powder.

2. **Learn the basics.** Fundamental techniques to master include sautéing, frying, and roasting; and knife skills like dicing and mincing.

3. **Start with simple recipes.** Many websites and online communities offer free recipes, but you can also borrow cookbooks from your library. Following recipes will give you a framework to experiment with different ingredients later.

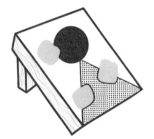

Cornhole

"It's just very straightforward but there's also a lot to it. A lot of strategy." *

—GAVIN HAMANN,
Student

GAMES/SOCIAL   COST: $$

Cornhole, also known as beanbag toss, is a lawn game that has become a staple at tailgates, family reunions, and backyard barbecues. The game involves two teams taking turns throwing fabric bags filled with corn kernels or beans at an inclined wooden platform with a hole at the far end. The objective is simple yet challenging: toss the bags into the hole to score points. There are several theories surrounding the origins of cornhole. One popular belief is that it originated in Germany in the fourteenth century and later brought to America's Midwest farming communities. Some claim that the game was invented or popularized in Chicago during the Prohibition era. Cornhole's relaxed pace allows for conversation and camaraderie, making it ideal for those who enjoy casual, outdoor activities with friends and family.

GET STARTED

1. **Buy the equipment and find a space.** Cornhole game sets typically include two cornhole boards and eight bags (four of each color). The ideal playing space for cornhole is outdoors on a flat surface with the boards approximately 27 feet (8.23 meters) apart.

2. **Play variations.** Traditional scoring is based on a cancellation system (that is, Team A scores 3 points, then Team B scores 1 point, so Team A is awarded 2 points). Other scoring variations include cumulative scoring, or speed scoring, which imposes a time limit per turn.

* *Olivia Young, "Colorado Students Receive First Ever Cornhole College Scholarships: 'We Were Shocked,'" CBS News, February 19, 2024, https://www.cbsnews.com/colorado/news /colorado-students-receive-first-ever-cornhole-college-scholarships/.*

Cosplaying

"I took apart clothes from my closet to hand-sew my first cosplay and fell in love with the creative process. When I wear my cosplays I feel invincible and get to truly come out of my shell."

—DR. RACHEL KRENEK,
Enrollment and Marketing Specialist

FASHION/BEAUTY   COST: $$

The term "cosplay" was coined by a Japanese reporter named Nobuyuki Takahashi in 1983 to capture the essence of costuming and play that he witnessed among fans of manga and anime—Japanese-style graphic novels and animated films or series. Dressing up to pay homage to favorite characters in media can be traced back earlier to the 1930s when the first science fiction conventions took place in the United States. Cosplaying has continued to grow as a dedicated hobby among different fandoms around the world. The goal of cosplaying is to portray a character as accurately and authentically as possible, from nailing the details of the costume itself but also in the embodiment of a character's speech, mannerisms, and expressions.

GET STARTED

1. **Choose your character.** A character can be from a TV show, book, or video game, or even from obscure media like a commercial or a mascot.

2. **Buy or create your costume.** Some people enjoy searching for a costume to buy, but a strong draw of cosplaying is the opportunity to practice resourcefulness and craft your own costume.

3. **Attend conventions and connect with others.** Cosplaying boasts a huge, supportive community. Conventions and other media-specific gatherings are a great place to connect with other cosplayers.

Creating Memes

*"I love memes as an art form, because in order to be successful, they usually have an unexpected juxtaposition of text and image that manages to creatively convey a relatable experience."**

—EVE PEYSER,
Writer

TECH   COST: $

Creating memes is a hobby that has rapidly gained popularity in the digital age. It is an art form that blends humor, culture, and commentary using images, text, or videos. Memes often reflect current trends, societal issues, or universal experiences, making them relatable and shareable. The concept of a "meme" was first coined by Richard Dawkins in his 1976 book *The Selfish Gene.* Dawkins presented it to describe an idea, behavior, or style that spreads within a culture. However, the modern internet meme as we know it originated in the early 2000s with the advent of social media and online forums.

GET STARTED

1. **Understand current trends.** Memes can span a variety of topics from current events to specific media franchises or social phenomena. Spend time on various social media platforms to understand what is trending and popular and what resonates most with people.

2. **Learn basic graphic editing.** You can easily edit graphics with an online tool like Canva or search directly for meme generators. The visual component of your meme does not need to be elaborate; the witty commentary and content are what makes a meme popular.

* *Eve Peyser, "How Sex Memes Helped Me After a Breakup,"* Cosmopolitan, *April 27, 2016, https://www.cosmopolitan.com/lifestyle/a57588/how-sex-memes-helped-me-after-a-breakup/.*

Crocheting

"A neighbor taught me to crochet, and I took to it immediately, making scarves, blankets, and other items. I love to crochet hats for myself and have a wide assortment of colors and yarns."

—CANDICE SABATINI,
Beauty Editor

FIBER ARTS   COST: $

Crocheting is a fiber art craft accomplished with the use of a single hooked needle and yarn. Initially, crocheting was known as crochet lace in nineteenth-century Europe because the focus was on creating fine lacework. Similar to knitting but with distinct differences, crocheting often comes easier for new learners because it involves working with one stitch at a time versus rows of stitching, making it easier to spot and correct mistakes. The stitches in crocheting also tend to be bulkier, lending itself to denser and more durable projects like dolls, rugs, and heavy blankets. Crocheting can be enjoyed individually or in a social setting, making it ideal for introverts and extroverts alike.

GET STARTED

1. **Gather the materials.** To start, you will need a crochet hook, which comes in various sizes to accommodate different yarn weights. Medium-weight yarns are great for newbies.

2. **Master the basics.** The fundamental stitching techniques of crocheting include the chain stitch, single crochet, and double crochet.

3. **Follow guided projects or classes.** Find books or online tutorials to start or join a local in-person class for guidance. You will likely start with simple patterns for dishcloths, potholders, and mug cozies before you can advance to items like hats, doilies, and dolls.

CrossFit

*"Every day I show up to a workout I'm not sure
I can do and have to focus and fight my way
through it. I know I can get through difficult things
in life because I do difficult things one breath at a
time every single day."*

—NOEL KILLEBREW,
Web Designer

PHYSICAL FITNESS   COST: $$$

CrossFit is often described as a lifestyle rather than just a fitness regimen. It boasts a holistic approach to health and athleticism, combining elements from high-intensity interval training, Olympic weightlifting, plyometrics, powerlifting, gymnastics, calisthenics, strongman exercises, and other workouts. This eclectic mix results in a training program that aims to build strength and conditioning through extremely varied and challenging workouts. CrossFit was developed in the late 1990s by Greg Glassman, a former gymnast, and officially became a brand in 2000 in Santa Cruz, California. Over time, CrossFit evolved from a simple exercise program into a competitive sport with its own marquee events like the CrossFit Games. CrossFit's appeal lies in its community spirit and the emphasis on improving functional fitness that supports real-life movements and activities.

GET STARTED

1. **Join a local box.** CrossFit is a branded system with trainers certified in their unique fitness regimen style, and their gyms are known as boxes. This reflects the no-frills, utilitarian design of their gyms.

2. **Start slow.** CrossFit can be adapted to different fitness levels but is generally an intense workout. Most boxes offer introductory classes and assessments; use these to gauge your current fitness level and familiarize yourself with the basics.

Cross-Stitching

"It's a very relaxing hobby with low costs and skill level to enter. I find that it clears the mind of chaos and allows me to work on practicing patience and peace."

—JEN TE,
Artist

FIBER ARTS   **COST: $**

Unlike embroidery's freehand style, cross-stitching features ×-shaped stitches and relies on a grid pattern where each stitch is aligned with the weave of the fabric. The origins of cross-stitching trace back to the Middle Ages with evidence of its practice found across diverse cultures in China, the Middle East, and Europe. Cross-stitching requires minimal tools and is accessible to beginners yet offers limitless potential for complexity and artistic expression. It is distinct from other fiber arts in its technique and aesthetic, where each stitch contributes to a larger image similar to pixels in a digital picture.

1. **Choose a pattern and gather supplies.** Patterns range from traditional motifs to contemporary designs and can be found in books or online. You'll need cross-stitch fabric that features the even weave grid squares like Aida cloth, a pair of embroidery scissors, and an assortment of colored embroidery floss according to your design. You will also need an embroidery hoop to keep your fabric taut and a cross-stitch needle that features a blunt tip and a long, large eye. Depending on the pattern you choose, you might be able to buy a kit that includes all the materials you need.

2. **Master the stitch.** The cross-stitch is essentially threading an X-shape per square. For example, you might move from the bottom-left of a square to the top-right and proceed to bottom-right and top-left to complete a stitch.

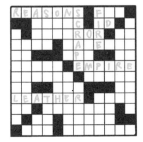

Crossword Puzzles

"As a kid, I would watch my dad painstakingly pencil in letter after letter in the giant grid, and triumphantly smirk when finishing the NYT Sunday puzzle. He passed the paper over to me to work on the less intimidating Quick Crossword, and I was hooked."

—ASHA GWIN,
Event Manager

EDUCATIONAL   COST: $

Crossword puzzles stand as a hallmark of mental exercise and leisure. Distinguished by their grid of white and black squares, the white spaces become a playground for words that intersect and interlock, each defined by clues ranging from the straightforward to the enigmatic. The genesis of the modern crossword puzzle is credited to Arthur Wynne, a journalist from Liverpool, England. In December 1913, Wynne published what he called a "Word-Cross" puzzle in the *New York World* newspaper. Swiftly captivating the public's imagination, the crossword puzzle burgeoned into a global phenomenon, cementing its place in newspapers and journals worldwide. Crossword puzzles are particularly appealing to those with a love for words, a knack for trivia, and an appetite for cognitive challenges.

GET STARTED

1. **Begin with simple puzzles.** As traditional printed newspapers decline, you can still find an abundance of crossword puzzles online or in books. Start with easy puzzles to build familiarity with common clue patterns.

2. **Expand your vocabulary.** The more robust your vocabulary, the greater success you will have in solving crossword puzzles. Reading and playing word games can help in addition to keeping up with current events and popular culture since many crossword clues often crossover with trivia knowledge.

Crystal Growing

"My [high school chemistry] teacher asked us to prepare copper sulfate salt. I thought it would look like a handful of sand. I was shocked when she showed us brilliant blue crystals that had formed over the weekend." *

—CHASE LEAN,
Student

EDUCATIONAL   COST: $$

Crystal growing involves dissolving a chosen substance in water or another solvent and then allowing it to recrystallize over time. The results are stunning—geometric crystal formations not only fascinate but educate observers. The roots of crystal growing as a scientific study can be traced back to early alchemists and natural philosophers who observed and documented crystallization processes. As advancements in chemistry and the availability of various chemicals grew, crystal growing also blossomed into a widespread modern hobby.

GET STARTED

1. **Select a starter kit.** The easiest way to begin is with a crystal growing kit, which typically comes with an instruction manual and includes chemicals like copper sulfate or borax, containers like beakers or petri dishes, and measuring equipment.

2. **Study the science.** Learn the fundamental concepts of solubility, saturation, and the components of different chemicals, which can influence the kind of crystallization that occurs.

3. **Experiment and share.** Experiment with different chemicals, dyes, and growth accelerators or modifiers to create different kinds of crystals. Keep your crystals or share them with others as gifts.

* Chase Lean, "I'm Obsessed with Growing Crystals at Home. Here Are 11 of the Most Beautiful Crystals I Managed to Grow," Bored Panda, June 3, 2022, https://www.boredpanda.com/im-obsessed-with-growing-crystals-at-home-here-are-11-of-the-most-beautiful-crystals-i-managed-to-grow/.

Cycling

"When I'm cycling, particularly when I've found my rhythm on a long ride, my mind is exclusively engaged in the activity, and all the other concerns in life fade away."

—JASON LANZA,
Motion Graphics Production Artist

PHYSICAL FITNESS   COST: $$

Cycling is an activity where speed and balance converge to create an exhilarating experience. From casual rides through verdant parks to stationary bicycles in fitness classes, cycling encompasses a spectrum of experiences, each unique in its appeal. The inception of cycling is often credited to Baron Karl von Drais (1785–1851), a German inventor who introduced the *Laufmaschine* (running machine), an early form of the bicycle. While this rudimentary design lacked pedals, it laid the foundation for what would evolve into the modern bicycle. For some, cycling offers a rush of adrenaline through winding roads or rugged trails. For others, it's the serene joy of a leisurely ride. Cycling is a hobby that appeals to the adventurous and the health-conscious, offering both a form of exercise and an avenue for exploration.

GET STARTED

1. **Choose the right bicycle.** Bicycles vary in tire width, tread, and so on to accommodate the primary type of terrain you intend to navigate. If you prefer indoor cycling, most gyms and community centers offer equipment and classes that accommodate all levels.

2. **Invest in proper gear.** Prioritize safety and comfort with a well-fitting helmet, fitted and breathable clothing, and chain lubrication.

3. **Practice basic maintenance.** Familiarize yourself with essential maintenance tasks like tire inflation and brake checks to lengthen the health of your bicycle.

Darts

*"It's good just to get out and meet people, talk to people, and spend a night with friends."** *

—ROB AMBROSE,
Counselor

GAMES/SOCIAL   COST: $

Darts is a game of skill that involves throwing small, pointed missiles called darts at a circular target that is typically affixed to a wall. Traditionally played in pubs and taverns, it has evolved into a beloved pastime and competitive sport, adored by many for its simplicity yet challenging nature. Darts trace back to medieval England and is believed to have evolved from soldiers throwing short arrows at the bottom of casks or tree trunks. As these objects dried, they would create sections that were later used as scoring areas. Darts is traditionally a social game but can be equally enjoyed as a solitary pastime. It's an attractive hobby for those who love games of skill, precision, and strategy.

GET STARTED

1. **Join a community.** Darts is a common game offered in bars, leagues, and other social communities. Consider joining games in these settings before investing in your own set.

2. **Acquire the equipment.** You can invest in a dart game set that comes with a dartboard and darts. Traditional dartboards are made of bristle boards, but electronic versions also exist.

3. **Learn the rules and scoring.** There are different scoring methods based on game variations. The most popular is starting with a score of 501 and racing to reduce it to zero; the closer to the bullseye, the higher your score.

---

* *Fran Perritano, "Darts Leagues Are a Cure for the Wintertime Blues," Observer-Dispatch, February 1, 2010, https://www.uticaod.com/story/news/education/graduation/2010/02/02/darts-leagues-are-cure-for/44876527007/.*

Decoupage

*"I live on the banks of the Shenango River.
I collect leaves and decoupage them on note
cards to share the peace and beauty of the river
with whomever I send them to."*

—BARBARA L. GEARY,
Retired Teacher

ART   COST: $

Decoupage is a craft that involves the artful arrangement of paper cutouts
to transform ordinary objects into visually captivating pieces. This technique, which can bestow new life upon anything from small trinkets to
large pieces of furniture, captures the essence of upcycling with an artistic
twist. The roots of decoupage are believed to be in East Siberian tomb
art, where nomadic tribes used cut-out felts to decorate the tombs of their
deceased. However, it was in seventeenth-century Europe, notably France
and Italy, where the craft flourished. Originally, decoupage was a method
of replicating hand-painted lacquer work from Asia, an endeavor made
popular among the upper classes. Its name, derived from the French word
decouper, meaning "to cut out," elegantly summarizes the core of this craft.

GET STARTED

1. **Gather the supplies.** The main materials used in decoupage are
   paper and fabric cutouts. Start with basic supplies like scissors,
   glue, and varnish, and choose a surface to decorate, such as a
   wooden box, picture frame, or vase.

2. **Prepare your materials.** Make sure to clean the surface of your
   chosen materials. Experiment by laying out your cutouts into a
   design before applying with adhesive.

3. **Seal and finish.** Apply several coats of varnish or lacquer, allowing sufficient drying time between each coat. This seals the
   decoupage, adding durability and a polished look to your item.

Diamond Painting

ART   COST: $

Diamond painting is the craft of placing tiny, shiny resins or "diamonds" onto a sticky canvas to form vibrant, patterned images. It marries the ease of paint-by-numbers with the charm of cross-stitching, offering a unique and mesmerizing way to create sparkling, mosaic-like artwork. Though this activity emerged as a craft hobby from Asia in the early 2000s, there are striking similarities with the process of Huichol beadwork, which is created by pressing colorful beads into beeswax spread over wooden sculptures and other objects. The Huichol, an Indigenous people of Mexico, practice their beadwork as a form of spiritual and cultural expression with patterns depicting mythological deities and natural elements. Diamond painting, on the other hand, is commercially rooted and features patterns that range from city scenes to cartoon figures. Diamond painting is an ideal hobby for those who appreciate meticulous, detail-oriented crafts.

GET STARTED

1. **Choose a kit.** You can start by purchasing a diamond painting kit, which comes in varying sizes and difficulty levels. These kits provide all the materials you need, and you can choose them based on the pattern you wish to complete.

2. **Create a workspace.** It's easier to proceed when you organize your diamonds by color and clear out space dedicated to your piece to avoid losing track of your tiny diamonds.

Digital Illustrating

"What's good about digital drawing is that everybody can do it. You don't have to be a professional artist or enroll in an art class and buy expensive tools. Also, it has no mess at all."*

—HAIDE,
Housewife and Mother

ART   COST: $$

Digital illustrating emerged in the 1980s alongside the rise of personal computing. Pioneers like Alvy Ray Smith, a cofounder of Pixar, and John Knoll, a creator of Photoshop, significantly contributed to its evolution. What began as pixel-based creations has evolved into sophisticated artworks with limitless potential for modifications and versatility thanks to advancements in software and hardware. Digital illustrating appeals to individuals who value flexibility and the ability to experiment without the constraints of traditional materials. The undo button embodies the forgiving nature of digital art, inviting both seasoned artists and novices to explore and create fearlessly. You can switch between styles like watercolor to oil painting with a simple click.

GET STARTED

1. **Choose your tools.** Begin with a basic drawing tablet or a stylus-equipped tablet. Popular choices for beginners are the Wacom Intuos or Apple iPad. Software choices range from professional-grade programs like Adobe Photoshop to more user-friendly apps like Procreate.

2. **Learn and practice.** Explore online tutorials or enroll in digital art courses to familiarize yourself with your chosen software's functionality. Practice regularly and play around with different palette options to build up your skills.

* *https://steemit.com/hobbyhub/@ediah/digital-drawing-is-my-hobby*

Disc Golf

"It's a fun way to get some light exercise and spend time outdoors and can be played any time the weather is nice. It's also very inexpensive and requires much less space than traditional golf."

—DREW KENNEDY,
Food Service

GAMES/SOCIAL   COST: $

Disc golf is an engaging recreational activity that blends elements of Frisbee and golf. Picture a traditional golf course, and instead of clubs and balls, players use flying discs and aim to complete each "hole" by throwing them into a metal basket. Disc golf emerged in the late 1960s and early 1970s in the United States, although its exact origins are often debated. George Sappenfield, a Californian recreation counselor, is credited with introducing the concept of playing golf with a Frisbee in 1965. The first formal disc golf course was established in Pasadena, California, in 1975, and the game has since spread globally with courses found in parks, recreational areas, and dedicated disc golf facilities. Most courses are free to play, making disc golf an affordable hobby. Often played in groups, the game's social aspect makes it a favorite for social gatherings.

GET STARTED

1. **Acquire a disc.** Although inspired by the Frisbee, the discs used in disc golf are smaller in diameter, heavier, and have a more streamlined, aerodynamic design. You can purchase a basic disc golf set, which includes a driver, a mid-range disc, and a putter. Each type of disc is designed for specific parts of the game, much like golf clubs.

2. **Find a course.** Look for a local disc golf course. Many public parks have them, and they are often free to use. Course maps and hole descriptions will guide you through the game.

DJing

"Once a frequent club DJ, I now see it as a hobby in my older years. Instead of big crowds, I find joy in sharing music with loved ones or enjoying it alone."

—JORDAN TAYLOR,
Video Producer

MUSIC   COST: $$$

DJing ("DJ" being short for "disc jockey") is the art of mixing and manipulating music to create a seamless flow of tunes. DJing is not simply playing songs but involves mindfully selecting tracks, blending them together, and adding in unique sound elements. DJing originated in the 1940s when radio disc jockeys played phonograph records. Pioneers like DJ Kool Herc and Grandmaster Flash revolutionized the art during the 1970s when they introduced techniques like break beat DJing and scratching. These innovations laid the foundation for modern DJing and influenced countless genres from hip hop to electronic dance music. You'll love DJing if you enjoy exploring different musical genres and have a keen understanding of rhythm and melody.

GET STARTED

1. **Choose your style and gear.** The two main styles of DJing are electronic and vinyl. Electronic DJing requires a mixer, turntables, and software like Serato or Traktor. Vinyl DJing is an analog approach and requires a physical collection of records.

2. **Build and organize your music library.** If you choose vinyl DJing, you can start building your collection by visiting record stores. For electronic DJing, platforms like Beatport, iTunes, and Bandcamp offer a vast selection of tracks for purchase. Organize your music by creating playlists based on genre, mood, or key.

Dollhouses

"I love it more than I imagined I would. At first, I worked on it during weekends, but now it's become a fantastic focus of my day." *

—JACQUELINE GREENWOOD,
Retired

ART   COST: $$

The origins of dollhouses date back to the sixteenth century in Europe, initially designed as display cases for adults. They were often used to showcase wealth and were elaborately decorated to mirror full-sized homes. By the eighteenth century, dollhouses became more accessible and started to find their way into children's playrooms. Dollhouses have resurged as a hobby for adults who are drawn to the charm, nostalgia, and complexity of these miniature worlds. Dollhouses involve creating, collecting, and decorating small-scale houses, making them as realistic and detailed as possible. It's a world where interior design, architecture, and storytelling converge.

GET STARTED

1. **Choose a dollhouse.** Miniature kits where you construct dollhouses from scratch have become popular and range in designs from bakeries to greenhouses. You can also purchase a traditional preassembled house.

2. **Gather the materials.** Many kits contain all the tools you need for assembly. Additional materials and accessories will depend on how you want to decorate your house (such as fabrics for curtains, miniature furniture, wallpapers, and so on).

3. **Research designs.** Research interior decorating styles for inspiration and guidance. Consider choosing specific themes or historical eras for your design.

* *Gayle Macdonald, "Dollhouses Are the Ultimate Pint-Size Pandemic Hobby," The Globe and Mail, April 7, 2021, https://www.theglobeandmail.com/life/home-and-design/article-dollhouses -are-the-ultimate-pint-size-pandemic-hobby/.*

Domino Toppling

"I like the artistry of it. It's like when you look at any great painting, it's not just thrown together. It's a meditative thing."*

—JARED LYON,
Web Developer and Programmer

TOYS   COST: $

The game of dominoes is believed to have been invented in China during the thirteenth century and involves matching rectangular tiles according to the number of dots they have. When the game was introduced to the Western world, arranging domino tiles upright into a patterned chain with the intent of toppling them in a cascading display became a popular hobby solely for entertainment purposes. During the late 1990s, a domino enthusiast named Robin Paul Weijers from the Netherlands established Domino Day, which introduced a competitive edge to the hobby through record-breaking toppling events. The current world record (since 2009) for most toppled dominoes stands at 4,491,863 tiles.

GET STARTED

1. **Acquire a domino set and create a workspace.** Most domino tiles are available in wood or plastic and come in various colors. Create enough space where you can arrange your design with minimal disturbance.

2. **Design your layout.** Start practicing with basic layouts that involve straightforward lines and simple curves. As you progress, you can play with more advanced layouts, like spirals or multiple split and merge pathways.

* *Greg Livadas, "RIT Employee Shows Off Toppling Talents on 'Domino Masters,'"* Rochester Institute of Technology, *March 21, 2022, https://www.rit.edu/news/rit-employee-shows-toppling-talents-domino-masters.*

Double Dutch Jump Roping

*"It takes you back to childhood. Back to a time when there's no stress, no bills, no issues when you're a kid jumping rope."**

—PAMELA ROBINSON,
Stay-at-Home Mom

GAMES/SOCIAL   COST: $

Double Dutch jump roping is a dynamic activity that involves two long jump ropes turning in opposite directions, with one or more players jumping in and out of the ropes. The origins of Double Dutch are commonly traced back to early Dutch settlers in New York during the colonial period. The name "Double Dutch" is believed to have originated as a term of derision by the English toward the Dutch. However, it was in the playgrounds of New York City where Double Dutch flourished, particularly within Black communities. By the 1970s and 1980s, it evolved into a popular pastime and competitive sport, gaining popularity in schools and neighborhoods across the United States.

GET STARTED

1. **Join a group or class.** Double Dutch requires at least three people, so it is best learned in a group setting. Look for local clubs, community centers, or classes that offer Double Dutch.

2. **Learn the basics.** Start by practicing the timing and rhythm required to jump in and out of the ropes. This can be done by observing and then trying to enter the ropes when they are open. Dedicate time to also learn how to turn the ropes in a consistent rhythm.

* *Cheryl Corley, "Jumping for Joy and Sisterhood, the 40+ Double Dutch Club Holds a Playdate for Women," NPR, September 20, 2023, https://www.npr.org/2023/09/20/1198675138 /jumping-for-joy-and-sisterhood-the-40-double-dutch-club-holds-a-playdate-for-wom.*

Drag

"I started by performing in drag at a regional theater called Arizona Broadway Theatre. I fell in love with the art form and haven't stopped since."

—CODY PETIT,
Actor and Singer

FASHION/BEAUTY   COST: $$

Drag is a vibrant and expressive performance art where individuals dress and perform in gender-exaggerated manners, typically opposite to their everyday gender identity. Performers—known as drag queens or drag kings—blend theatricality, fashion, and self-expression to create elaborate personas with distinctive makeup, costumes, and personalities. The early practices of drag can be traced back to Shakespearean theater where male actors played female roles, since women were not allowed on stage. Contemporary drag emerged in the early twentieth century, particularly in underground LGBTQ+ communities. It was a form of expression and defiance in a society that was often unwelcoming.

GET STARTED

1. **Research and learn.** Start by exploring the history of drag and watching performances by various drag artists. This can provide inspiration and help you understand the culture and diverse styles within the drag community.

2. **Experiment with makeup and costume.** Drag makeup is often bold and theatrical, and costumes range from glamorous to satirical. Practice and experiment with makeup techniques and costume design.

3. **Develop a persona.** Create your drag persona. This includes not just the physical appearance but also the character's name, backstory, personality, and performance style.

Dragon Boating

"Each seat has a specific skill but only together can we win the race. I get so much cultural pride when I think I'm doing something that was invented two thousand years ago by my Chinese forbearers!"

—MARIAN LIEN,
Educator and Community Advocate

GAMES/SOCIAL   COST: $$

The roots of dragon boating are steeped in Chinese history, tracing back over two thousand years to the southern provinces of China. The legend surrounding the sport is linked to the famous Chinese poet and politician Qu Yuan, whose death in the Miluo River inspired local villagers to race out in their boats to retrieve his body. This act of communal effort is said to have inspired the spirit of dragon boat racing. Dragon boating continues as a cultural tradition in China, but has since transformed into a competitive and recreational sport enjoyed worldwide. Dragon boating involves a long, slender boat, usually adorned with a dragon's head and tail, navigated by a team of paddlers who move in unison to the rhythm of a drum.

GET STARTED

1. **Join a club or team.** Dragon boating is a team sport requiring at least twelve people (ten paddlers, one drummer, and one steerer). Search for local dragon boating clubs or community groups. Note that dragon boating usually takes place on rivers or lakes.

2. **Train consistently.** Regular training sessions with your team will build fitness, improve technique and timing, and foster team dynamics. Together you can look forward to participating in festivals and competitions, which are not only about racing but celebrating the cultural aspects of the sport with specific foods, performances, and rituals.

Driving

"I love driving—virtually and IRL. I felt that I found a hobby that puts my brain 'in the zone' or the mental state of flow." *

—BALAJI DAMODARAN,
Software Engineer

NATURE/OUTDOOR   COST: $$

The first automobile was invented in the late nineteenth century by Karl Benz in Germany. As cars became more accessible and road networks expanded, driving for pleasure emerged as a popular pastime. It was no longer just a means of transportation but a source of freedom, exploration, and expression. Driving as a hobby transcends the routine of simply getting from point A to point B. Whether it's the serenity of a country road, the challenge of a twisting mountain pass, or the adrenaline rush of a racetrack, driving can provide an escape and a new way to engage with the world from behind the wheel. Driving is a hobby that can be both meditative and thrilling, deepening a love and appreciation of the open road.

GET STARTED

1. **Choose your driving adventure.** If scenic driving is your preference, plan routes that offer beautiful landscapes and interesting stops. For track or performance driving, look for local tracks or events that cater to amateurs.

2. **Gas up!** Remember to keep your tank filled and identify gas stations along the way. Learning basic car maintenance skills, like changing a flat tire, can also prove helpful.

3. **Stay environmentally conscious.** Consider eco-friendly or fuel-efficient vehicles and eco-driving practices like smooth acceleration and reducing idling.

* *https://www.balaji.dev/2022/11/28/driving.html*

Drone Flying

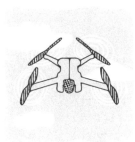

"I got into drone flying when I was pursuing travel photography. I love seeing a different perspective on the world and beautiful sites."

—KAREN THI,
Content Creator

TECH   COST: $$$

Flying drones is a hobby that combines a love for technology and the thrill of flight. It involves operating small, unmanned aerial vehicles (UAVs) for recreational purposes. These drones are equipped with rotors for propulsion and stability and are controlled remotely by hobbyists who often capture breathtaking aerial photographs and videos in the process. Drones were initially created for military applications but became accessible and affordable for civilian use by the early 2000s. Piloting drones is attractive to people who enjoy the outdoors, photography or filmography, and the challenge of developing a technical skill.

GET STARTED

1. **Learn local regulations.** Drones are subject to various regulations depending on your location. It's crucial to familiarize yourself with these rules, which might include registration requirements, no-fly zones, and altitude limits.

2. **Choose a drone.** Start with a basic model that is durable and easy to control. Some examples include the latest versions of the DJI Mini, Ryze Tello, or Holy Stone HS100.

3. **Practice in an open space.** Spend time understanding your drone's controls and capabilities. Start in an open, safe area like a backyard to practice takeoff, hovering, gentle turns, and landing.

Drum Circles

"I was gifted a drum and then attended a drum circle, and I was immediately hooked. They're healing for the body and the brain."

—SYDNEY STEPHENSON,
Therapist

MUSIC   COST: $

A drum circle is a communal gathering where people come together to create rhythm and harmony using drums and other percussive instruments. Often led by a facilitator who guides the group in rhythm and tempo, it's an immersive experience that revolves around spontaneously creating music in a circle. The origins of drum circles are rooted in traditions that span across African, Native American, and Asian communities, where drumming was a fundamental part of ceremonies and rituals. These ancient practices laid the groundwork for the modern drum circle, which has evolved into more of an informal gathering in public spaces to encourage unity through music.

GET STARTED

1. **Find a local drum circle.** Many communities have local drum circles that meet regularly. Websites, social media groups, and community centers can be great resources to find one near you.

2. **Acquire an instrument.** While traditional drums are commonly used, any percussion instrument can contribute to a drum circle. Some lower-cost instruments for beginners are wood blocks, bongos, or a djembe.

3. **Learn basic rhythms.** Practice basic drumming techniques and rhythms. There are many online tutorials and classes that can help beginners get started, but you can also practice by playing along to songs to familiarize yourself with keeping a beat.

Dumpster Diving

"The thrill, the rush, you never know what you're gonna find." *

—YARROW FIRST-HARTLING,
Mother

HOME   COST: $

Dumpster diving is the practice of sifting through commercial or residential waste to find items that are still useful or valuable. It's a hobby that combines elements of treasure hunting, recycling, and frugal living. The concept of dumpster diving gained momentum in the 1980s and 1990s, particularly within the environmentalist and anti-consumerist movements. It combats the problem of waste and consumerism, and it is also a practical means of saving money or finding goods to resell.

GET STARTED

1. **Know local laws.** In some areas, it's perfectly legal, while in others, it may be restricted or prohibited. Avoid trespassing onto private properties.

2. **Prioritize safety and hygiene.** Wear protective clothing like long-sleeved shirts that you don't mind getting dirty, gloves, and sturdy shoes. Bring tools like a flashlight and a grabber or stick. Be mindful of hygiene and safety, especially when handling discarded items.

3. **Start with retail and grocery locations.** Many divers find success behind stores or supermarkets, as they often discard items that are near or slightly past their sell-by dates but are still perfectly usable.

* *"Maryland Mom Picks Up New Pandemic Hobby: Dumpster Diving,"* CBS Baltimore, *May 28, 2021, https://www.cbsnews.com/baltimore/news/maryland-mom-picks-up-new-pandemic-hobby-dumpster-diving/.*

Dungeons & Dragons (D&D)

"It's like having an adventure in another world while hanging with your friends in this one."

—ADAM J. N. KEENE,
Storyteller

GAMES/SOCIAL   COST: $

Dungeons & Dragons (D&D) is a fantasy tabletop role-playing game (RPG) where players create their own characters—ranging from wizards and warriors to rogues and clerics—and embark on imaginary adventures within a fantasy setting. Guided by a narrative provided by the Dungeon Master or Dungeon Magi (DM), who acts as the game's referee and storyteller, players navigate through these adventures, making choices and rolling dice to determine the outcomes of their actions. Created in the United States during the early 1970s by Gary Gygax and Dave Arneson, it rapidly grew from a niche hobby into a cultural phenomenon.

GET STARTED

1. **Gather game supplies and a group.** Beginners can acquire a starter set that includes a rule book, premade characters, and a set of polyhedral dice (dice of various shapes, each with a different number of faces) used to make decisions in the game. You can play with just two players, but the recommended number is at least four to five.

2. **Create your characters and embark on a campaign.** Each player creates a character using guidelines from the chosen rule books, deciding on aspects like race, class, and background. A "campaign" in D&D refers to a continued storyline or adventure that can last for a single session or extend into weeks and even years. Campaigns are worlds typically built by the DM while players' choices can significantly impact what happens.

Eastern Calligraphy

"The beauty of calligraphy goes beyond the visual elegance of the characters; it lies in the profound meanings of the words I bring to life on paper."

—RAN YANG,
Professor

ART   COST: $$

Eastern calligraphy is a cultural and spiritual practice that originates from the Shang Dynasty of China (1600–1050 BCE) and includes influences and iterations from Japan, Korea, and Arabic-speaking regions. Eastern calligraphy emphasizes mindfulness and a harmonic connection to nature. The ink is traditionally a solid stick made from pine soot that artists grind on an ink-stone with water to achieve a desired consistency. The ink-making process, combined with a conscious awareness of body positioning and keeping the brush held in an upright manner, serve as meditative rituals. Eastern calligraphy can include motifs and imagery to represent the natural world, and many of its characters and symbols are rich with philosophical significance.

GET STARTED

1. **Gather the materials.** You will need a calligraphy brush, ink, and paper. Most inks are made from soot and can be searched as *sumi* or *sumi-e* ink or *meok*. Search for *xuan, washi,* or *hanji* papers.

2. **Choose a style.** Eastern calligraphy styles are distinguished by different cultural, historical, and linguistic traditions. Learn more about the backgrounds, characters, and philosophies of each and choose the one that resonates with you most.

3. **Set an intention.** Many approach Eastern calligraphy with the intent to internalize the meaning behind the written character or to release an emotion.

Embroidery

"Embroidery is a solitary activity; just you and the thread, over and over. It taught me to give myself grace and patience."*

—EVA RECINOS,
Arts and Culture Journalist

FIBER ARTS   COST: $

Tracing the origins of embroidery takes us back thousands of years, with evidence of hand-stitched embellishments found in ancient civilizations across the globe from China and Egypt to Scandinavia and South America. Distinct from sewing, where the purpose is primarily functional, embroidery involves decorating fabric with a needle and thread or yarn. The fabric itself becomes an integral part of the art with every stitch adding to the texture and depth of the final piece. It's a versatile fiber art, allowing for a variety of techniques and materials—like silk, wool, or metallic threads—and can range from simple designs to complex, multicolored masterpieces.

GET STARTED

1. **Gather the essentials.** Start with basic supplies like embroidery needles, embroidery floss, a hoop to keep your fabric taut, and a piece of plain fabric like cotton or linen. Many starter kits include most of these tools and materials.

2. **Learn basic stitches.** Begin by learning a few fundamental stitches like the running stitch, backstitch, and satin stitch. Seek online tutorials and books for guidance.

3. **Start simple.** Beginner embroidery projects include stitching a monogrammed handkerchief, simple floral embroidery on tote bags, or embellishments on fabric bookmarks.

*   *https://www.refinery29.com/en-us/embroidery-hobby-coming-out-bisexuality*

Engraving

"Laser engraving and cutting is a hobby I do in the cool months. It's fun to make things for special occasions and humbling when called upon to remember those who have passed." *

—CHARLES COZAD,
Manager Solution Architecture

ART   COST: $$

Engraving is the process of using special tools to etch, carve, or cut designs into hard surfaces like metal, glass, or wood. From the intricate armor of medieval knights to the delicate embellishments on Victorian glass, engraving has historically served not only as an artistic expression but also as a practical method for recording information and decorating objects. Engraving as a modern hobby continues to captivate those who appreciate detailed, hands-on work. It challenges individuals to develop steadiness, precision, and fine motor skills, which can both feel meditative and be an exercise in patience and focus.

GET STARTED

1. **Select your engraving tools.** You can start with traditional engraving hand tools like gravers and burins or invest in an electric engraving pen, which requires less manual effort. There are engraving starter kits that include a variety of bits and stencils.

2. **Practice on cheap materials.** Practice on smaller pieces of wood and cheap metals like aluminum and copper. This is an economical way to hone your skills and familiarize yourself with the nuances of working with different materials before advancing onto larger projects or more expensive surfaces.

---

* *https://www.linkedin.com/posts/charlescozad_laser-engraving-and-cutting-is-a-hobby-i-activity-7106159214816858112-Cwck/*

Entertaining/Hosting Dinner Parties

"I love hosting because food and warm welcomes are ways that I show love."

—COURTNEY WILLIAMSON,
Medical Device Entrepreneur and
Real Estate Investor

HOME   COST: $$$

Entertaining or hosting dinner parties is an art that blends culinary skills, social grace, and creative planning. It involves inviting guests into your home and providing them with a meal accompanied by engaging conversation and a warm, welcoming atmosphere. Hosting dinner parties can be traced to the elaborate feasts of Roman banquets and the refined gatherings of the Chinese and French aristocracy. These events were social and cultural experiences as well as opportunities to display wealth, status, and taste. The hobby of hosting dinner parties appeals to those who take pleasure in the details—curating menus, decorating spaces, and creating an atmosphere that makes guests feel special.

GET STARTED

1. **Master basic cooking skills.** You can choose to hire a caterer for your party, but entertaining is traditionally rooted in personally cooking meals for your guests. Practice your culinary techniques and learn to master a few go-to recipes.

2. **Learn table settings and decor.** Understand the basics of setting a table and creating an inviting dining environment. You can range from elegant and formal to casual and cozy.

3. **Plan and organize.** Good planning includes deciding on a menu, sending out invitations, and considering any dietary restrictions of your guests. Preparation can make the difference between a relaxed host and a stressed one.

Entertainment Memorabilia

"You build relationships with other collectors and often share in the excitement of helping that community plug holes in their collections."

—ADAM TAYLOR,
Film Industry

COLLECTING   COST: $

Collecting entertainment memorabilia provides a way of immersing yourself in an extended reverence of a cherished form of media. Entertainment memorabilia includes a wide array of items related to film, television, music, or other forms of popular culture. They can include posters, autographs, scripts, figurines or toys, and props or costumes. Collecting these forms of memorabilia is a particularly enjoyable hobby for dedicated fans of specific franchises. What sets apart entertainment memorabilia collecting from other collecting hobbies is the strong sense of fandom and emotional connection to a chosen niche. It is a hobby that doubles as a love language, keeping your relationship to a specific form of media active and alive.

GET STARTED

1. **Choose your fandom.** Focusing on a specific TV show, band, or film that you feel strongly drawn to can help you start building a unique and quality collection.

2. **Define display and storage spaces.** Consider what kinds of display apparatuses showcase your collection best. For items you would rather keep hidden, invest in reliable storage units that keep them protected from wear and tear.

3. **Join a community.** Search for events, conventions, or online forums where you can connect with other fans who share your enthusiasm and may be able to share tips on where to look for items to add to your collection.

Entomology

"I became fascinated with bugs when I moved to the country as a kid. There's always some new fact to learn, behavior to observe, and new species to discover, even in your own backyard!"

—OWEN MCNAMARA,
Front End Web Developer

COLLECTING   COST: $$$

Entomology is the scientific study of insects. As a hobby, it involves observing, collecting, and studying insects to unravel the mysteries of their behaviors, life cycles, and roles in the ecosystem. The origins of entomology as a systematic study can be traced back to the times of Aristotle and Pliny the Elder, who made early contributions to the field. However, it was not until the Renaissance and the subsequent periods of scientific enlightenment that entomology emerged as a formal discipline. For hobbyists, entomology satisfies a curiosity about the natural world, a love for detailed observation, and an interest in biological sciences.

GET STARTED

1. **Study first.** Start with books, online resources, and local nature groups to build a foundational understanding of entomology.

2. **Observe, collect, and document.** Spend time in nature observing insects. Parks, gardens, and even urban areas can be rich with insect life. Observation is a key part in understanding and appreciating their world. If interested in collecting, invest in basic entomology tools like nets, containers, and a magnifying glass. Keep a journal to document your findings.

3. **Join a community.** Local or online entomology groups can offer valuable insights, support, and opportunities to participate in citizen science projects.

Environmental Restoration

*"[My kids and I] started talking about how dirty the river is and how we should pick it up, and one thing led to another and we just started cleaning it up."**

—ALEX WHITTAKER,
Marine Mechanic

VOLUNTEERING   COST: $

Environmental restoration is a proactive and impactful hobby that involves rejuvenating and preserving natural habitats. It entails actively participating in efforts to repair ecosystems that have become degraded, damaged, or destroyed. Environmental restoration can include a variety of activities, such as planting native species, removing invasive plants, cleaning up polluted areas, and working to improve the health of rivers, forests, and other ecosystems. If you are passionate about nature conservation and are willing to invest time and effort into making a positive difference, environmental restoration can be a deeply fulfilling hobby that offers a hands-on approach to improving the planet's health.

GET STARTED

1. **Educate yourself.** Take time to learn about local ecosystems, native species, and the specific challenges they face. Understanding the science behind restoration and the most urgent needs in your area can help you take informed and effective action.

2. **Volunteer with local organizations.** Many communities have groups focused on environmental restoration and provide ample opportunities for volunteers.

* Susannah Sudborough, *"This Family Has a New Hobby—Removing Trash from the River."* The Enterprise, *October 7, 2020, https://www.enterprisenews.com/story/news/local/2020 /10/07/taunton-family-has-new-hobby-removing-trash-from-river/114539034/.*

Esports

"You get to make more friends, new friends that share the same interest in games as you." *

—JEREMY GARCIA,
Student

TECH   COST: $$$

Esports (short for electronic sports) is a rapidly growing hobby that stands at the intersection of competitive gaming and spectator sports. It involves organized, multiplayer video game competitions, often professional, where players and teams battle against each other in popular games. Esports started gaining traction in the late 1990s and early 2000s and has since catapulted in popularity, especially in countries like South Korea, China, and the United States where professional esports leagues and players garner as much fervor from fans as traditional sports. Esports appeal to those who enjoy mastery of a game, the excitement of competition, and being part of a passionate community.

GET STARTED

1. **Choose a game.** Popular esports titles include *League of Legends, Counter-Strike: Global Offensive,* and *Dota 2,* among others. Each game has its own set of rules, strategies, and community.

2. **Practice and join a community.** Spend time learning your game's mechanics and strategies, and watch how professional players and teams play. Engage with the game's community through online forums, social media, and local or online gaming groups. This can provide opportunities to participate in amateur tournaments.

---

* Scott German, *"Esports Matches Turn Hobby into Competition for Some Fairfax Co. Students,"* WTOP News, *November 2, 2020, https://wtop.com/fairfax-county/2022/11 /esports-matches-turn-hobby-into-competition-for-some-fairfax-co-students/.*

Extreme Ironing

"I like the idea of taking a landscape that might have been shot 1,000 times before and making it unique with some ironing. Plus, it always makes people smile!" *

—JACK NICHOLS,
Photographer

NATURE/OUTDOOR   **COST: $$**

Invented by Phil Shaw of Leicester, England in 1997, extreme ironing is a quirky blend of adventure and domestic chore that turns the mundane task of ironing into an adrenaline-pumping activity. This hobby involves taking an ironing board, iron, and a few wrinkled garments to remote or extreme locations and ironing them there. Extreme ironists have ironed atop mountains, underwater, while parachuting, and in countless other unconventional settings. It's a whimsical fusion of extreme sports and performance art, showcasing a blend of humor, danger, and the satisfaction of well-pressed clothing.

GET STARTED

1. **Choose your ironing equipment.** A portable ironing board and iron are essential. Ensure the iron can be used in a variety of settings, possibly a cordless or travel iron.

2. **Practice safety and start small.** Begin in a local park or a backyard to get a feel for the activity. Safety is key. As you become more comfortable, start pushing your adventurous limits to a hilltop, beach, or any place that adds an exhilarating element of the outdoors.

3. **Document and share.** Take photos or videos and join online communities to connect with fellow extreme ironers around the world.

* *Scott Sistek, "'Extreme Ironing' Adds Challenging Wrinkle to a Simple Hike," CBS 21, August 22, 2017, https://local21news.com/news/offbeat/photos-extreme-ironing-adds -challenging-wrinkle-to-a-simple-hikes.*

Fanfiction Writing

"Looking back on my teen years, I realize I loved fanfiction because I love writing. Through this creative expression, I discovered I can enjoy writing and use it as a skill in my adult life." *

—KATIE REDEFER,
Reporter

ART   COST: $

Fanfiction writing is a creative and engaging hobby of crafting stories using characters, settings, and plot elements from existing works of fiction like books, movies, TV shows, or video games. The roots of modern fanfiction can be traced back to the science fiction fandoms of the twentieth century, particularly with the advent of *Star Trek* in the 1960s. Fans of the show began writing their own stories and sharing them in fanzines. These fan-created narratives can follow the canonical storyline, branch into alternate universes, or explore "what if" scenarios. It's a way for fans to extend their favorite fictional worlds and express their creativity.

GET STARTED

1. **Choose a fandom.** Start with a universe you love and are familiar with. Read fanfiction created by others in your fandom to gain inspiration and insight into the style, range, and genres that resonate with readers.

2. **Write and share.** Begin with a short story or a specific scene. Focus on expressing your ideas and enjoying the process. Platforms like FanFiction.net, Archive of Our Own, or Wattpad are great places to share your work, receive feedback, and connect with other fanfiction writers.

* Katie Redefer, "Read It and Weep: Writing Fan Fiction Shaped My Adolescence," The Berkeley Beacon, *January 29, 2019, https://berkeleybeacon.com/read-it-and-weep-writing -fan-fiction-shaped-my-adolescence/.*

Fansubbing

"I ended up significantly improving my Chinese reading, listening, and comprehension skills after fansubbing three full-length Chinese/Taiwanese TV series by myself so I could share the stories I loved with people who didn't know Mandarin."

—VAY CAO,
Program Manager

TECH   **COST: $**

Fansubbing is the practice of creating unofficial subtitles for foreign-language TV shows, movies, and other video content. An unpaid labor of love, these subtitles are produced by dedicated fans who are fluent in both the source and the translation languages. Its origins can be traced back to the 1980s when Japanese anime grew in popularity. International fans would transcribe and translate dialogue and then burn subtitled episodes onto VHS tapes to distribute to fellow fans who didn't understand the Japanese language. Fansubbing has existed in a legal gray area. Fansubbers argue that their work falls under the fair use doctrine, and many copyright holders allow fansubbing, understanding its role in helping to promote their content. As more streaming services and production companies provide official subtitles to meet growing demand, fansubbers still help in making niche and older content accessible to international audiences.

GET STARTED

1. **Choose your niche.** Start with the language(s) you know or want to learn and choose content that captivates you.
2. **Respect copyright and distribution laws.** Focus your fansubbing hobby on content available in the public domain. The digital library Internet Archive has an open access database. You can also search for Creative Commons content, which allow legal reuse and translation.

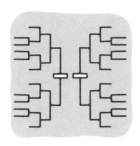

Fantasy Sports

"Two of my leagues are with friends and family that are spread out around the country. Fantasy football is a catalyst for communication and a means to interact with them each football season."

—JOE FRATENA,
Multimedia Communications Producer

GAMES/SOCIAL   COST: $

Fantasy sports is a strategic hobby where participants create virtual teams composed of real-life players from a specific sport, such as football, baseball, or basketball. It's a blend of sports knowledge, statistical analysis, and a bit of luck. Participants act as team managers, making decisions on player selection, trades, and lineups, all in a quest to outscore their competitors in the fantasy league. The concept of fantasy sports began in the United States, with fantasy golf in the late 1950s. However, it truly took off with fantasy baseball in the 1980s when author Daniel Okrent and his friends formulated the first set of fantasy baseball rules. The advent of the internet in the 1990s and 2000s further contributed to the explosion of fantasy sports, making it easier to track stats and manage teams.

GET STARTED

1. **Choose a sport.** Start with a sport you are already knowledgeable about or are interested in learning.

2. **Join a league.** A league is comprised of participants who compete against each other. You can join an existing league or create your own. There are many websites and apps offering various formats and league types.

3. **Draft and manage your team.** Throughout the season, you'll make decisions on who to start, sit, trade, or pick up from free agency. Stay informed and active to ensure success for your fantasy team.

Felting

*"I discovered needle felting as I was researching
different stop motion puppet techniques. I was
exposed to wool sculptures and fell in love with
this medium."*

—MARIEKE VAN DER MAELEN,
Miniature Model Maker

FIBER ARTS   COST: $

There are two main types of felting: wet felting and needle felting. Wet
felting uses water, soap, and agitation to entangle and compact wool fibers
together. Needle felting, on the other hand, employs a barbed needle to
interlock wool fibers, allowing for detailed sculptural work. Felting predates
spinning and weaving and is one of the oldest forms of making textiles.
Historical records and archaeological finds suggest that felting was known
in Central Asia as far back as 2,500 years ago. It played a crucial role
in the everyday life of nomadic tribes, who used the craft to make yurts,
rugs, and clothing. The process of turning loose wool into a structured
form through matting, condensing, and pressing the fibers can feel both
fascinating and therapeutic.

GET STARTED

1. **Choose your method and gather supplies.** Wet felting is great
   for larger projects like scarves or hats, while needle felting is
   suited for detailed sculptures and decorations. For wet felting,
   you'll need wool roving (unprocessed wool fiber), warm water,
   soap, and a flat surface for rolling. For needle felting, you'll
   need wool roving, felting needles, and a foam pad.

2. **Learn fundamental techniques.** There are many online tutorials,
   books, and workshops that can teach you the basic techniques
   of each felting style. Wet felting involves layering, applying soap
   and water, and fulling. Needle felting requires a felting tool,
   which is used with a straight up-and-down motion.

Fight Choreography

"It's really a combination of ballroom dance and sleight of hand."*

—MERON LANGSNER,
Playwright

PHYSICAL FITNESS   COST: $

Fight choreography involves creating coordinated sequences of staged combat for public entertainment or personal recreation. It's not just about simulating fights, but also about storytelling and expressing character through dynamic physical action. Fight choreography can cover a wide range of combat styles from sword fighting to street brawling. Fight choreography originated during the early days of theater, but it catapulted into an art form with the advent of cinema. It continues to grow in popularity thanks to fans of action movies and franchises who film and share their fight scenes online.

GET STARTED

1. **Build foundational skills and understanding.** You should have a fundamental understanding of a fighting style and techniques through martial arts classes, dance, or stage combat workshops. Study existing fight scenes in movies and plays to understand how fights are structured and executed. If you plan to film your fights, pay attention to pacing, camera angles, and how the fight serves the bigger story.

2. **Practice safety.** Prioritize safety and clear communication. Practicing with experienced individuals or under supervision is recommended.

*   *Suzanne Yeagley, "Meron Langsner, Choreographing Fights," McSweeney's Internet Tendency, February 13, 2012, https://www.mcsweeneys.net/articles/meron-langsner-choreographing-fights.*

Fire Spinning

"Immediately after my first 'burn,' I knew I was hooked. My favorite thing about being a fire performer is the ability to show people something they may have never seen before."

—JOEY LYNN TOMKO,
Claims Field Property Adjuster

PHYSICAL FITNESS   COST: $$$

Fire spinning is a captivating performance art that combines elements of dance, juggling, and the ancient allure of fire. Practitioners, often referred to as fire dancers or spinners, wield emblazoned tools such as staffs or hoops in a choreographed dance, creating a mesmerizing spectacle of light and motion. Fire spinning has roots in traditional Maori culture, where *poi* (balls on cords) were used in dance and storytelling. Fire spinning fuses danger with beauty, demanding both physical skill and artistic expression. It attracts individuals who are drawn to unique forms of physical artistry and anyone fascinated by the primal allure of fire.

GET STARTED

1. **Start with non-fire props.** It's essential to practice with LED poi, flags, or unlit staffs to build skill and confidence in handling the equipment.

2. **Learn safety precautions.** Understanding and adhering to safety measures cannot be overstated. This includes using proper fuel (like white gas), having fire extinguishing equipment on hand, and never spinning alone.

3. **Take lessons and practice regularly.** Learning from experienced fire spinners is invaluable. They can provide guidance on techniques, safety, and performance tips.

Fishing

"I found fishing to be a therapeutic experience for me because it got me out of my mind for a while." *

—HAROLD SKELTON,
U.S. Air Force Veteran

NATURE/OUTDOOR   COST: $$

Fishing offers a chance to disconnect from the hustle of daily life and immerse oneself in nature. The anticipation and thrill of the catch coupled with the peacefulness of being near water provide a unique form of relaxation and satisfaction. Fishing can range from a casual, recreational pursuit to a competitive sport; and it encompasses various techniques from simple rod-and-line fishing to more complex methods like fly fishing or deep-sea fishing. It requires patience and persistence, and is most suited to those who enjoy spending time outdoors and appreciate wildlife.

GET STARTED

1. **Consider local regulations.** Different areas have specific fishing regulations regarding licenses, catch limits, and conservation practices. It's important to be informed and compliant with these rules before starting.

2. **Gather the equipment.** The type of equipment you'll need will depend on the fishing method you use and your target fish species. Basic fishing equipment includes a fishing rod, reel, line, hooks, and bait.

3. **Start small.** Start by fishing in local ponds or lakes and gradually explore larger locations and different techniques. Practice is key in developing skill and intuition in fishing.

---

* Angelica Stabile, "Fishing Trips for Veterans: Nonprofit Boosts Heroes' Mental Health with 'Calming Experience,'" Fox News, August 9, 2023, https://www.foxnews.com/lifestyle/fishing-trips-veterans-nonprofit-boosts-heroes-mental-health-calming-experience.

Flag Football

"I've just always loved football, and I think [there are] a lot of women and girls that love football. An opportunity for them to enter into the sport with a more equitable kind of physical prowess is really exciting."*

—KARISSA NIEHOFF,
Nonprofit CEO

PHYSICAL FITNESS   COST: $

Flag football is a dynamic and engaging team sport that shares many similarities with traditional football but with a key difference: instead of tackling, players pull flags attached to their opponents' belts to end a play. Flag football was created as an alternative to tackle football in military training during World War II, allowing American soldiers to play football without the high risk of injury. As a noncontact variation, flag football makes the game safer and more accessible. Flag football teams and fields are also generally smaller and have simplified rules. This hobby is great for anyone who enjoys physical fitness, team sports, and strategy.

GET STARTED

1. **Learn the rules.** Familiarize yourself with the specific rules of flag football, which can vary slightly depending on the league or organization.

2. **Gather equipment or join a league.** The minimum number of players needed to play a game is eight, with four members per team. You can invest in a flag football set that comes with belts, cones, and flags. Otherwise, consider joining a local league or community group. Many cities have recreational leagues that are open to all skill levels.

---

* *Stephen Borelli, "'These Girls Can Be Pioneers': Why Flag Football Is Becoming So Popular with Kids," USA Today, October 22, 2023, https://www.usatoday.com/story/sports/2023/10/22/flag-football-why-sport-is-becoming-so-popular-with-girls-kids/71270522007/.*

Flash Mobbing

*"That's the beauty of a flash mob. You can join in whenever you want."**

—CRISTINA GIBSON,
Public Health

GAMES/SOCIAL   COST: $

Flash mobbing is a spontaneous performance art where a group of people abruptly assemble in a public place, perform something predetermined like a choreographed dance, and then quickly disperse. These performances are typically organized through social media or other digital means and are known for their surprise element, often leaving unsuspecting bystanders delighted and amazed. The concept of the flash mob was created in 2003 by Bill Wasik who, at the time, served as senior editor of *Harper's Magazine*. The first official flash mob took place at a Macy's department store in Manhattan and involved participants behaving in a synchronized, unusual manner. Since then, the idea has evolved to include flash mob singing, dancing, instrumental performance, and even cause-based flash mobs that raise awareness about important issues.

GET STARTED

1. **Join a group.** Many cities have groups that organize regular flash mobs. While they're usually free to join, there may be associated costs like travel or costume expenses.

2. **Learn the choreography and follow the plan.** Once you've joined a group, you'll need to learn the dance. This often involves watching tutorial videos or attending practice sessions. Being able to thoroughly understand and follow the plan is critical to the success of a flash mob performance.

---

* Leslie Moses, *"Savannah Flash Mob Dance Crew Puts Joy in Their Boogie,"* Savannah Now, *September 17, 2016, https://www.savannahnow.com/story/news/2016/09/17/savannah-flash -mob-dance-crew-puts-joy-their-boogie/13915914007/.*

Flower Arranging/ Ikebana

"I spend a good chunk of each day staring at a screen for work. The opportunity to build and piece together a gorgeous and tactile arrangement is hugely rewarding and just plain fun."*

—TABIA YAPP,
Talent Agency Owner

ART   COST: $$

Flower arranging, or floral design, involves the thoughtful composition of flowers and foliage to create visually appealing arrangements. This hobby spans various styles and methods, each with its unique philosophy and aesthetic. One of the most renowned methods is *ikebana,* the Japanese art of flower arranging. Dating back to the seventh century, ikebana is a disciplined art form steeped in the philosophy of bringing together nature and humanity. Ikebana focuses on minimalism, emphasizing shape, line, and space. In contrast, Western styles of flower arranging, which have roots in ancient Egyptian, Greek, and Roman cultures, tend to be fuller and more intensive with color. Flower arranging, in its many forms, offers a serene yet creatively stimulating hobby.

GET STARTED

1. **Learn a style.** Begin by exploring various flower arranging styles to see which resonates with you most.

2. **Gather the materials.** Some essential tools include floral shears, a vase or container, and floral foam. Select a range of flowers and foliage by considering the texture, color, and shape for your chosen style.

---

* Kirsten Judson, "Stressed Out? Try Flower Arranging," Shondaland, *April 29, 2020, https://www.shondaland.com/live/body/a32307676/stressed-out-try-flower-arranging/.*

Flower Pressing

"I got into the hobby as a way to make space and time in my grieving of family death. It's made me appreciate the small things in life that tend to go unnoticed or taken for granted—it's literally made me 'stop and smell the roses.'"

—JULIE LEE,
Artist

NATURE/OUTDOOR   COST: $

Flower pressing is the art of preserving flowers and foliage by drying and flattening them. This technique not only maintains the color and shape of botanical elements, but also transforms them into lasting keepsakes that can be used in various crafts, such as personalized stationery, wall art, or decorations. The practice of flower pressing has been around for centuries, with its origins tracing back to the ancient technique of drying plants for medicinal purposes. It became particularly popular in Victorian England as part of the era's fascination with botany. Flower pressing is a meditative hobby, allowing you to preserve the fleeting beauty of flowers in a form that lasts for years.

GET STARTED

1. **Select your flowers.** Choose fresh flowers and foliage that are not too bulky or moist. Flat-petaled flowers and leaves work best.

2. **Gather the supplies.** You will need absorbent paper like parchment or blotting paper and a heavy book or flower press.

3. **Press your flowers.** Place your flowers between two sheets of absorbent paper, then place them inside the book or flower press. Add more weight if using a book. It can take a few weeks for your flowers to fully dry. Once your flowers are pressed and dried, you can use them in various crafts like making bookmarks and greeting cards to decorating frames.

Foam Carving

"It's easy, it's fast, it's fun, and you can just let your imagination go and play and have a great time."*

—ROBERT TOLONE,
Artist

ART   COST: $$

Unlike traditional carving materials like wood or stone, foam is much softer and easier to manipulate, making it an ideal medium for both beginners and experienced artists. Foam carving grew in popularity with the advent of modern foam materials like polystyrene and polyurethane foam, but its rise can be attributed to expanding DIY culture and cosplay communities, where foam has become a staple material for creating intricate costumes and props. One of the major draws of foam carving is its accessibility. The materials and tools required are relatively inexpensive and easy to handle compared to other sculpting mediums. It's a·wonderful outlet for hobbyists who enjoy crafting and using a unique medium that's both forgiving for beginners and versatile enough for elaborate projects.

GET STARTED

1. **Gather the materials.** You'll need craft foam sheets or blocks, a cutting mat, and sharp knives or blades (like utility knives or craft knives). Hot wire cutters and glues designed for foam can also be useful.

2. **Learn the basics.** Familiarize yourself with basic foam-carving techniques like cutting, shaping, and gluing. Online tutorials, books, or local craft workshops can be excellent resources for beginners.

* *https://youtu.be/i0tYIP2vYF4?si=gjcXDM3UtLvJ84rq*

Food Rescuing

*"I love giving back to my local community by filling plates of food insecure people, rather than filling landfills."** *

—MISSY BREEN,
Volunteer

VOLUNTEERING   COST: $

Food rescuing, or food recovery, involves salvaging edible food that would otherwise be wasted and redirecting it to those in need. Food rescuing encompasses a variety of activities from collecting unsold or excess food from restaurants and supermarkets to harvesting surplus from farms and gardens. The goal is to minimize food waste and contribute to community well-being by ensuring that nutritious food reaches those who might otherwise go without. Food rescuing appeals to those who are passionate about environmental sustainability, community service, and addressing food insecurity.

GET STARTED

1. **Research local opportunities.** Look for food banks, shelters, community kitchens, or local nonprofits engaged in food rescuing. Understand their needs and how you can contribute.

2. **Start your own food rescue.** Though most areas should have existing food recovery programs that you can support, you can also start your own food rescue by establishing relationships with local supermarkets, restaurants, farms, and other food suppliers. Learn about their surplus food situations and how you can help in redistributing these resources.

---

* *Kelli Goes, "Food Rescue US Gets Fresh Food (That Would Go to Waste) to Those in Need," The Zebra, February 5, 2024, https://thezebra.org/2024/02/05/food-rescue-us-gets-fresh-food-that-would-go-to-waste-to-those-in-need/.*

Foraging

*"In an ever modernizing world, foraging provides an opportunity to recall the simplicity of survival."**

—DANIEL WOOD,
Visual Journalist

NATURE/OUTDOOR   COST: $

Foraging is the practice of searching for and harvesting wild food resources. This includes identifying and collecting edible plants, herbs, fruits, nuts, mushrooms, and even some types of seaweed. It's a way to connect with nature and gather food in its most natural and unprocessed form. Foraging has experienced a renaissance in modern times as people seek to reconnect with nature, understand the origins of their food, and explore sustainable living practices. It appeals to those who have a love for the outdoors, an interest in botany and natural history, and a desire for a hands-on approach to sourcing food.

GET STARTED

1. **Join a community.** Begin by learning from experienced foragers through guided walks, workshops, community groups, or online resources. Connecting with experienced foragers can help deepen your understanding around local regulations and which plants are safe to eat, which is critical to foraging successfully.

2. **Start local.** Familiarize yourself with a few common edible plants that are easy to identify and abundant in your area. Books and apps on local flora can be invaluable resources.

* Analise Ober and Arielle Retting. "From Cycling to Foraging, Here's What We Were Really into This Year." NPR, December 24, 2022, https://www.npr.org/2022/12/24/1145202216 /favorite-hobbies.

Fossicking

"It becomes addictive, immersing yourself in nature and uncovering the beauty of natural sapphires."

—DR. DAVID MILJAK,
Research Program Director

NATURE/OUTDOOR   COST: $$

Fossicking, also known as prospecting, involves searching for precious stones, minerals, and other geological treasures in their natural environment such as old mines, riverbeds, and natural geological formations. It's a blend of exploration, patience, and a touch of luck. The term "fossicking," meaning "rummage," likely originated from Cornish miners who immigrated to Australia during the gold rushes of the 1850s. The activity echoes similar practices around the world from panning for gold in American rivers during the nineteenth century to searching for amber along the Baltic coast. Fossicking is an enthralling adventure into the world of mineral and gem hunting, often leading enthusiasts to remote and picturesque landscapes.

GET STARTED

1. **Understand laws and regulations.** Fossicking laws vary by region. Ensure you have the necessary permissions or licenses, and always respect private property and protected areas.

2. **Learn the basics.** Take time to study the basic principles of geology and mineralogy to help you identify potential fossicking sites and the types of minerals or gems you might find there.

3. **Gather the equipment.** You'll need basic tools like a pick, shovel, sieve, and a strong container to hold your finds. A good guidebook on minerals and gems can also be invaluable.

---

* *Keirissa Lawson and David Miljak, "Chasing Beauty: Fossicking for Sapphires," CSIRO, February 18, 2024, https://www.csiro.au/en/news/All/Articles/2024/February/Sapphire-fossicking.*

Freestyling

"You can resolve emotional pain only if you confront it directly and make sense of what you feel. That's what hip hop allows for— making sense of the feelings we often hide from ourselves."

—DUKE ROLDY,
Entrepreneur

GAMES/SOCIAL   COST: $

Freestyling emerged as a key component of hip-hop culture during the 1970s in the United States. It's a form of spoken art that involves improvising lyrics and rhymes on the fly, usually to a beat. The spontaneous nature of freestyling showcases a rapper's quick thinking, creativity, and verbal dexterity. Freestyling within the context of hip hop became a way for individuals to express themselves and address social issues in a creatively powerful manner. Freestyling as a hobby provides a unique opportunity to sharpen and share one's personal wit and ingenuity, attracting anyone with a love for language and wordplay.

GET STARTED

1. **Absorb the culture.** Immerse yourself in hip-hop music and culture. Listen to skilled freestylers to understand different styles and the nuances of rhythm and rhyme.

2. **Develop your improvisational skills.** Practice improvising raps on a variety of topics. Start by picking random subjects or use freestyle prompts. The key is to let go of the fear of making mistakes and to focus on the flow of words.

3. **Engage in freestyle sessions.** Observe or participate in freestyle sessions, battles, or cyphers. Engaging with other freestylers can provide inspiration, feedback, and a sense of community.

Fursuiting

"Being able to portray a character has proven to be a fantastic outlet and form of self-expression that I can share with the public."

—KIRE,
Student Pilot

GAMES/SOCIAL   COST: $$$

Fursuiting is an expressive hobby deeply rooted in the furry fandom, a community where individuals create and embody anthropomorphic animal characters known as fursonas. Fursonas allow participants, commonly referred to as "furries," to explore various aspects of identity and creativity in a highly personalized way. Many hobbyists craft their fursuits by hand—full-body costumes designed to bring their fursonas to life. Emerging in the 1980s in the United States, fursuiting and the furry fandom evolved from the intersection of science fiction and fantasy fandoms, animation, and comic book cultures. It grew organically as a distinct subculture with its own conventions, art, and social gatherings. Distinct from general cosplay, fursuiting is characterized by its emphasis on original characters.

GET STARTED

1. **Participate in the furry culture.** Begin by connecting with the furry community online and attending furry conventions and local meetups. This will offer insight into the culture and help build meaningful connections.

2. **Create a fursona.** Develop your own unique anthropomorphic character. Consider attributes like appearance, traits, and backstory, which will inspire your costume design.

3. **Use your crafting skills or commission a suit.** Learning about costume construction is part of the journey. Many furries find joy and fulfillment in the creative process of bringing their original fursonas to life.

Galanthomania

"I can think of few more pleasurable gardening activities than searching out their noses as they erupt from the ground. There can be no better sign that the days are getting longer." *

—ANDY BYFIELD,
Nonprofit Founder

NATURE/OUTDOOR   COST: $

Galanthomania centers around the passion for collecting and cultivating snowdrops, known scientifically as *galanthus*. Snowdrops are among the first flowers to bloom at the end of winter between late January and early March, and herein lies the essence of Galanthomania: the joy of observing and nurturing harbingers of spring. The hobby involves seeking out, growing, and sometimes trading rare and diverse varieties of snowdrops. Primarily a seasonal hobby for year-round gardeners and nature enthusiasts, Galanthomania is defined by a sense of anticipation as each new variety blooms, signaling the end of winter and the promise of spring.

GET STARTED

1. **Learn about snowdrops.** Study the different species and varieties of snowdrops. They are native to regions in Europe and the Middle East but are also cultivated in North America and other regions that experience cold winters.

2. **Join a community.** Connect with other Galanthophiles through clubs, online forums, and garden societies. These communities can offer trading opportunities and the chance to participate in snowdrop events like garden shows and snowdrop walks.

---

* Andy Byfield, "Why Do Snowdrops Set My Pulse Racing?," The Guardian, *January 22, 2013,* https://www.theguardian.com/lifeandstyle/gardening-blog/2013/jan/22/snowdrops-galanthus.

Gelatin Art

"They're bodily and shuddery and sloppy and bouncy, but they're also crystalline and perfect. And it's the way they hold opposites within their texture that is so appealing to us."

—FREDDIE MASON,
Creative Strategist

FOOD   COST: $

Gelatin art, or Jell-O art, transforms a clear gelatin base into a canvas of colorful and intricate designs that include flowers, abstract patterns, and even detailed landscapes. Gelatin art is characterized by its translucent texture and three-dimensional effect, creating a unique perception of depth and realism. It is created by using scalpels and culinary syringes to inject colored gelatin into a clear base. The origins of gelatin art can be traced back to the nineteenth century with its roots in traditional aspic and jelly-making techniques used in European fine dining. The modern resurgence of gelatin art started to gain popularity in Mexico and Eastern Europe in the late twentieth century, seen as both a therapeutic and challenging blend of culinary skill and creative expression.

GET STARTED

1. **Learn gelatin.** Start by understanding the fundamentals of gelatin preparation. Experiment with basic shapes and colors. Using Jell-O packets can be an easy way to start.

2. **Gather the materials.** Essential tools include syringes, needles of various sizes for injecting the colored gelatin, and molds for shaping the base. Though gelatin art is about creating patterns into a clear base, you can also start by learning how to layer and embed objects into Jell-O.

* *Elyssa Goodman, "Jell-O Is Cool Again—This Time as Edible Art," Bustle, December 27, 2022. https://www.bustle.com/life/jello-art.*

Genealogy Mapping

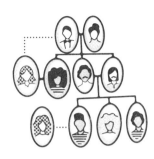

"I love the wonder and mystery of searching for my ancestors who have passed and discovering the stories of their lives, which continue to flow through my own veins."

—RICK TERRIEN,
Entrepreneur

INTROSPECTIVE   COST: $

Genealogy mapping brings family histories to life with visual maps that illustrate one's ancestral origins, migrations, and connections. By placing ancestors within specific geographic contexts, it provides a clearer understanding of their journeys, experiences, and the historical events that might have influenced their lives. The practice of tracing family history is ancient, but the specific integration of mapping into genealogy gained traction with the advent of digital tools and online databases. This hobby suits those with an interest in history, geography, and storytelling. It's particularly rewarding for individuals who enjoy detective-like research, piecing together clues from the past to form a cohesive narrative.

GET STARTED

1. **Emotionally prepare.** Digging into personal history can be both fascinating and emotional. Consider checking in with friends, family, or a professional counselor for support.

2. **Gather information.** Start by compiling as much information as you can about your ancestors. If you don't have access to family lineage information, DNA testing services like 23andMe or AncestryDNA can help. This is your map, so feel free to be creative. You can even make a map of your chosen family.

3. **Utilize mapping tools.** You can make a map by hand or use digital tools to help. Some common online tools include MyHeritage, Family Historian, or Google Earth and Google Maps.

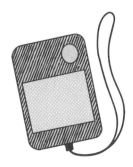

Geocaching

"I discovered new places, geocaches I never knew existed in familiar places, and a community of fellow treasure-hunters all around me."

—R. BUTINA,
Graphic Design Student

NATURE/OUTDOOR   COST: $

Geocaching is an outdoor recreational activity where participants use GPS devices or smartphone apps to locate hidden containers, known as geocaches, at specific coordinates all around the world. The hobby originated in May 2000 in the United States with the first documented placement of a GPS-located cache created by Dave Ulmer, a computer consultant. He hid a container in the woods of Oregon and posted the coordinates online. The concept quickly caught on, evolving into the global game of geocaching we know today. Geocaching combines elements of hiking, puzzle-solving, and exploration. The activity can be tailored to various levels of physical ability and interest from easy-to-find urban caches to more challenging rural locations.

GET STARTED

1. **Learn to navigate.** First, familiarize yourself with a chosen GPS device or geocaching app on your smartphone. Some geocachers enjoy developing traditional orienteering skills by using a compasses and physical maps.

2. **Create an account.** Sign up for a free account on a geocaching website or app. This will give you access to the coordinates of geocaches around the world.

3. **Start local and log your find.** Start with a cache that has a lower difficulty rating and is close to your location. Look for hints or logs from previous finders to help you, and keep track of your progress by signing the logbook or exchanging trinkets.

Ghost Hunting

"I had multiple paranormal encounters that shook me but also led me to start researching more. I love listening to the stories of others who went through something like I did and letting them know they aren't alone."

—ADAM CHIZMAR,
Animation Business Owner

GAMES/SOCIAL   COST: $

Ghost hunting involves investigating locations reported to be haunted by spirits or paranormal phenomena. Participants, often armed with various equipment, seek to gather evidence of ghostly presences, such as unexplained sounds, visual anomalies, or temperature changes. Figures like Harry Price in the early twentieth century were pivotal in popularizing the pursuit of paranormal investigation using scientific methods and equipment like infrared photography and fingerprinting kits. Modern ghost hunting often blends these scientific approaches with a more sensationalized quest for supernatural encounters influenced by pop culture and media.

GET STARTED

1. **Prioritize safety and respect**. Always prioritize safety, especially when exploring unfamiliar locations. Research ethical practices and approach this hobby with respect for the sites and for any potential spirits you encounter.

2. **Choose a location**. Start with local haunts or well-known paranormal sites. Learn about the history of the location and any reported ghost sightings or stories associated with it.

3. **Acquire the equipment.** A flashlight, camera, voice recorder, and EMF (electromagnetic field) detector can be helpful for detecting potential paranormal activity and documenting experiences.

Gilding

*"I incorporate gold into my art because it allows me to blend history with modern art pieces."**

—BARBARA BALDWIN,
Retired

ART   COST: $$

Gilding, the art of applying thin layers of gold leaf or gold paint to surfaces, is a craft that transforms ordinary objects into striking pieces imbued with luminosity and elegance. The roots of gilding trace back to ancient civilizations, with examples found in Egyptian tombs, Byzantine icons, and Chinese lacquerware. Practitioners of gilding meticulously apply gold to various materials—including wood, metal, glass, and even paper—creating works that range from decorative art pieces to ornate furniture. Gilding requires patience, precision, and a gentle hand, making it well-suited for individuals who enjoy meticulous crafts and have an appreciation for classic aesthetics.

GET STARTED

1. **Learn the basics.** There are different methods of gilding, each offering a unique aesthetic and learning experience. Oil gilding and acrylic gilding are forgiving methods suggested for beginners.

2. **Gather the supplies.** You'll need basic supplies like gold leaf sheets, gilding adhesive, a soft brush, and a gilder's tip for picking up and laying the gold leaf. Be sure to prepare a clean, dust-free workspace when you're ready to start.

---

* Julianna Ems, "Edgemere Resident Celebrates National Hobby Month with Gold Leaf Artwork," Leading Age Texas, January 31, 2024, https://www.leadingagetexas.org/news/663852/Edgemere-resident-celebrates-National-Hobby-Month-with-Gold-Leaf-Artwork-.htm.

Gingerbread House Construction

"I was channel surfing and on the Food Channel saw the national gingerbread competition held in Asheville. I told myself, 'I can do that.'" *

—ANN BAILEY,
Artist

FOOD   COST: $$

Gingerbread house construction involves designing, baking, and decorating edible houses made from gingerbread dough. The practice of making gingerbread houses became popular in Germany during the sixteenth century. The tradition is thought to have been inspired by "Hansel and Gretel," the famous fairy tale by the Brothers Grimm in which two children come across a house made entirely of treats deep in the forest. Though predominantly a seasonal craft, many enthusiasts enjoy building gingerbread constructions year-round.

GET STARTED

1. **Master recipes.** The recipe you choose should be based on whether you want to consume your piece or leave it out for display. Recipes with a high flour content are great for providing sturdiness and structure to your pieces. Learn recipes for royal icing to use as adhesive for your house. You can also use melted chocolate or candy melts.

2. **Design your house.** Sketch out your house or use a template available in books or online. Rehearsing your design with cardboard or foam can help ensure that your baked pieces will fit together.

3. **Learn ways to display.** Keep your piece away from humidity, secure it to a stable base, and use a sealant spray.

* Nancy Pardue, "Sweet Ambition," Cary Magazine, October 28, 2015, https://www.carymagazine.com/features/sweet-ambition/.

Glassblowing

"Well, it's hot, first of all. Real hot. From the start, you just see molten glass. As you go through the process, you start to see something you created. It's so awesome and unique."*

—MATTHEW JUDON,
American Football Player

ART   COST: $$

Picture a glassblower at the furnace, a glowing, honey-like blob of glass at the end of their pipe. They skillfully blow air into the pipe while turning and shaping the malleable glass, transforming it into stunning vessels, sculptures, or decorative items. The roots of glassblowing stretch back to the first century BCE, likely originating in the regions of Syria and Palestine. As the art spread throughout the Roman Empire, glassware flourished in both commonplace and artistic contexts. Learning to shape a fluid, dynamic material into a solid form is as challenging as it is captivating and offers a fiery allure for hobbyists who enjoy hands-on creative activities and mastering a unique skill.

GET STARTED

1. **Participate in a workshop.** Glassblowing is typically taught by an experienced glassblower in a specialized space equipped with furnaces and related tools and materials. Search for glassblowing studios in your area; many offer introductory courses and workshops that teach basic techniques and safety protocols.

2. **Join a community.** Stay connected with other glassblowers or a local glass art community who can provide support, inspiration, and opportunities to learn and share techniques and ideas.

---

* Dan Roche, *"Matthew Judon Finds a New Passion—Glass Blowing,"* CBS News, July 24, 2023, https://www.cbsnews.com/boston/news/matthew-judon-patriots-gather-glass-blowing-studio-providence-nfl-training-camp-retire-in-new-england/.

Go-Karting

"Karting helps a lot in building self-confidence; you become smarter and more attentive at the same time, you temper your character." *

—**ECATERINA MOROSEVICI**,
Student

COMPETITIVE   **COST: $$**

Go-karting is an exhilarating motorsport where participants race in small, low-slung vehicles on a track. Unlike more complex motorsports, go-karts are simple: four wheels, an engine, a steering wheel, and basic controls. Art Ingels, often hailed as the father of go-karting, built the first kart in 1956. Using a simple frame and a lawnmower engine, Ingels crafted a vehicle that sparked a worldwide phenomenon, leading to the formation of organized races and karting associations. Go-karting stands apart from other motorsports due to its accessibility and focus on grassroots racing. It offers an adrenaline rush and a taste of motorsport without the intimidating complexity and expense of professional racing.

GET STARTED

1. **Visit a local track.** The best place to try out go-karting is by visiting a local track that offers rental karts and introductory sessions. Most charge by number of races for a day of fun, but some offer monthly memberships.

2. **Join a club or league.** If available in your area, consider joining a go-karting club where you can gain valuable insights into driving techniques and kart maintenance. Leagues may require higher skill levels but will introduce you to the competitive side of go-kart racing.

---

* *"Go-Karting Is an Art of Resilience That Brings Together Enthusiasts from Both Banks of the Nistru River,"* UNDP, *February 13, 2024, https://www.undp.org/moldova/stories/go -karting-art-resilience-brings-together-enthusiasts-both-banks-nistru-river.*

Golfing

"I'm not good at golf, but I like to golf. Someday, I want to be good at golf. That's something I'd like to do." *

—DAN LANNING,
American Football Coach

PHYSICAL FITNESS   COST: $$

Golfing is a game of precision, patience, and strategy. The objective of this sport is to hit a small ball with a club into a series of holes on a large course in as few strokes as possible. Unlike many sports, golf is not confined by a standardized playing area; every golf course has its own unique challenges, from sand traps to water hazards. The origins of golf are widely debated, but the modern game as we know it was shaped in Scotland during the Middle Ages. By the fifteenth century, the game had become so popular in Scotland that it was temporarily banned because it was a distraction from military training.

GET STARTED

1. **Take lessons.** There are a lot of nuances to golf culture and technique. Group clinics can be a cost-effective way to learn the game and build a solid foundation in the basics of grip, stance, swing, and etiquette.

2. **Start at a driving range.** A driving range is a facility dedicated solely to the practice of swinging. It's a great place to start because you can rent equipment and hit numerous balls without the pressure of playing a full round of golf, which can usually take a few hours.

---

*   Kaiden Smith, *"Dan Lanning Identifies Golf as a Hobby He Would Like to Be Good At,"* Oregon Ducks, *October 12, 2023, https://www.on3.com/college/oregon-ducks/news/oregon-ducks -head-coach-dan-lanning-reveals-desire-to-improve-golf-game-team-impact/.*

Graffiti Art

"Graffiti is one of the few tools you have if you have almost nothing. And even if you don't come up with a picture to cure world poverty you can make someone smile while they're having a piss."

—BANKSY,
Artist

ART   COST: $$

Graffiti art is the practice of creating visual artwork in public locations, usually with spray paint and markers on walls and other surfaces. It's an art form that allows for raw expression, often characterized by its bold colors, dynamic lettering, and sometimes controversial messages. While its legality is debated, many cities have designated spaces for this art form, recognizing its cultural significance. The contemporary style of graffiti art most recognized today began to take shape in the 1960s and 1970s in New York City, primarily on subway trains and later spreading to city walls. It often serves as a voice for the voiceless, a form of social and political commentary, and an assertion of identity.

GET STARTED

1. **Know the laws.** It's important to know where you can legally create graffiti art. Look for legal walls or art spaces specifically designed for this purpose.

2. **Learn the culture.** Understand the various techniques and terminologies like tagging, bombing, and piecing. Always show respect for the community and other artists. Graffiti art is as much about the unwritten rules of the street as it is about creativity.

3. **Gather the materials.** Invest in quality spray paints, markers, and nozzles. Different caps produce different spray patterns, allowing for variation in line work and fill-ins. Always use a mask or respirator and gloves when painting. Eye protection is also advisable.

Gymnastics

"I do improvised dances including gymnastics with background music, doing acrobatics. I really enjoy when I do it; it frees me from stress. I relax without thinking about what to do."*

—ANGELY ALBARRAN,
Nurse

PHYSICAL FITNESS   COST: $$

Gymnastics encompasses a wide range of activities, including floor exercises and apparatus work like the rings, bars, and beam. The sport is distinguished by its unique combination of dynamic and static skills, dance elements, and acrobatics. Gymnastics was included in the first modern Olympic Games in 1896. Friedrich Ludwig Jahn (1778–1852), known as the father of modern gymnastics, played a pivotal role in its development, establishing several key apparatuses still in use today. Gymnastics offers a fulfilling path to physical fitness and artistic expression, representing the pinnacle of what the human body can achieve with dedication and practice.

GET STARTED

1. **Find a class.** The availability of adult gymnastics classes has been increasing, part of a growing trend of adults participating in activities previously considered primarily for younger individuals. Take beginner's lessons to learn basic skills like rolls, handstands, and cartwheels.

2. **Condition your body.** Gymnastics requires strength, flexibility, and endurance. Cross-train by practicing a fitness regimen that helps to build these attributes. Pilates, yoga, and bodyweight training are great complements to gymnastics training.

---

*   *https://ecency.com/hive-168869/@angely11c3/gymnastics-my-favorite-hobby*

Ham Radio

"I like working with a base level technology and learning about the mechanics of different transmission types and frequency ranges."

—HANK BUTINA,
Student

TECH   COST: $$$

Amateur or ham radio is the use of radio frequencies to communicate for noncommercial purposes. The origin of the name "ham radio" likely came from professional telegraphers in the late nineteenth century using "ham" pejoratively to describe amateur operators. Despite the prejudice, hams played significant roles during World War I and World War II by assisting in emergency communications and espionage. An educational hobby perfect for those interested in the confluence of tech, communication, and electronics, modern-day hobbyists enjoy the ability to connect with others globally and experiment with both the hardware and different modes of communication involved in operating a ham radio.

GET STARTED

1. **Get a license.** Licensing requirements for amateur radio vary by country, with different class levels determining your bandwidth (meaning local versus international) and depth of knowledge and responsibilities.

2. **Choose your equipment.** Beginners typically start with a hand-held transceiver, but there are a variety of communication modes to explore that include voice, digital, and Morse code. Depending on which you're most interested in, the type of equipment you'll want to invest in will differ.

3. **Join a community.** Ham radio is all about connection, so joining a club of hobbyists will significantly help you progress on your journey.

Handbell Choir

"A lot of people traditionally think of [handbell music] as exclusive to churches, but in our spring concert last year, we played Taylor Swift, we played Imagine Dragons, we played La La Land. We're modernizing handbells." *

—AVA SOLIS,
Student

MUSIC   COST: $$$

Handbell choir, or campanology, is the harmonious collaboration of individuals each holding a handbell and creating a rich tapestry of melodies and harmonies together. Each ringer is typically responsible for a specific set of notes and works in concert with the group to perform music ranging from classical compositions to modern arrangements. The result is a symphony of bells, each contributing their unique timbre to the collective performance. The origin of handbell ringing is often traced back to seventeenth-century England, where bell ringers in churches would practice with handbells before performing with the larger tower bells. The allure of a handbell choir lies in its communal spirit and the enchanting, crystalline sound produced. It's a hobby that offers both a musical challenge and the opportunity for social interaction.

GET STARTED

1. **Seek out a local choir.** Joining an established group is a great way to learn. Many communities, schools, and churches host handbell choirs and welcome new members.

2. **Learn the basics.** Learn the fundamental techniques of handbell ringing, such as the proper way to hold the bell, the basic ring, and the damping technique to stop the sound.

*   Haley Zimmerman, "How the College's Handbell Choir 'Modernizes the Handbell,'" The Williams Record, November 8, 2023, https://williamsrecord.com/465120/features/how-the -colleges-handbell-choir-modernizes-the-handbell/.

Heels Dance

"My heels journey has been one of pushing my comfort zone—physically, mentally, and spiritually—through movement, in safe spaces, to learn tools to apply in the real world."

—OLIVIA M. RYAN,
Licensed Massage Therapist

PHYSICAL FITNESS   **COST: $$$**

Heels dance combines the poise of upright postures with the edgy dynamics of hip hop and jazz. It is characterized by a focus on femininity, empowerment, and a bold attitude, as dancers strut and gyrate to the rhythm, exuding confidence and embracing their sensuality. The distinctive feature, as the name suggests, is that the dance is performed in high-heeled shoes, which adds an element of challenge and a distinctive aesthetic to the movements. Heels dance has gained prominence over the last few decades, evolving from the influence of commercial dance and the rise of pop culture icons who often perform in heels. What draws people to heels dance is its liberating and expressive nature. It is for those who wish to nurture their self-confidence and embrace a powerful aspect of their persona.

GET STARTED

1. **Choose your heels and attire.** Comfortable and supportive high heels are a must. Start with a lower, thicker heel and work your way up to higher, thinner heels as you become more comfortable. Since floorwork is often incorporated in heels dance, investing in knee pads can be helpful. Prioritize comfort when it comes to your attire but choose something that makes you feel sexy and boosts your confidence.

2. **Take a class.** Look for dance studios that offer heels dance classes. These classes are tailored for dancing in heels and will provide a safe environment to learn the basics.

Herbalism

"By incorporating homemade blends of teas, tinctures, balms, and vapors into my life, I feel part of an ancient friendship between plants and people that nourishes and heals us all."

—CHRIS LIPPERT,
Experience Designer

EDUCATIONAL   COST: $

Herbalism is the art and science of using plants for their therapeutic properties. It's a practice as ancient as humanity itself—from the healing traditions of Ayurveda in India to the herbals of traditional Chinese medicine—where knowledge of the medicinal uses of herbs has been passed down through generations. Herbalists cultivate, collect, study, and prepare plant-based remedies, ranging from simple teas and tinctures to complex salves and supplements. It appeals to those who are self-directed learners, who have a passion for plants and their uses, and who seek a more naturalistic approach to health care.

GET STARTED

1. **Educate yourself.** Start with reputable books or courses on herbalism to understand the basics of plant properties, safety, and remedy preparation.

2. **Begin an herb garden.** Growing your own herbs is a fulfilling way to connect with the practice. Start with easy-to-grow varieties like mint, basil, or chamomile.

3. **Harvest and experiment.** Learn when and how to harvest different parts of plants. Begin with simple preparations like infusions (teas) or decoctions (simmered herbs).

4. **Join a community.** Connect with other herbalists through online forums, local clubs, or classes where you can share knowledge, ask questions, and find support.

Hikaru Dorodango

*"It is truly an otherworldly artifact from this world. I would describe the process of crafting a hiraku dorodango as mindless mindfulness."**

—JOSH BURKER,
Entrepreneur

ART   COST: $

Hikaru dorodango, a term that translates to "radiant mud dumpling," is a traditional Japanese craft that turns ordinary soil into a polished, lustrous orb through patience and meticulous care. It begins with shaping mud by hand into a sphere, then continually coating it with fine soil and polishing the form until it gleams. The practice, which has roots in the playground pastimes of Japanese children, has evolved into a form of meditative art that reflects the *wabi-sabi* aesthetic—finding beauty in simplicity and impermanence. Hikaru dorodango offers a tactile connection to the Earth element and stands as an antidote to haste, inviting practitioners to slow down and savor the satisfaction of crafting something truly unique with their own hands.

GET STARTED

1. **Gather the materials.** All you need is some dirt, water, and a flat surface. Choose a dirt type that has a mix of sand and clay for cohesion.

2. **Form the ball.** Mix the dirt and water together to form a malleable mud. Shape it into a sphere with your hands, adding more soil as needed to maintain its shape and density.

3. **Dry and polish.** Allow the ball to dry slightly, then begin the polishing process by dusting it with fine, dry soil. This step is repeated many times to achieve the characteristic shine.

---

* *Josh Burker, "Hikaru Dorodango," Josh Burker's Blog of Musings, June 15, 2016, http://joshburker.blogspot.com/2016/06/hiraku-dorodango.html.*

Hiking

"Always loved walking through the forest as a kid. Now being able to travel and hike everywhere from Washington to Peru, I can say it's such a refreshing way to experience a new place."

—PATRICIA HAFLEY,
Project Manager

PHYSICAL FITNESS   COST: $

Hiking is the leisurely, paced exploration of landscapes ranging from undulating countryside to mountainous terrain. Hiking for pleasure and exploration gained popularity in the eighteenth century with the Romantic movement. It was during this period that natural scenery became appreciated for its aesthetic and spiritual value, leading more people to seek out the experience of wandering through the wilderness. The allure of hiking lies in its simplicity and the manifold experiences it offers. The hobby calls out to those who feel the pull of the outdoors, find tranquility in the rustle of leaves, and revel in the quiet challenge of a long climb. It's a natural fit for those who seek respite from the clamor of urban life and yearn to disconnect and immerse themselves in the serenity of the natural world.

GET STARTED

1. **Research and equip yourself.** Start by researching local hiking trails suitable for your fitness level. Equip yourself with a good pair of hiking shoes, appropriate clothing for the weather, and a backpack with essentials like water, snacks, and a first-aid kit. Always let someone know where you're going and when you expect to return.

2. **Leave no trace.** Embrace the principles of outdoor ethics by minimizing your impact on the environment. Stay on trails, pack out what you pack in, and respect wildlife and other hikers.

Historical Reenactment

"After attending Abraham Lincoln's 200th birthday celebration, I became enthralled with the idea of impersonating this great man."

—DUKE THOMPSON,
Music School President

GAMES/SOCIAL   COST: $$

Historical reenactment is the act of recreating events from the past as accurately as possible, often by dressing in period costumes, using era-appropriate tools and technology, and following the social customs of the time. Participants, known as reenactors, might simulate famous battles, everyday life, or pivotal historical moments, aiming to bring history to life in a tangible, experiential way. The origins of historical reenactment as a hobby are rooted in the commemoration of military events. One of the most significant early reenactments was the staging of the Battle of the Nations at Leipzig in 1813 to celebrate its centennial. Historical reenactment is a hobby well-suited to people who enjoy acting and storytelling, and those who appreciate the artistry involved in replicating period attire and artifacts.

GET STARTED

1. **Choose an era.** Select a time period that fascinates you. Research the significant events and daily life of the era to find a focus for your reenactment.

2. **Join a group.** Look for local reenactment societies or groups that share your interest. They can offer resources, support, and events where you can participate.

3. **Acquire proper attire.** Start assembling your costume and any paraphernalia you might need. This can be a gradual process, and many reenactors take pride in crafting their own attire and accessories.

Hitting Mung

"I wanted to be able to press the stop button and take a moment for myself, but I feel like I constantly have to do something. In this space, the rule is that I must do nothing." *

—JAE-HWAN JUNG,
Skincare Brand Owner

INTROSPECTIVE   COST: $

The Korean concept of *mung* is often described in the context of *mung-ttaerigi*, literally translating to "hitting mung," which means "to space out" or "to stare blankly." Hitting mung has surged in South Korea as a wellness practice to counter the high-pressure, fast-paced lifestyle that characterizes much of its modern society. To hit mung is to mentally pause and achieve an idle state. It's a momentary disengagement from the world, often accompanied by a blank facial expression, where one's gaze is fixed on nothing. Distinct from daydreaming, hitting mung centers in a lack of thought rather than letting the mind wander in imagination.

GET STARTED

1. **Decide on a place.** Set aside time and space to be completely undisturbed. The concept of hitting mung can be reached through a repetitive task like washing dishes, but it's really about doing nothing, like sitting on a park bench or staring out a window.

2. **Release guilt.** Living in cultures where productivity is so highly valued, there can be a tendency to feel guilty about being blank and doing nothing. Hitting mung is not laziness or wasted time, but practiced as an essential component of a healthy mental life.

* *Michelle Ye Hee Lee, "'Hitting Mung': In Stressed-Out South Korea, People Are Paying to Stare at Clouds and Trees," The Washington Post, November 25, 2021, https://www .washingtonpost.com/world/2021/11/25/korea-stress-relax-pandemic/.*

Hobbyhorsing

*"The normal things, that normal girls like,
they don't feel like my things."* *

—FANNY OIKARINEN,
Student

GAMES/SOCIAL   COST: $

Hobbyhorsing is a whimsical and imaginative sport that simulates the elegance of equestrian events, such as dressage and show jumping, but instead of riding live horses, participants compete with hobbyhorses—a crafted horse's head attached to a stick. Finland has seen a surge in the popularity of hobbyhorsing after gaining wider attention through social media and a 2017 documentary titled *Hobbyhorse Revolution.* This film not only highlighted the skill and dedication involved in the sport but also the sense of empowerment and community it fosters among its participants. Hobbyhorsing offers a unique blend of fantasy and athleticism that harks back to the innocent joy of childhood games, yet stands firmly in the arena of adult hobbies.

GET STARTED

1. **Choose your horse.** You can purchase a premade hobbyhorse, but crafting one personal to you is part of this hobby's enjoyment. The head can be sewn from fabric or carved from wood, adorned as elaborately as you wish, and mounted on a stick with the appropriate length for your height.

2. **Learn about equestrian arts.** Study the basics of equestrian movement and terminology. Study the gaits, jumps, and dressage movements to accurately simulate them.

* *Ellen Barry, "Finland's Hobbyhorse Girls, Once a Secret Society, Now Prance in Public,"*
The New York Times, *April 21, 2019, https://www.nytimes.com/2019/04/21/world/europe
/finland-hobbyhorse-girls.html.*

Hockey

"Every day is a great day for hockey."

—MARIO LEMIEUX,
Former NHL Player and Member of
the NHL Hall of Fame

PHYSICAL FITNESS   **COST: $$$**

Hockey is a high-energy team sport where two teams vie to score goals by hitting a small puck or ball with a stick. There are many different variants of the sport, but the two main popular styles are played on ice or a field. On ice, players don skates, adding an exhilarating layer of speed and grace to the game. In field hockey, players maneuver on grass or turf, showcasing strategic play and agility. Both sports have ancient roots, with variations played across the globe for centuries. Modern ice hockey crystallized in Canada in the late 1800s, while field hockey's contemporary rules were formalized in England around the same time. Hockey's major draws are its pace, teamwork, and the sheer thrill of play. It's a hobby that can challenge the body and engage the mind, offering a unique blend of competitive excitement and community belonging.

GET STARTED

1. **Choose a style.** Decide between ice hockey or field hockey. Each has its own charm and challenges.

2. **Equip yourself.** For ice hockey, essential equipment includes skates, a helmet, padding, and a stick. For field hockey, you'll need a stick, protective gear, and suitable footwear.

3. **Learn the basics and join games.** Mastering the foundational skills of skating (for ice hockey), stickhandling, passing, and shooting will set you up for success. Find a local league or pickup group to start playing. There's no better way to improve and enjoy the sport than by being part of a team.

Home Café

"I love home café videos—watching and making them. I know I still have to improve, but it's such a fun journey!" *

—AQALILI AZIZAN,
Blogger

FOOD   COST: $$

The concept of a home café transcends the traditional visit to a local coffee shop, bringing the essence and ambiance of a café into the home. It's an art form where coffee and tea making intertwine with home decor. The hobby of home café grew prominent in South Korea due to the country's deep appreciation for café culture and its innovative beverage trends, including the viral sensation of dalgona coffee—a whipped coffee concoction made by vigorously mixing instant coffee with sugar and water. Dalgona coffee became emblematic of the home café movement during social distancing periods of the COVID-19 pandemic, representing a shift toward inventive home-based hobbies.

GET STARTED

1. **Gather the essentials.** Invest in a reliable coffee or tea maker, a frother, a selection of your favorite coffee beans or tea leaves, and glassware and utensils.

2. **Learn drink recipes and techniques.** Whether it's mastering the pour-over technique or the art of latte frothing, adding different recipes and skills to your arsenal is part of the joy of this hobby.

3. **Design your space.** Create a nook with elements of your favorite café. This could mean adding indoor plants, selecting themed coasters, or displaying coffee-table books. Incorporate elements that resonate with your style to create an atmosphere that complements the sensory experience of making coffee and tea.

*   *https://www.aqasnote.com/banana-smoothie-recipe/*

Horseback Riding

*"Horses are the most wonderful animals and so much of riding is about your mutual respect and connection to them. Despite their size, they are kind and therapeutic to be around."** *

—AOIFE CAFFREY,
Wedding and Event Planner

NATURE/OUTDOOR   COST: $$$

The origins of horseback riding can be traced back over four thousand years to Central Asia. Horseback riding has evolved from a survival skill to an element of warfare, a tool for agriculture, a sport, and finally a cherished hobby. Horseback riding encompasses both the control and guiding of a horse as well as the art of maintaining balance and harmony with the animal's movements. It's an activity characterized by the profound connection between rider and steed, offering a unique blend of sport, art, and companionship. Horseback riding is a journey that rewards the rider with both moments of exhilaration and tranquility.

GET STARTED

1. **Take lessons.** Begin with lessons at a reputable stable to learn the basics of horse care, handling, and riding technique under the guidance of experienced instructors.

2. **Acquire appropriate attire.** Invest in the proper attire and equipment for safety and comfort like a well-fitting helmet, riding boots, and fitted clothing.

3. **Get to know horses.** Spend time with horses outside of riding to understand their behavior and build trust, which is just as critical as mastering the reins.

* Jo Linehan, "Why I Love . . . Horse Riding," The Irish Times, October 13, 2018, https://www.irishtimes.com/life-and-style/health-family/fitness/why-i-love-horse-riding-1.3651736.

Hula Hooping

"It's a fun, stimulating activity that temporarily takes my mind off life's stresses." *

—ZAINAB KWAW-SWANZY,
Mathematician and Product Manager

PHYSICAL FITNESS   **COST: $**

Hula hooping, also known as hooping, is a dynamic activity where an individual twirls a hoop around their waist, limbs, or neck. The modern incarnation of the hobby incorporates elements of dance, acrobatics, and rhythmic gymnastics to form an expressive and often mesmerizing art form. The modern hula hoop was popularized in the 1950s by Richard Knerr and Arthur "Spud" Melin, founders of the Wham-O toy company. Knerr and Melin trademarked the name "hula hoop" due to the hoop's hip-swinging action that they believed resembled the Hawaiian hula dance. Hooping is a playful fusion of fitness and self-expression well-suited for those who enjoy dance, movement, and the carefree spirit of youth.

GET STARTED

1. **Choose a hoop.** Larger, heavier hoops rotate more slowly and are ideal for novices, while smaller, lighter hoops require more skill and speed.

2. **Master the basics.** Begin with waist hooping, focusing on maintaining a rhythmic rocking motion. As you gain confidence, you can experiment with moving the hoop up and down your torso and other body parts.

---

* *https://gal-dem.com/crochet-pickles-hula-hooping-are-we-keeping-up-the-lockdown-hobbies-once-were-allowed-outside/*

Hunting

"I am very fond of hunting, and there are few sensations I prefer to that of galloping over these rolling limitless prairies, with rifle in hand, or winding my way among the barren, fantastic and grimly picturesque deserts of the so-called Bad Lands . . ."

—THEODORE ROOSEVELT,
Twenty-sixth President of the United States

`NATURE/OUTDOOR`   `COST: $$$`

Hunting is an intricate dance between humans and nature, requiring patience, knowledge of the wilderness, and respect for the environment and wildlife. While it originated out of necessity and is deeply rooted in human history, controversy surrounding hunting is multifaceted, touching on moral, ecological, and economic concerns. Modern hunting is regulated with laws to ensure sustainable practices, but dialogue continues as societies seek to balance the interests of hunters, wildlife conservation, and wildlife protection advocates. Some use hunting to connect with a primal aspect of human nature, while others use it to play an active role in wildlife management and habitat preservation.

GET STARTED

1. **Educate yourself.** Learn local laws and regulations. Oftentimes you will need to register and obtain a license. Complete a hunter education course to learn about safety, responsibilities, conservation, and other ethical principles to guide you.

2. **Acquire the appropriate gear.** Depending on the type of hunting you choose (that is, bow or rifle), the required gear will vary. However, the basics include suitable clothing, weaponry, and navigation tools.

3. **Seek mentors.** Experienced hunters can provide invaluable knowledge and insight that only comes from years of practice.

Hydroponics

*"Seed. Germinate. Pollenate. Love.
That's all it takes."**

—JOSEPH R. CERVANTES, SR.,
Life Safety Expert

NATURE/OUTDOOR   COST: $$$

Hydroponics, which roots itself in the Greek words *hydro* for "water" and *ponos* for "labor," is a method of growing plants without soil. Though the term was coined by Dr. William Frederick Gericke of the University of California in 1929, its lineage can be traced back to the fabled Hanging Gardens of Babylon and the Floating Gardens of the Aztecs. Hydroponics systems work by providing plants the nutrients they need from a water-based solution, allowing them to grow in spaces where traditional agriculture might falter. Urban dwellers are drawn to it for its space efficiency, making fresh produce available in the smallest of apartments.

GET STARTED

1. **Research first.** There are many different types of hydroponics systems, from simple countertop kits to more complex setups. Take time to research and understand the basics of nutrient solutions, lighting, and pH balance.

2. **Start small.** Begin with a basic system with a single plant type like herbs or lettuce. A smaller scale can help you learn the ropes without becoming overwhelmed.

3. **Monitor and maintain.** Regularly check your plants for growth, health, and nutrient levels. Unlike traditional soil gardening, precision is key to plant vitality in hydroponics.

---

*   *https://www.linkedin.com/posts/josephrcervantessr_seed-germinate-pollenate-love-thats
-activity-7109178484299624449-dSDE/*

Ice Sculpting

"It's something that I can get kind of really engaged in, I can spend a couple hours on it and it doesn't feel like I'm working." *

—DENZIL BARKLEY,
Trades Instructor

ART   COST: $$$

Transforming ice into intricate sculptures is not only mesmerizing to watch but also provides a unique blend of physical activity and artistic expression. Historically, ice sculpting began as a practical technique in ancient China for creating ice lanterns during winter festivals. Over centuries, it evolved from these utilitarian origins into an artistic hobby. The allure of ice sculpting lies in its blend of impermanence and spectacle. Unlike sculpting in wood or stone, ice sculpting is a race against time. Additionally, its translucent nature requires consideration of light and its interaction with the sculpture. The fact that these works of art last only as long as the temperature allows adds a layer of appreciation for the moment and the skill it requires.

GET STARTED

1. **Educate yourself.** Begin by watching videos and attending events to observe the techniques used by seasoned sculptors.

2. **Create a workspace and gather tools.** Basic tools include chisels, ice saws, molds, and a melting iron for finer details. Use gloves to protect your hands and work in a space where the ice can melt without causing damage to the area.

3. **Start small.** Practice on manageable blocks that you can store in your freezer. A beginner ice sculpting project is themed ice cubes that look like different geometric shapes.

* Mélanie Ritchot, *"Iqaluit Ice Sculptor Carves Out New Hobby,"* Nunatsiaq News, *March 8, 2022, https://nunatsiaq.com/stories/article/iqaluit-ice-sculptor-carves-out-new-hobby/.*

Ice Skating

"I started ice skating when I was eight and just fell in love from the first time I stepped foot on the rink. My favorite thing is how freeing it is when you glide with the wind through your hair and feel all your worries melt away."

—CHELSEA BOWMAN,
Personal Trainer

PHYSICAL FITNESS   **COST: $**

Picture a vast, mirror-like expanse of ice and individuals with skates dancing across its surface, some leisurely, others with the speed and agility of athletes. This enchanting activity of ice skating has roots in Scandinavia around 3000 BCE when skates were made from the rib bones of elk, oxen, or reindeer and strapped to the feet to cross frozen lakes and rivers. By the nineteenth century, with the advent of indoor ice rinks, skating became a year-round pastime and spread to other parts of the world. Ice skating is a hobby that caters to many, encompassing a variety of styles from figure skating to speed skating and ice hockey. It offers a perpetual winter playground for those who love the thrill of gliding on ice.

GET STARTED

1. **Find a rink.** Locate a local rink where you can rent skates and enjoy time on the ice. Many also offer lessons so that you can master basics like the proper stance, how to fall safely, and how to glide and stop.

2. **Dress appropriately.** Wear warm, comfortable clothing that allows for movement, and don't forget gloves to keep your hands warm and protected.

3. **Invest in your own skates.** Over time, investing in your own skates becomes more cost-effective compared to renting. In general, prioritize comfort and strong ankle support in the skates you purchase.

Improv

"What I love most are the people I met on my first day of class and the continued relationships I've built over the years that relish in being in the moment and having fun."

—MARY C. PARKER,
JEDI Consultant and Life Coach

GAMES/SOCIAL   COST: $

Improv, short for improvisational theater, is the art of creating a spontaneous performance without scripted dialogue. Performers craft scenes relying on their wit, cues from fellow players, and suggestions from the audience. Improv is hinged on the pivotal philosophy of "Yes, and . . . ," which promotes affirmative collaboration and idea building. Modern improv began to take shape in the 1920s and 1930s with avant-garde experiments and games by theater practitioners like Viola Spolin (1906–1994), who is often considered the mother of improvisational theater. Her techniques were developed further by her son, Paul Sills, in the 1950s and 1960s, leading to the formation of influential improv comedy troupes like The Second City in Chicago. The charm of improv lies in its unpredictable nature and the communal experience it fosters. It's about enriching life with the ability to adapt and to create something extraordinary from the ordinary.

GET STARTED

1. **Watch a performance.** Watch a live improv performance to familiarize yourself with the energy and skill involved.

2. **Join a community.** Join a local improv troupe or find beginner's classes and workshops to learn the fundamental principles of improv. Attend classes regularly to hone your wit and reflexes. Let go of fear and be in the moment to enjoy the flow that happens between you and your improv peers.

Indoor Gardening

"Gardening is a tranquil refuge where we plant the seeds of peace and nurture the blossoms of serenity, cultivating not just a garden, but a sanctuary for the soul."

—ALLEN GEARY JR.,
Principal Architect

NATURE/OUTDOOR   COST: $$

The concept of a dedicated indoor space for growing plants took off in the nineteenth century with the advent of the glasshouse. Indoor gardening purifies the air, enhances the aesthetics of a home, and offers a therapeutic respite from the hustle of daily life. It can often bypass the restrictions of seasons, allowing gardeners to grow certain plants year-round. Indoor gardening is not just about potted plants on a windowsill; it's a meticulous process of nurturing and growth, creating controlled environments to grow herbs, flowers, and even vegetables under your roof. Indoor gardening is suited to those who find joy and pride in the persistent patience required to see a seed blossom under their care.

GET STARTED

1. **Choose the right plants.** Research plants that thrive indoors and match your home's light levels. Some require bright light, while others can grow in low-light conditions.

2. **Gather the supplies.** Get pots with drainage holes, quality potting soil, a watering can, and a spray bottle for misting (if needed). Consider purchasing grow lights if natural light in your space is scarce.

3. **Learn basic care.** Understand the watering and feeding needs of your plants. Overwatering is a common mistake, so ensure you're familiar with the signs of both underwatering and overwatering.

Indoor Wall Climbing

"Climbing is a great way to connect with your inner self and your physical limits, while learning that you possess a surprising amount of grit and determination."

—KATELYN,
Communications and Outreach

PHYSICAL FITNESS   COST: $$

Indoor wall climbing is a physically demanding yet exhilarating hobby that involves climbing artificial structures designed to mimic the experience of outdoor rock climbing. These structures, known as climbing walls, are embedded with a variety of holds and grips, simulating different rock textures and challenges. Climbers use their strength, endurance, and problem-solving skills to navigate routes marked out on these walls, aiming to reach the top without falling. The first modern climbing gym appeared in the United Kingdom in the 1960s and was initially conceived as a way for climbers to train during offseasons or when outdoor conditions were unfavorable.

GET STARTED

1. **Find a climbing gym.** Locate a gym near you that offers indoor climbing facilities. Most gyms provide various climbing routes for different skill levels.

2. **Take an introductory course.** Many gyms offer beginner courses that teach basic climbing techniques, safety procedures, and how to use the equipment.

3. **Acquire the gear.** You will need climbing shoes, a harness, chalk, and sometimes a belay device (used to manage rope tension). Many gyms offer most of these items for rent, but you may want to eventually invest in your own equipment.

Investing

"Some people online shop and wake up the next morning not knowing what shopping receipts are going to be in their email inbox, and I wake up with investment confirmations in mine!"

—CASSIE BRKICH,
Owner of Design and Marketing Business

EDUCATIONAL   COST: $

For the hobbyist, investing transcends the mere increase of wealth. Picture the satisfaction of nurturing a garden; in investing, your assets are the seeds from which your financial future blossoms, but the joy of tending to this garden is found in the journey, not just the harvest. The establishment of the first public stock exchange in Amsterdam in the seventeenth century marked a significant evolution in the practice of investing, allowing it to become more structured and accessible. Hobbyist investors often find pleasure in the research and analysis that investing requires, delving into company reports and economic data with the zeal of a detective unraveling a mystery.

GET STARTED

1. **Accrue knowledge.** Immerse yourself in the world of finance through books, courses, and reputable financial news sources to build a solid foundational knowledge.

2. **Start with simulations.** Simulation platforms like Investopedia Stock Simulator or HowTheMarketWorks allow you to invest virtual money and experience the market's dynamics without financial risk.

3. **Define your philosophy.** Develop an investment philosophy that resonates with your personal beliefs and goals, whether it's supporting sustainable businesses or focusing on long-term growth.

Jewelry Making

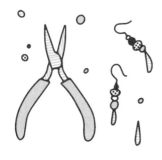

"I find that jewelry making can be really calming when I'm going through my anxiety. I also have ADHD, so it allows me to keep my hands busy and my mind clear."

—CAIT BENTLEY,
Customer Service Representative

ART   COST: $$

Involving the design and assembly of adornments such as necklaces, bracelets, and earrings, jewelry making is a process that can be as simple as stringing beads onto a wire or as complex as casting metal and setting stones. The art of jewelry making dates back thousands of years, with the earliest known pieces being created by ancient civilizations like the Egyptians. One of the major attractions of jewelry making is the ability to create personalized pieces that express individual style or carry personal significance. It also offers a tangible sense of accomplishment when turning raw materials into beautiful, finished pieces. Jewelry making is a meditative process that can feel both relaxing and invigorating and appeals to anyone looking to explore their creative side.

GET STARTED

1. **Gather the supplies.** Assemble a basic toolkit that includes wire cutters, pliers, beads, clasps, and wires. Begin with inexpensive materials and then move on to more costly items as your skills improve.

2. **Learn basic techniques.** Start by learning simple techniques such as wire bending, beading, or working with findings. Online tutorials, books, and community workshops can be great resources. Look for inspiration in nature, fashion, or historical pieces. Sketch out designs or play with your materials to create unique patterns and shapes.

Jigsaw Puzzles

"Puzzles are the polar opposite of how I am in my day-to-day life. They allow me quiet and help me avoid overstimulation while simultaneously keeping my mind active and working."

—CHRISTOPHER OLPP,
Chef and Photographer

`INTROSPECTIVE`   `COST: $`

Jigsaw puzzles are a timeless and engaging hobby that offers a dual nature of being both stimulating and relaxing. John Spilsbury, a London-based mapmaker, is credited with inventing the first jigsaw puzzle in 1767. Typically made from cardboard or wood, each jigsaw piece is a small part of a larger image ranging from famous artworks and scenic landscapes to complex patterns and photographs. Requiring patience and concentration, completing a jigsaw puzzle can be a great way to sharpen cognitive skills like visuospatial reasoning and short-term memory. It's a great hobby for those who enjoy methodical, thoughtful activities and the satisfaction of seeing a project through to completion.

GET STARTED

1. **Choose a puzzle and workspace.** Start with a puzzle that matches your interest in terms of complexity and image. Find a comfortable and well-lit area with a large flat surface. Consider a puzzle mat or board for larger puzzles as they can take several days to complete.

2. **Develop a strategy.** Most enthusiasts start by sorting pieces by color, pattern, or edge. Jigsaw puzzles are as much about the journey as the destination, so take your time and enjoy the process of gradually seeing the picture come together.

Jiu-Jitsu/BJJ

"Jiu-jitsu is very empowering. I can defend myself and control another person even if they are bigger than me."

—GINA TALLARICO,
Software Engineer

PHYSICAL FITNESS   COST: $$

Jiu-jitsu originated from Japan during the late nineteenth century as a comprehensive combat art that included striking techniques, but the iteration that most people around the world have come to recognize since the 1990s is Brazilian jiu-jitsu (BJJ). Developed by members of the Gracie family from Brazil, BJJ is a ground-based grappling art with techniques focused on control, submission, and escape. BJJ equips you to defend against opponents of all shapes and sizes by leveraging your body weight and positioning. Combined with strengthening situational awareness and mindset control, BJJ is a popular choice for self-defense, especially against sexual assault. BJJ requires joining a school and engaging in close physical contact with different training partners.

GET STARTED

1. **Research the school's affiliation and instructor.** Lineage, the line of instructors and students that trace back to the founding Gracie family, is valued in BJJ schools. Some prominent BJJ affiliations include the International Brazilian Jiu-Jitsu Federation (IBJJF) and Gracie Barra.

2. **Wear a *gi*—or not.** The traditional BJJ *gi*, or kimono uniform, is comprised of a heavy cotton jacket and pants. Gi practice is great for beginners to get used to gripping and moving opponents. In no-gi practice, you wear a rash guard or spandex shirt. Some schools train in both.

Judo

"I was often paired with men who were twice my size and weight. The only solution was to keep trying new moves and not be idle. Judo taught me to keep trying something else, and in doing so you will find a solution." *

—ANDREA GOODWIN,
Healthcare Executive

PHYSICAL FITNESS   COST: $$

The origins of judo can be traced back to late nineteenth-century Japan, crafted by Jigorō Kanō, a martial artist and educator. He distilled the ancient techniques of jiu-jitsu into a new martial art that focused not only on self-defense but also on personal character, mental discipline, and moral behavior. It is a martial art style characterized by throws and take-downs, emphasizing the efficient use of balance and leverage. The objective in judo is to either throw or take down an opponent to the ground, immobilize or otherwise subdue them with a pin, or force them to submit with a joint lock or a choke. Judo is rooted in philosophies like *Jita-Kyoei*, "mutual welfare and benefit," and *Seiryoku Zen'yō*, "maximum efficiency with minimum effort."

GET STARTED

1. **Find a *dojo*.** Research local judo clubs (or *dojos*) with certified instructors to join. A good dojo will welcome beginners, prioritize safety, and offer a structured learning path.

2. **Invest in gear.** Purchase a *judogi* (judo uniform), which is designed to withstand the rigorous pulling and grappling of the sport.

3. **Train regularly.** Consistently attend classes to master the fundamentals. Progress in judo is marked by a colored belt system, which serves as a rewarding signifier of advancement.

* https://www.linkedin.com/pulse/how-judo-has-shaped-my-life-andrea-goodwin/

Jump Roping

"Jump roping, the endorphins and energy that happens to you when you're jumping—it's a mood booster." *

—ALYSIA MATTSON,
Commercial Real Estate Agent

PHYSICAL FITNESS   COST: $

Jump roping is a playground staple, a boxer's drill, and a fitness enthusiast's go-to exercise all rolled into one. It can be performed individually or with a group, and it ranges from simple, steady-paced skipping to complex tricks and stunts that require agility, timing, and coordination. Variations of jump roping began in ancient China and Egypt, where vines were used instead of ropes for play and for athletic training. Jump roping can be a high-intensity workout that enhances cardiovascular fitness, tones muscles, and improves balance and coordination. It's a perfect hobby for individuals looking for a fun and low-cost way to stay active.

GET STARTED

1. **Buy a jump rope.** Find a jump rope that's the correct length for your height and has comfortable handles. A general rule is that the rope should reach your armpits when you stand on its center. Lighter ropes made of PVC or vinyl are great for speed, while weighted ropes are used to build strength and intensify a workout.

2. **Choose a space.** Find a flat, open area with a suitable surface like a gym floor, wooden deck, or grass. Avoid concrete, as it's hard on the joints and can wear out your rope quickly.

---

* *Hannah Kanik, "This Seattle Woman Is on a Pandemic-Inspired Mission to Get Everyone to Jump Rope," The Seattle Times, December 2, 2020, https://www.seattletimes.com/life /fitness/this-seattle-woman-is-on-a-pandemic-inspired-mission-to-get-everyone-to-jump-rope/.*

Karaoke

"Karaoke is just fun. You can sing out your joy no matter how good or bad your voice is because your joy will override any flaw."

—CAROLINE CHOE,
Chef and Artist

GAMES/SOCIAL   COST: $

Karaoke is a form of entertainment that allows individuals to sing to instrumental versions of popular songs while following lyrics on a screen. A Japanese drummer named Daisuke Inoue was one of the first to invent an early iteration of a karaoke machine in 1971, but Filipino entrepreneur Roberto del Rosario would be the one to patent the system in 1975. He also coined the term "karaoke"—a portmanteau of the Japanese words *kara*, meaning "empty," and *okesutora*, or "orchestra"—to refer to the absence of a lead singer. Karaoke has become a popular bar recreation around the world, where patrons participate by singing in front of others on an open-mic stage. Private room karaoke also exists for those less inclined to sing in front of strangers.

GET STARTED

1. **Find a karaoke venue.** Many bars host karaoke nights that are free for patrons. If the bar scene isn't for you, search for private karaoke rooms in your area. Private rooms are usually priced by time, but some places charge by the song.

2. **Look for karaoke videos or buy a machine.** Invest in your own machine or follow karaoke videos online. You can find basic karaoke machines for under $100, or search YouTube for free karaoke videos. Both options allow you to host karaoke sessions in the comfort of your own home.

Karate

"I became interested in karate after taking a women's self-defense class. Karate has improved my self-confidence, strength, flexibility, and social health. It's challenging and fun!"

—PATTY TRAN,
Artist and Retail Sales Associate

PHYSICAL FITNESS   COST: $$

Karate is a martial art distinguished by its emphasis on striking techniques and a philosophical approach rooted in the Okinawan tradition. The practice involves a balanced array of punches, kicks, and open-handed techniques like palm-heel strikes. Karate practitioners, or *karateka*, also train in *kata*—choreographed patterns of movements that encapsulate the art's defensive and offensive techniques. Originating from the Ryukyu Kingdom, now part of Japan, karate's development was influenced by various forms of Chinese kung fu. The founder of Shotokan karate, Gichin Funakoshi (1868–1957), played a significant role in popularizing karate in mainland Japan.

GET STARTED

1. **Find a dojo.** Many dojos offer trial lessons or the opportunity to observe a class so you can better understand their teaching style and atmosphere.

2. **Acquire the proper gear.** You will need a karate *gi* (traditional uniform), a white belt, and potentially mouthguards and hand wraps for protection during sparring sessions.

3. **Train regularly and embody its principles.** Approach karate with humility and openness. Understand that karate is not just about physical training but also about personal growth.

Kayaking

"I was a terrible swimmer and had zero athletic stamina. Kayaking enabled me to push out on the water with very little effort, and my friends and I would paddle our way to escape to nature."

—ITHA YI CAO,
Nonprofit Director

PHYSICAL FITNESS   **COST: $$**

Kayaking is the practice of navigating waterways using a small, narrow watercraft propelled by a double-bladed paddle. In a kayak, you sit just above the waterline with your legs stretched out before you, rhythmically slicing the water with your paddle as you glide forward. Kayaking traces back thousands of years to the Inuit and Aleut tribes of the Arctic North America. They crafted the first kayaks out of driftwood and whalebone, stretching animal skins over the frame to create a waterproof vessel that was perfect for hunting due to its stealth and maneuverability. Today, kayaking beckons adventurers of all kinds. It is a hobby that offers a unique vantage point to experience the tranquility of nature, the excitement of exploring inaccessible areas, or the adrenaline rush of whitewater rapids.

GET STARTED

1. **Join a community.** Connect with a local kayaking club or group where you can rent equipment and take classes to learn fundamental paddling techniques, safety procedures, and how to effectively maneuver your kayak. Experienced paddlers can also help you learn the best spots to paddle.

2. **Start on calm water.** Begin on a calm body of water to practice and build your confidence before moving on to more challenging environments.

Kek Lapis Sarawak

"When it comes to authenticity, it's not about where the cake is baked, but the craft of baking and the ingredients that go into making kek lapis.*"**

—MAK KAH KEIN,
Business Owner

(FOOD)   (COST: $$)

Kek lapis Sarawak, or Sarawak layer cake, comes from the Malaysian state of Sarawak and is a delicacy that is as much a feast for the eyes as it is for the palate. Its origins trace back to the Dutch colonial period in Indonesia when a layered cake known as *spekkoek* was created. "Spekkoek" translates to "bacon cake" in Dutch, referring to its dark and light layers resembling layers of fat and meat in bacon. Kek lapis is distinguished by its vibrant, alternating layers that represent the colorful fabric of Sarawak's culture. Crafting it is a meticulous process, requiring patience and precision as each layer is individually baked to create a harmonious blend of flavors and a visually stunning effect.

GET STARTED

1. **Study the craft.** Understand the layers and how to bake them evenly. Familiarize yourself with the traditional flavorings that go into the cake. There are many resources from cookbooks to online tutorials that offer insights into the process.

2. **Gather the equipment and start simple.** Precise measuring tools and pans are essential for achieving the perfect layers that define kek lapis Sarawak. Invest in an oven thermometer or baking stone to better manage and control your oven's temperature. Begin with simpler recipes to master the basics.

---

* Chitra Santhinathan, "Kek Lapis Sarawak, the World's Most Intricate Layer Cake," AirAsia, January 11, 2022, https://www.airasia.com/play/assets/blt345641e95c1451dc/kek-lapis-sarawak-the-worlds-most-intricate-layer-cake.

Kendo

"Kendo is meditative and spiritual in ways that are different from everything else that I do, and I'm honored to have learned from such a distinguished martial art."

—ANDREW HANLIN,
Zamboni Driver

PHYSICAL FITNESS   COST: $$

Kendo, translating to "way of the sword," is a Japanese martial art that epitomizes the practice of swordsmanship. It originated from the samurai who developed *kenjutsu*, a method of sword fighting for combat. As the need for these skills in battle waned, kenjutsu gradually transitioned into today's form of kendo, focusing on self-improvement and spiritual discipline. Kendo is practiced by wearing protective armor and using bamboo swords called *shinai*. It is distinguished from other martial arts by its strict codes of respect and etiquette. Kendo practitioners, known as *kendoka*, learn not only to strike effectively but also to maintain a calm mind and composure under pressure.

GET STARTED

1. **Research dojos.** Look for a Kendo dojo or club that not only fosters technical skills but the values and etiquette of the art as well.

2. **Use the appropriate gear.** Initially, beginners may only need comfortable clothing for practice. As you progress, investing in the proper *bogu* (armor) and shinai (bamboo sword) will be necessary.

3. **Understand the commitment.** Kendo is a journey of personal development that requires a disciplined approach. Regular attendance is essential to the progress of your technique and understanding of the art.

Kite Flying

*"I'm at peace when I'm flying. It's something unique that I do."** *

—LARRY DAY,
Retired

NATURE/OUTDOOR COST: $

Kite flying is a pastime that dates back over 2,500 years with its origins often attributed to China. Chinese philosophers Mozi and Lu Ban are considered among the first to document kite designs in the fifth century BCE, using materials like silk fabric and bamboo. Kite flying has become a universally appealing hobby, embraced by all ages and cultures around the globe. It's a creative outlet for those who enjoy crafting, and an aerodynamic puzzle for those intrigued by the physics of flight. For those who enjoy the outdoors, it offers a serene way to connect with nature. For the competitive spirit, there are kite-fighting and sport-kiting events.

GET STARTED

1. **Select your kite.** Begin with a simple and sturdy single-line kite. Diamond-shaped or delta kites are recommended for their ease of flying.

2. **Learn basic techniques.** Familiarize yourself with the fundamental techniques of launching and controlling your kite. Open fields, beaches, or parks with consistent winds and free of obstructions are ideal locations. Remember to always be aware of your surroundings, including weather conditions, power lines, trees, and other flyers. Safety should be your top priority.

* Melissa Kossler Dutton, "Kite Flying Hobby Gives Lift to Enthusiasts Both Young and Old," The Columbian, May 13, 2018, https://www.columbian.com/news/2018/may/13/kite-flying-hobby-gives-lift-to-enthusiasts-both-young-and-old/.

Knitting

"I love knitting because it's a really wonderful balance between being productive and meditative repetition."

—TIFFANIE BEDERMAN,
Nonprofit Leadership

FIBER ARTS   COST: $

Knitting is the craft of creating fabric by interlocking loops of yarn with two long needles that are usually made of wood but can also be made of metal or plastic. Knitting is free-form. It can be picked up and put down at leisure, making it an ideal companion for quiet evenings or moments of reflection. The precise origins of knitting are veiled in history, but fragments of knitted fabrics have been found in Egypt dating back to the eleventh century. Knitting has evolved naturally over time in diverse cultures, where it has served a utilitarian necessity and a form of artistic expression. The major draws of knitting include the satisfaction of creating something functional and beautiful by hand, the therapeutic rhythm of the needles, and the infinite variety of projects one can undertake.

GET STARTED

1. **Gather the supplies.** Start with a pair of knitting needles (size 8 is a good starting point) and some medium-weight yarn.

2. **Learn the basics.** Master the two foundational stitches—the knit stitch and the purl stitch. Begin with a simple project like a dish-cloth or scarf to perfect the basics.

3. **Join a community.** Communities of fellow knitters are great places to share patterns and techniques. Find knitting communities at local libraries, knitting supply stores, coffee shops, or even online.

Knotting

"Focusing on the sensation of the rope between my hands while I figure out my next move helps ward off distraction. It's a means to create my own controlled calm." *

—SERENA COADY,
Writer

INTROSPECTIVE   COST: $

Knotting is the art of tying knots in a purposeful and methodical way to create both practical objects and decorative pieces. This craft transforms simple lengths of cord, string, or rope into intricate patterns and structures through a series of loops, bends, and wraps. The resulting creations can range from functional items like hammocks and fishing nets to ornamental designs like wall hangings and jewelry. Ancient civilizations had their own knotting traditions, evident in the artifacts of Egyptians, Greeks, and Incas, to name a few. Knotting can be meditative and relaxing, offering a form of tactile mindfulness that detaches one from the digital whirl of modern life.

GET STARTED

1. **Gather the materials.** Begin with some basic cords or ropes. Paracord is a popular choice for novices due to its strength and versatility.

2. **Learn the basics.** Familiarize yourself with fundamental knots like the square knot, the bowline, and the sheet bend. There are excellent online resources, books, and videos dedicated to teaching these skills.

* *https://www.self.com/story/knot-tying*

Kombucha Brewing

"It takes me around ten days to make a single batch, so it definitely passes the time. Anyone could do it really . . . It's black tea with a lot of sugar." *

—AMOS ARMONY,
Student

FOOD   COST: $

Kombucha brewing is the art of fermenting sweetened tea using a symbiotic culture of bacteria and yeast, commonly abbreviated and referred to as a SCOBY. This living home brew turns the initial sugary tea into a slightly tangy, effervescent beverage teeming with probiotics. The genesis of kombucha is claimed by various cultures, including Chinese, Russian, and Korean. Kombucha brewing is distinct from other fermentation activities due to the use of the SCOBY. Each batch is a continuation of the last, as part of the SCOBY and starter liquid is carried over, creating a lineage of brews connected through time.

GET STARTED

1. **Gather the supplies.** You'll need a large glass jar, a cloth cover, and a rubber band to get started. Ensure everything is sterile to avoid contamination. Purchase a SCOBY from a reputable source or obtain one from a fellow brewer.

2. **Prepare the tea.** Brew a batch of tea, sweeten it while still hot with sugar, and allow it to cool to room temperature. Then introduce the SCOBY and starter liquid. Cover the jar with cloth and seal it with a rubber band.

3. **Ferment and monitor.** Place the jar in a warm, undisturbed area and wait as the kombucha ferments.

* Lily Stein, "On Baking Blogs, Kombucha Breweries, and Shrinky Dinks: Creativity in the Time of COVID," 34th Street Magazine, *April 13, 2020, https://www.34st.com/article /2020/04/baking-blogs-kombucha-breweries-shrinky-dinks-painting-art-creativity-covid -penn-quarantine.*

K-Pop Dancing

"I have been really having a good time doing it because I've never done anything like that before." *

—NIA GRIFFIN,
Student

DANCE   COST: $

K-pop dancing is an energetic and highly expressive form of dance that accompanies the genre of Korean pop music known as K-pop. The choreography is often tightly synchronized and performed with precision, mirroring the exact movements seen in K-pop music videos. Emerging from South Korea in the 1990s, K-pop and its distinctive dance style have become a global phenomenon, thanks in part to the international reach of social media and platforms like YouTube. It's a vibrant expression of fandom, as dancers emulate the moves of their favorite K-pop stars, but it's also a way to engage in vigorous physical activity and creative expression.

GET STARTED

1. **Learn the music.** Begin by listening to a variety of K-pop tracks. Watch the accompanying music videos to familiarize yourself with the style and energy of the dance.

2. **Practice the moves and join others.** Start with beginner-friendly choreography tutorials available online. Many K-pop dance covers include step-by-step instructions. Join a local dance class or find a community of K-pop enthusiasts. Sharing the experience with others can provide motivation and enhance the joy of learning.

---

* *Erin Martin, "Student-Led K-Pop Dancing N'Singing Club created at Elon University,"* Elon News Network, *March 31, 2023, https://www.elonnewsnetwork.com/article/2023/03/elon -university-student-led-created-k-pop-dancing-singing-club-burst-bubble.*

Lampworking

"A friend taught me how to make glass beads after she took a class on it."

—DAWN WALLHAUSEN,
Editor

ART   COST: $$

Lampworking is a form of glassblowing that utilizes a torch to melt rods and tubes of clear and colored glass. Once in a molten state, the glass is formed by blowing and shaping with tools and hand movements to create an array of objects from beads and figurines to intricate art pieces. Distinct from traditional glassblowing, lampworking operates on a smaller scale and allows artists to work closely with the material. The roots of lampworking reach back to ancient Syria in the first century BCE. It flourished in Italy during the fourteenth century, particularly in Murano. Lampworking is a hobby well-suited for those with a steady hand and a large measure of patience. The nature of working with molten glass provides a meditative yet exciting process that combines precision with spontaneity.

GET STARTED

1. **Educate yourself.** Start with a class or workshop to learn the fundamentals of lampworking, including how to safely light and adjust the torch, manipulate the glass, and understand the cooling process to prevent cracking.

2. **Invest in equipment.** Basic tools include a torch suitable for lampworking, glass rods, a marver, tweezers, mandrels, and safety equipment like goggles. You will want to work in a space with proper ventilation.

Lapidary Arts

"It's fascinating what's inside these rocks when you cut them and polish them." *

—DAVID GILL,
Family Doctor

ART   COST: $$$

Lapidary arts involve the craft of working with precious stones. From cutting and polishing to carving and setting, this ancient practice transforms rough mineral and rock specimens into glittering gemstones and intricate jewelry. The lapidary arts have deep roots stretching back to ancient civilizations of Mesopotamia, Egypt, and the Indus Valley. Adjacent to jewelry-making activities, lapidary work zeroes in on the transformation of raw, natural materials into polished, cut, and shaped gemstones.

GET STARTED

1. **Educate yourself.** Begin by learning about different types of stones, their properties, and how they respond to cutting and polishing. Books, online resources, and local gem and mineral clubs can be great sources of knowledge.

2. **Focus on a category.** There are a few different categories of the lapidary arts that you can choose to focus on from faceting (gem cutting) to tumbling (polishing stones in a barrel).

3. **Gather the supplies.** Basic tools include a trim saw for cutting stones, grinding wheels of various grits for shaping, and a polishing machine for finishing. Start with inexpensive or common stones like agate, jasper, or quartz.

---

* *Dan McGarvey, "These Calgary Hobbyists Polish Fossils and Make Jewelry Out of Rocks— and Their Numbers Are Doubling," CBC News, December 25, 2021, https://www.cbc.ca /news/canada/calgary/rock-lapidary-club-calgary-alberta-1.6285965.*

LARPing

"Some play for the physical side of it, others for costumes, but for me, it has always been about telling an immersive story with friends."

—CHARLIE HENSLEY,
Video Game Designer

GAMES/SOCIAL   COST: $$$

LARPing, or live action role-playing, is an immersive role-playing experience where participants physically act out their characters' actions in a fictional setting. Participants dress in costume, use props, and interact with each other in character to create a shared storytelling adventure. Elements of LARP are rooted in historical reenactment and improvisational theater, but it began taking its modern form in the 1970s alongside the rise of tabletop role-playing games like Dungeons & Dragons. It has since evolved into a worldwide phenomenon with various genres ranging from medieval fantasy to futuristic science fiction. LARPing blends creative expression, strategic gameplay, and social interaction.

GET STARTED

1. **Research and connect.** Begin by exploring the multitude of LARP genres and find one that resonates with you. Online resources and local gaming communities can provide valuable information.

2. **Create a character.** Develop your character by considering their backstory, motivations, and goals. This process will guide your interactions and decisions during LARP events.

3. **Buy or create your gear.** Acquire or craft a costume that reflects your character. Props and attire can be simple at first, evolving as you become more involved in the hobby.

Latte Art

"I was curious about how foam was created for lattes and cappuccinos and searched online for ways to do it at home. Through my research, I discovered 3D latte art." *

—DAPHNE TAN,
Artist

FOOD   COST: $$$

You can enjoy an iced one, but lattes are traditionally hot coffee beverages made by combining espresso with steamed milk. Latte art began gaining popularity in the 1980s and 1990s in North America as baristas honed their skills for latte art competitions that started to emerge during this time. The original method of creating latte art is free-pouring steamed milk into a cup with espresso and creating patterns like hearts, rosettes, and swans based on wrist movements and angles. Other forms of latte art include using toothpicks to etch or draw elaborate scenes onto the latte's surface with espresso or food coloring and creating three-dimensional sculptures with milk foam.

GET STARTED

1. **Invest in an espresso machine.** Check your local coffee shops for workshops or classes as an economical way to start. Otherwise, invest in your own espresso machine, making sure it includes a steam wand.

2. **Master the basics.** Practice steaming your milk to a temperature range of 150°F to 155°F (65°C to 68°C). This is the optimal temperature to yield a velvety texture perfect for creating latte art.

3. **Save your leftovers.** Freeze your leftover coffee and milk in popsicle or ice cube trays to use in smoothies or cocktails!

---

* *"Artist Daphne Tan Has Shot to Fame by Creating Amazing Frothy 3D Sculptures Out of LATTE,"* SWNS, *October 20, 2017, https://stories.swns.com/news/artist-daphne-tan-has-shot-to-fame-by-creating-amazing-frothy-3d-sculptures-out-of-latte-90152/.*

Lawn Mower Racing

"It's about winning, but I can't stress enough how good the sportsmanship is."*

—JOHNNY WILSON,
Former Mayor

GAMES/SOCIAL   COST: $$$

Lawn mower racing is a motorsport that transforms the common household gardening appliance into a competitive racing machine. Lawn mower racing took off in the United Kingdom in 1973 as a response to the rising costs of motorsport racing; the British Lawn Mower Racing Association was pivotal in the hobby's growth and establishment. The hobby involves modifying lawn mowers with enhancements to the engine, suspension, and wheels, then racing them around a prepared track, usually on grass or dirt. It's a community-centric hobby, bringing together people who enjoy tinkering and mechanical challenges with those who appreciate the camaraderie and excitement of racing.

GET STARTED

1. **Research and connect.** Lawn mower racing clubs and associations can provide guidance on regulations, safety, and event schedules. You can also consider starting something local with your neighbors.

2. **Choose and modify a mower.** Acquire a suitable lawn mower, which can often be a used one. Ensure that it meets the specifications for the racing class you're interested in and upgrade it according to racing guidelines and regulations.

*   *Tammy Keith, "Guy Mayor Rides Harleys, Races Mowers," Arkansas Democrat Gazette, July 21, 2013, https://www.arkansasonline.com/news/2013/jul/21/guy-mayor-rides-harleys-races -mowers/.*

Learning a Language

"I love the quote: 'If you speak to a man in a language he understands, that will go to his head. If you speak to him in his language, that will go to his heart.' I want to build heart-to-heart connections."

—POIZUN WILLIAMS,
Social Media Marketer

EDUCATIONAL   COST: $

Learning a language is like unlocking the door to a new world. You can gain unique insights into the historical backgrounds and nuances of different cultures, broaden your world perspective, and widen your network of friendships. The most common spoken languages in the world include Mandarin Chinese, Spanish, English, Hindi, and Arabic. Fluency in any of these languages can also open you to different career opportunities. Consider learning nonverbal languages as well, like sign language or braille, which have their own national languages based on country or region.

GET STARTED

1. **Set small, achievable goals.** Learning a new language takes time, especially if you are interested in both written and conversational fluency. Commit to a regular routine to practice and set milestones to keep you motivated on your journey.

2. **Utilize resources.** There are a multitude of language-learning resources available from online courses and apps to textbooks and private tutors. Look to your local libraries and community centers too, which often provide free or low-cost classes.

3. **Immerse yourself.** Immersion is one of the quickest ways to pick up on a new language. Connect with language exchange partners online or through local groups and watch movies or listen to music in the language you're trying to learn.

Learning an Instrument

"In 1966, I applied for a job as a waiter at a banjo club, but the manager said he only needed banjo players. I lied and said I played, thinking, 'How hard could it be?'"

—CHRIS FENNIMORE,
Public Television Producer and Host

MUSIC   COST: $$$

Learning an instrument is a gratifying hobby for anyone who loves music and wants to build a creative skill. The primary categories of musical instruments are string, wind, percussion, keyboard, and brass. There are also hybrid and unconventional instruments like the theremin, which is an electronic instrument. Each style requires the mastery of different techniques like finger positioning, striking methods, or breath control. Learning any instrument will familiarize you with universal music principles like rhythm and timing, pitch and scales, harmony and chords, and notation. It requires the ability and willingness to invest in consistent practice but offers a sense of achievement, stress relief, physical coordination, and mental stimulation.

GET STARTED

1. **Choose your instrument.** Consider your musical preferences, physical capabilities, and the practicality of the instrument within your living space. Housing and transporting a harp will be very different from an ukulele!

2. **Use a guide.** Seek out an instructor or explore online tutorials, apps, and courses. A teacher can ensure that you're learning proper form and techniques unique to your instrument.

3. **Carve out a schedule.** Consistency with your practice will accelerate your progress. Your practice sessions don't need to be long; the important thing is to build a routine.

Leatherworking

"I went out to the store and bought a little leather wallet making kit. It saved my life. This outlet is why I have a family still, or a job or anything." *

—TONY FANTASIA,
Former Army Sergeant

ART   COST: $$$

Leatherworking is the craft of creating objects from leather through techniques such as cutting, dyeing, sewing, and stamping. Tracing its origins back to prehistoric times, leatherworking is one of the oldest crafts developed by humanity that emerged out of necessity. Traditionally involving animal hides, a growing facet uses vegan leather as an environmentally conscious option. Vegan leather includes materials made from synthetic compounds and plant-based resources like pineapple leaves, mushroom mycelium, or recycled plastic. Whether one works with traditional or vegan leather, leatherworking is a rewarding hobby that offers a tactile means of creating personal items that last.

GET STARTED

1. **Educate yourself.** Research the different types of leathers available and their properties. Understanding how vegan leather compares to animal leather will inform your crafting techniques and tool choices.

2. **Gather the supplies.** Invest in a basic set of leatherworking tools, which typically includes items like a cutter, needles, thread, and a few stamps or a mallet for embossing.

---

*   William Blankenship, *"PTSD and Leather: Army Vet Finds Healing through Handiwork,"* Military.com, *July 5, 2018, https://www.military.com/off-duty/2018/07/05/ptsd-leather-army -vet-finds-healing-handiwork.*

LEGO Building

"It's tough to find a hobby when your main creative outlet is also your career. LEGO building has sparked my creativity and helped me play again."

—RICKY WEBSTER,
Chef

TOYS   COST: $

A toy construction system invented by Ole Kirk Christiansen in 1932, the term "LEGO" derives from the Danish words *leg godt*, which translate to "play well." Comprised of colorful plastic building blocks ranging in various shapes and sizes, each LEGO piece features small studs or tubes that interlock with other pieces. You can find LEGO kits that have step-by-step instructions for a specific build or as sets of unassorted bricks that you can use to create whatever you want. LEGO building can feel meditative while encouraging you to tap into your imagination and problem-solving skills. Its simplicity and adaptability have led it to becoming a timeless hobby that can be enjoyed by both children and adults.

GET STARTED

1. **Choose a set.** Although you can start by playing with random LEGO bricks, you may want to choose a kit with a predetermined design to familiarize yourself with the building process. LEGO sets are marked with an age bracket and number of pieces to indicate their level of difficulty. As a beginner, you may want to choose a set with fewer pieces.

2. **Join and follow communities.** As you advance to more free builds and complex sets, consider joining online or in-person communities to share your creations and receive tips and resources. Some techniques you might learn from advanced LEGO builders include how to incorporate mechanical movement or lights into your design.

Letter Writing

"There is something very special about the sensory experience of letter writing: the unique handwriting, the choice of paper or card, the ability to add smells with a spray of perfume or little extras like stickers or magazine clippings."

—MANDY YOKIM,
Substitute Teacher

GAMES/SOCIAL · COST: $

The earliest recorded handwritten letter is attributed to the Persian Queen Atossa around 500 BCE. From the wax-sealed missives of the Middle Ages to the airmailed letters of the twentieth century, letter writing has been a constant in the shifting trends of communication technology. It offers various avenues for engagement, from crafting thoughtful messages to friends and family to reaching out to strangers who share similar interests. One avenue of letter writing is penpalling, where individuals exchange letters with others across the globe. Writing to individuals in prison is another avenue, often serving as a lifeline to the outside world for inmates. There are also organizations that use letter writing to comfort those who may be lonely, such as seniors in nursing homes or those in hospice care. Writing to someone can be a deeply fulfilling experience; it's an opportunity to enact kindness and potentially impact someone's life profoundly.

GET STARTED

1. **Choose your letter writing path.** Decide on the type of letter writing that interests you most, whether it's cultural exchange, supporting others, or creative correspondence.

2. **Connect with communities.** Utilize online platforms or community boards to find like-minded individuals or organizations that can connect you with pen pals, inmates, or others who would cherish receiving a letter.

Line Dancing

"You just get out there and do the moves you want to do, but you do them together." *

—NICK EBERT,
Student

DANCE   COST: $

Line dancing is a choreographed dance with a repeated sequence of steps in which a group of people dance in one or more lines, executing the steps simultaneously. It doesn't require a partner and is distinct from other dance forms by its uniformity and synchrony. Modern line dancing, especially in its association with country music, began to gain popularity in the 1970s and has since branched out to encompass a variety of musical genres. Line dancing is a social hobby by nature. Its ability to cater to all levels of dancing skill appeals to those who enjoy rhythm and movement but may be apprehensive about the close contact or the improvisational aspect of other forms of dance. Line dancing offers a structured way to enjoy dancing without the need to lead or follow a partner, making it a welcoming activity for novices and seasoned dancers alike.

GET STARTED

1. **Learn the basics.** Start with beginner-friendly dances. Many places offer lessons that focus on simple steps that form the foundation of many dances. You can also use online resources to help you master the moves at your own pace.

2. **Find a venue.** You can join others by looking for local community centers, dance studios, or country western bars that offer line dancing classes or nights.

* *Lindsey Hull, "There's Good, Clean Fun in Line Dancing," The Roanoker, August 29, 2023, https://theroanoker.com/blogging/behind-the-page/theres-good-clean-fun-in-line-dancing/.*

Linocut

"Linocutting brings me all the joy of creating art, but with the added bonus of being able to recreate it as many times as I want! And the process of cutting linoleum itself is so meditative and satisfying."

—ASHE,
Hair Stylist

ART   COST: $

Linocut is a printmaking technique that involves carving a design into a linoleum surface, leaving the parts of the image to be inked raised while the carved-out areas remain blank on the final print. Linocut found its footing in the early twentieth century as an offshoot of woodcut printing. It emerged as artists searched for a less laborious alternative to wood. Linoleum, initially used for flooring, proved to be a softer and more forgiving material. Linocut allows for bold and expressive lines, creating a uniquely striking contrast in the prints it produces. It's a hobby for those who delight in the tactile process of carving and the printmaking process. The carved linoleum block can also be used multiple times, allowing you to reproduce a piece of art without diminishing its qualities.

GET STARTED

1. **Gather the materials.** Essential tools you'll need include linoleum blocks or sheets, carving tools, printing ink, a brayer (roller), and paper.

2. **Learn the basics of carving.** Practice carving on a small piece of linoleum to get a feel for the material. Begin with simple shapes before progressing to more intricate designs.

3. **Experiment with printing techniques.** Apply ink with the brayer and make a few prints to understand how pressure and the amount of ink you use can affect the image.

Live Model Drawing

"Not only does figure drawing get your creative muscles going, the focus and challenge of capturing the 3D form in 2D, as well as capturing the human gesture in a short period of time, makes it almost like a Zen meditation."

—BARBARA B.,
Editor

ART   COST: $

Live model drawing is the practice of sketching a human subject in real-time as they pose. This art form often focuses on the study of how light and shadow interact on the curves and contours of the human figure. The discipline has roots that reach deep into the annals of art history, harkening back to the times of ancient Greece and Rome. The practice as we know it today was more formalized during the Renaissance when masters like Leonardo da Vinci and Michelangelo honed their craft through the study of live models. The allure of live model drawing lies in its raw authenticity; it captures the ephemeral nature of a moment and the individuality of the human body.

GET STARTED

1. **Gather the materials.** Start with basic drawing tools like pencils, charcoal, erasers, tortillons (blending tools), and paper.

2. **Find a class or workshop.** Many community centers, art schools, and studios offer live model drawing sessions. These guided environments provide structure and often include valuable feedback from instructors.

3. **Study anatomy.** Gaining a deeper understanding of anatomy by reviewing books or videos will enhance your ability to capture the human form with accuracy and insight.

Lock Picking

"There is no better feeling than when you crack the lock; it's phenomenal every time."

—CHRIS GILLOTTI,
IT Manager

EDUCATIONAL   COST: $

The oldest known lock and key device dates back over six thousand years and was found in the ruins of the ancient Assyrian empire. Lock picking evolved as a skill set over centuries, often being associated with locksmiths and espionage. It emerged as a modern hobby, intriguing those with an affinity for solving problems and who enjoy deconstructing how things work. It's particularly appealing to individuals who enjoy mechanical puzzles and possess a persistence in unraveling complex systems. The hobbyist lock picker takes pleasure in the tactile feedback of pins setting and the satisfaction of a lock releasing without the brute force of breaking or the original key. It's a practice that demands delicate manipulation, patience, and a keen awareness of tactile feedback and auditory cues.

GET STARTED

1. **Research local laws.** Before you start, understand the laws regarding lock picking in your area. In some jurisdictions, simply possessing lock picking tools without being a licensed locksmith can be considered evidence of criminal intent. Keep the practice private and confined to your own property.

2. **Buy the tools.** Purchase a basic set of lock-picking tools, which usually includes a variety of picks and a tension wrench.

3. **Start with easy locks.** Start with simple pin tumbler locks, which are easier to understand and manipulate. There are also clear practice locks that are transparent, allowing you to see the inner workings as you pick

Machine Learning

"I have always been interested in painting but not very good, so I started playing with computer-generated art. In the process of pursuing my hobby, I learned a ton about state-of-the-art AI/ML tooling." *

—BRAD FLAUGHER,
Lead Engineer

TECH   COST: $

Machine learning (ML) is a specific application of artificial intelligence (AI), where algorithms and data are provided for computers to learn on its own and make predictions. Instead of programming a computer with explicit instructions for every decision, you feed it data and let it infer the patterns and rules. The modern field of ML began in the 1950s by AI pioneer Arthur Samuel. Samuel created a checkers-playing program based in "reinforcement learning"—the program received feedback in the form of rewards or punishments (in this case, wins or losses in checkers) and would revise its actions to optimize reward. ML beckons those who are fascinated by the potential of AI, who relish logical challenges, and who are drawn to the intersection of technology and creativity.

GET STARTED

1. **Educate yourself.** Start with online courses or tutorials that cover the basics of machine learning. Many of these resources are free and can provide a solid theoretical foundation as well as practical skills.

2. **Join a community.** Platforms like GitHub, Kaggle, or Reddit have vibrant machine-learning communities where you can share your projects, get feedback, and learn from others.

* Sarah Huffman, *"How Does Music Relate to Coding? 5 Technologists on How Hobbies Influence Their Careers,"* Technical.ly, *July 19, 2022, https://technical.ly/professional-development/how-hobbies-help-tech-careers/.*

Macramé

"What I love most about macramé is how once you get good, you can start by following a design or pattern and then make it your own in so many different ways."

—HAILEY BROCKOPP,
Healthcare Operations

(ART)   (COST: $)

Macramé is the art of knotting string into patterns to make decorative items. While all macramé is knotting, not all knotting is considered macramé. Knotting can be purely functional, like tying a rope for securing objects, but macramé is decorative. Imagine taking strings or cords and, rather than weaving or knitting them, you tie them in various combinations to form intricate patterns and designs. These designs can range from simple to complex and can be used to create everything from wall hangings and plant hangers to jewelry and clothing. Macramé is believed to have started with thirteenth-century Arab weavers who would use excess thread along the edges of hand-loomed fabrics to create decorative fringes. It requires very few tools and can be done anywhere. The ability to start small and scale up as one's confidence grows makes it accessible for everyone.

GET STARTED

1. **Gather the supplies.** Start by choosing a macramé cord or yarn. There are many options available from cotton twine to more robust synthetic ropes, depending on the project you have in mind.

2. **Learn to tie knots.** The foundation of macramé is in its knots. Learn the basic ones—the square knot, the larks head knot, the half hitch—and you're well on your way to creating your first piece.

Magic

"The public sees only the thrill of the accomplished trick; they have no conception of the tortuous preliminary self-training that was necessary to conquer fear."

—HARRY HOUDINI,
Magician

GAMES/SOCIAL   COST: $

Magic as an entertaining performance art involving tricks, sleight of hand, and visual illusions. It likely originated in the sixteenth century when the publication of *The Discoverie of Witchcraft* (1584) revealed how certain feats of magic were performed. This era demystified the idea that magicians held supernatural powers and instead highlighted the skill and craft behind the art. The allure of magic lies in its capacity to invoke wonder and the joy of the unexplained. It's an act of storytelling where the magician's props and gestures weave narratives that defy logic and reality. Magic is a hobby for the curious, the creative, and the playful who love to engage and connect with others, bringing a sense of awe and delight.

GET STARTED

1. **Learn the basics.** Start with books or tutorials that introduce you to simple tricks and the fundamental principles of magic. Understanding the psychology behind magic is as crucial as mastering the tricks themselves.

2. **Practice and perform regularly.** Magic is an art of precision. Regular practice is necessary to hone the sleight of hand and other techniques that make the tricks appear effortless. Perform for friends and family. The feedback is invaluable, and the experience is critical for refining your skills.

Magic: The Gathering

"When I was in middle school, I started playing with my friend. I really like team strategy games and immersive high fantasy elements, which are the cores of this card game."

—MATTHEW BEDSOLE,
Corporate Counsel

GAMES/SOCIAL   COST: $

Magic: The Gathering is a collectible card game (physical and digital), where players take on the role of planeswalkers—powerful mages who summon creatures, cast spells, and duel against others in a battle of wits and strategy. The game was conceived by mathematician Richard Garfield and introduced by Wizards of the Coast, LLC in 1993. It quickly evolved from a simple card game to a cultural phenomenon, spawning a rich competitive scene and a vast, dedicated community. Magic: The Gathering is often hailed as the progenitor of modern trading card games, a blueprint that many others have followed but none have replicated in terms of depth and complexity.

GET STARTED

1. **Understand the rules.** Learn the fundamental principles of the game before you begin. Resources are available online, including tutorials and comprehensive rule books.

2. **Buy a starter deck.** Starter decks are curated to provide a balanced play experience for new players. They are an excellent way to learn the game mechanics without being overwhelmed by the vast card pool.

3. **Join a community.** Whether it's a local game store, school club, or online group, connecting with other players can provide support, learning opportunities, and friendship.

Mahjong

"It is such a joy to play Mahjong because it brings in conversation, strategy, and a great bonding time for everyone. Winning is fun and everyone wants to try again to see who will win next!"

—S.E. SONG,
Customer Success Manager

GAMES/SOCIAL   COST: $$$

Mahjong, a game often known for the clinking of bamboo tiles as hands shuffle them across a table, is a classic Chinese pastime that has transcended borders and generations. Mahjong is a game of skill, strategy, and a touch of chance, and is played with tiles adorned with Chinese characters and symbols. Four players sit around a square table with the objective to build sets with matching tiles. The aim is to outwit opponents through calculated moves and thoughtful tile selection. The roots of mahjong stretch back to the Qing Dynasty of the nineteenth century, with some legends suggesting even earlier origins. The game reached global popularity by the 1920s.

GET STARTED

1. **Acquire a set and learn the rules.** Begin with a traditional mahjong set, which includes 144 tiles. Each set usually comes with dice and, in some versions, chips or scoring sticks. Rule books are also often included. Understanding the objective and tile groupings such as chows (three consecutive numbered tiles), pungs (three identical tiles), and kongs (four identical tiles) is essential.

2. **Join a community.** Community centers, local clubs, and online platforms offer opportunities to play with others. Solo practice of tile arrangement and identifying potential winning combinations can also sharpen your game before you join a group.

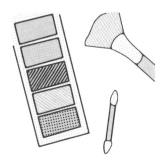

Makeup Artistry

"My favorite thing about doing makeup is helping people feel more confident in their own skin, while still being able to recognize themselves."

—MARENDA ZERONAS,
Domestic Engineer

FASHION/BEAUTY   COST: $$

Makeup has weaved its way through cultural and historical tapestries from the lead-based concoctions of the Elizabethan era to the red lips symbolizing Hollywood's golden age glamour. The ancient Egyptians used kohl to line their eyes, a practice that was both cosmetic and ritualistic, believed to ward off evil spirits. With the advent of social media, enthusiasts have been able to share a vast array of techniques and styles that transform the face, and sometimes body, into an artistic masterpiece. From enhancing natural features to creating elaborate designs for theatrical productions, makeup artistry can be as subtle or as dramatic as the artist decides.

GET STARTED

1. **Assemble a makeup kit.** Invest in an introductory set of quality makeup brushes and a palette that covers a broad spectrum of colors. Start with some essentials and gradually build your collection as you develop your skills.

2. **Study and practice.** Begin by studying the fundamentals of makeup, such as skin preparation, color theory, and the different purposes of each makeup product. Resources are abundant, from online tutorials to books. Beyond practicing on your own face, practice on friends and family who are willing to be your canvas and experiment with different styles and techniques.

Making Cosmetics

*"The fact that I take the time to take care of myself, and do my own products, helps me maintain sanity in hard times."**

—MATILDE MAGRO,
Regenerative and Sustainability Designer

FASHION/BEAUTY   **COST: $$$**

Making cosmetics is as much about aesthetics and sensory pleasure as it is about understanding the chemistry of ingredients and how they interact. You can concoct different blends of natural oils, pigments, and other ingredients to create personalized makeup, skincare, or lotions that are tailored to your specific needs and preferences. The craft of making cosmetics has seen a resurgence as people seek more control over the ingredients in their beauty products, driven by a desire for natural and organic alternatives to commercial offerings.

GET STARTED

1. **Educate yourself.** Learn about common cosmetic ingredients like essential oils, butters, and emulsifiers. It can be helpful to focus your research on a specific beauty product you're most interested in, such as body butters or face masks.

2. **Start with simple recipes.** Initiate your craft with straightforward recipes, such as lip balms or body scrubs, which require fewer ingredients and less complex methods. Some basic supplies you might need include carrier oils (coconut oil, olive oil, and so on), essential oils, waxes, and containers. Many of these items can be found online or at local health stores.

* *https://www.permaculturewomen.com/making-your-own-cosmetics/*

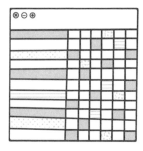

Making Spreadsheets

"I find spreadsheets calmingly structured, taking the chaos and unruliness of life and fitting it into a lovely grid of only right angles. More than data crunching, though, it's really a form of journaling that I find meditative and immensely satisfying.

—JON TAI,
Magician and Storyteller

EDUCATIONAL   COST: $

Spreadsheets are a way of organizing information in a digital grid-like document. They are most known as a diagnostic tool for businesses and financial professionals to perform calculations or to visualize data into charts and graphs. Interestingly, the first digital spreadsheet was created by and for hobbyists. VisiCalc, short for "Visual Calculator," was spreadsheet software invented in 1979 for the Apple II computer. VisiCalc became the catalyst that shifted microcomputers from a niche hobby to the ubiquitous system most of the world uses today. The versatility of spreadsheets is what makes it an unlikely but entertaining hobby. You can use spreadsheets to plan your meals or catalog your favorite films by year, genre, and personal rating scale.

GET STARTED

1. **Choose and learn your software.** The most widely used spreadsheet software include Microsoft Excel, Google Sheets, and LibreOffice Calc. Starting can be as easy as charting your data by columns and rows, but tapping into different resources can lead you to discover a world of unique formulas, sorting functions, and data filtering that can elevate your organizational experience.

2. **Create a simple project.** Beginner spreadsheet projects include building a song library, a water consumption log, or a budget tracker. More advanced projects might include a weather forecaster, recipe formulator, or itinerary optimizer.

Making YouTube Videos

"I noticed other people were living and having fun on YouTube, while I was sitting there watching them. I started a YouTube channel as an excuse to see what's out there in the world."

—TOM BARTINS,
Inside Sales Representative

TECH   **COST: $**

Created in 2005 as an online platform for sharing videos, YouTube has become the world's largest library of audiovisual information. You can easily discover and upload diverse content that ranges from comedic skits to how-to tutorials. There are other video-sharing platforms, like Vimeo, Twitch, and TikTok, each distinguished by specific niches, content styles, and audiences. YouTube has maintained its top position as a video-sharing platform because of its universally global reach, accessibility (free with ads), interactivity, search engine function, built-in video editor, and monetization. YouTube also allows a generous upload limit of fifteen minutes, while verified users can upload up to twelve hours of content.

GET STARTED

1. **Choose your niche.** Consider both your skills and interests. You can share your expertise on a subject or document your learning journey in a new field.

2. **Film, edit, and upload.** The minimum you will need to start is a camera or smartphone and an internet connection. Head to YouTube.com to create your free account and access basic editing tools within their platform. Take your time to invest in more complex gear and editing software like Adobe Premiere Pro or Final Cut Pro as you progress.

Meringue Art

*"I always followed a lot of cooking and baking accounts, but it was mostly the standard types of cakes, pastries, etc. I wanted to make food and desserts that would look cute or different than usual."**

—**AMY CHAO,**
Author

FOOD   COST: $$

Meringue art is the culinary craft of whipping sugar and egg whites into a light, airy confection that's then piped into various shapes and baked to crisp perfection. Meringue art dates to at least the seventeenth century, with some accounts attributing its invention to a Swiss pastry chef named Gasparini. Over time, it has traversed across Europe, becoming a staple in French, Italian, and Swiss confectionary arts. As a modern hobby, artists use social media to spearhead the latest trends of crafting meringue art into adorable figures like corgi butts and cartoon characters. Meringue art combines the piping techniques of cookie decorating with the three-dimensional form of cake art on a small scale.

GET STARTED

1. **Gather the supplies.** Invest in quality piping bags and a variety of nozzles. You'll also want gel food coloring and silicone mats for your baking trays.

2. **Practice and learn from others.** Meringue can be very tedious to master. Learn the basics, understanding how to achieve stiff peaks and the right consistency for piping. Begin with simple shapes and patterns like rosettes, stars, or even letters to help build the skills needed to move on to more elaborate designs. Watch tutorials, attend a class, or join a baking community to further your progress.

---

* Brandy Arnold, "Everyone Is Talking About These Floating Meringue Animals and I'm Obsessed," Totally the Bomb, *https://totallythebomb.com/floating-meringue-animals.*

Metal Detecting

"A man who had lost his ring messaged me, asking whether I could help him, as the ring was very important to him. I thought, 'This is my chance to do something different and special.'" *

—HASAN ZAHEER,
Engineer

NATURE/OUTDOOR   COST: $$

Metal detecting combines the lure of exploration with the thrill of discovery. Participants use a handheld device known as a metal detector, which emits an electromagnetic field to sense metallic objects hidden in the ground. When the device passes over a metal object, it sends a signal—often an audible tone or visual cue—suggesting where to dig. An inventor named Dr. Gerhard Fischer is often credited with creating the first handheld metal detector, which he also patented in 1931. Since then, advancements in technology have turned metal detecting into a popular pastime for history buffs, adventure lovers, and those who simply enjoy a good mystery.

GET STARTED

1. **Examine local laws.** Before you start, understand local regulations regarding metal detecting. Some areas may be off-limits or require permits.

2. **Choose the right equipment.** Research and invest in a metal detector that fits your budget and the type of detecting you want to do. Beginners may opt for simpler, more user-friendly models like the Garrett ACE Series.

3. **Start local.** Start in your own backyard or a local park (with permission) to get a feel for your detector.

*   Anu Prabhakar, "From Geocaching to Metal Detecting, Meet UAE Residents with Unusual Hobbies," Kahleej Times, *December 25, 2023, https://www.khaleejtimes.com/long-reads/from -geocaching-to-metal-detecting-meet-uae-residents-with-niche-interests-and-unusual-hobbies.*

Meteorology

"All of a sudden, this huge Haboob dust storm came towards me, and I was fascinated with it. I was like, how did that happen? And I was hooked from that moment." *

—SARAH HASAN AL-SAYEGH,
Accountant

`EDUCATIONAL`   `COST: $`

Meteorology is the study of the atmosphere, weather processes, and patterns. For the hobbyist, it involves tracking and analyzing weather conditions, learning about atmospheric phenomena, and may even include contributing to citizen science projects. The origins of meteorology can be traced to Aristotle's treatise titled *Meteorologica* (340 BCE), which attempted to tackle a range of natural phenomena, combining observational insights with philosophical speculation. Meteorology is an engrossing pursuit for the naturally curious.

GET STARTED

1. **Research and learn.** Study basic meteorological principles. There are numerous resources available, from online courses to local community college classes.

2. **Invest in equipment.** Purchase a personal weather station. This can be as simple as a thermometer and barometer or as complex as a full home setup that measures rainfall, wind speed, and more.

3. **Observe and record.** Document weather patterns, significant weather events, and seasonal changes in a journal. Over time, you'll start to notice trends and understand the local climate.

---

* Nadia Leigh-Hewitson, "This Storm Chaser Captures Stunning Photographs of Extreme Weather," AccuWeather, September 21, 2023, https://www.accuweather.com/en/severe-weather/this-storm-chaser-captures-stunning-photographs-of-extreme-weather/1581049.

Miniature Cooking

"It relieves stress. And then it's satisfying to feel like you've created something small." *

—ALEX APOSTOL,
Call Center Agent

ART   COST: $$

Miniature cooking is a delightful blend of culinary art and the whimsical world of miniatures. Imagine creating an entire meal, but on a scale so small it could be served on a dollhouse table. This unique hobby involves crafting tiny dishes, often cooked with real ingredients and functional miniature cooking implements. The result is a fully edible plate of food, identical to its life-sized counterpart, just significantly smaller. Miniature cooking has grown as a modern hobby thanks to its internet fame. Through various online and social media platforms, miniature cooking has captivated a global audience with the charms of creating and sharing deliciously diminutive dishes.

GET STARTED

1. **Gather the tools.** Purchase miniature kitchen tools and cookware, which can be found in specialty craft stores or online. You can also improvise with items found around the house. Tea candles are usually the primary heat source used in miniature cooking.

2. **Start simple.** Choose simple recipes with fewer ingredients to practice your skills. Something as straightforward as tiny sandwiches or mini pancakes can be the perfect starting point.

---

* Racquel Quieta, "LOOK: A Functional Miniature Kitchen That Makes Edible Miniature Food," GMA Entertainment, February 10, 2021, https://www.gmanetwork.com/entertainment/celebrity life/hobbies/74127/look-a-functional-miniature-kitchen-that-makes-edible-miniature-food/story.

Miniature Pottery

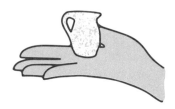

"I really wanted to make something like tiny ceramics and I had this small lump of clay at home and had a last-minute thought—'What if I made everyone a tiny object instead of a Christmas card?'" *

—**VERONIKA MCQUADE**,
Graphic Designer

ART   COST: $

Miniature pottery is the art of shaping and creating pottery on a tiny scale. The pieces are fully crafted with the same techniques as full-sized pottery, but they're small enough to fit in the palm of your hand or even on the tip of your finger. This craft requires steady hands, patience, and a passion for detail. For some, the appeal lies in the cuteness factor associated with all things miniature. Additionally, miniature pottery offers a unique way to dabble in the art without having to commit to the more extensive process and resources required for traditional pottery.

GET STARTED

1. **Acquire the supplies.** Start with polymer clay, which can be baked in a home oven. You'll also need a set of small sculpting tools, which can be found in craft stores. You can also purchase a miniature pottery wheel set that comes with all the tools you need.

2. **Master the basics.** Familiarize yourself with the fundamentals of pottery through classes, online tutorials, or pottery books.

3. **Practice and connect with others.** Patience is crucial, as working on a miniature scale can be challenging. Engaging with a community of enthusiasts can be a valuable resource for tips, inspiration, and feedback on your creations.

---

* Adita Bora, "Graphic Designer Makes Adorable Mini Ceramic Souvenirs for Her Colleagues Instead of Christmas Cards," Upworthy, April 25, 2023, https://scoop.upworthy.com/graphic-designer-makes-adorable-mini-ceramic-souvenirs-for-colleagues-597564.

Miniature Tree Cultivating

*"Creating an ancient tree is a challenge that has become an addiction."**

—ROGER SNIPES,
Financial Manager

NATURE/OUTDOOR   COST: $$$

The two most popular methods of miniature tree cultivation are bonsai and penjing. The term "bonsai" is from Japan and translates to "planted in a container," but the practice of shaping tiny trees originated in China during the Tang Dynasty (618–907 CE) and is called *penjing*, meaning "potted scene." Both penjing and bonsai center around ideas of harmony, balance, and the interconnectedness between humanity and nature. Penjing depicts landscapes with miniature trees and can include other elements like rocks, water, or figurines. Bonsai focuses on a single tree, emphasizes simplicity, and is influenced by the Zen Buddhist idea of pursuing enlightenment.

GET STARTED

1. **Choose your trees.** Select a tree species that resonates with you and suits your local climate. Common choices for bonsai include juniper, pine, and maple. Ficus, Chineste elm, and banyan are common species for penjing.

2. **Acquire the essential tools.** Basic tools include concave cutters, pruning shears, wire cutters, wire, and bonsai or penjing pots and containers.

---

* Pat Munts, "Gardening: Careful Pruning, Shaping an Ancient Art: Bonsai Sale Will Show-case Area Hobbyists' Work," The Spokesman-Review, *July 18, 2019, https://www.spokesman .com/stories/2019/jul/18/gardening-careful-pruning-shaping-an-ancient-art-b/.*

Mixology

*"I'm motivated by the belief that it's possible for everyone to create happy hour at home— no matter the size of their living room or their budget."** *

—CAMILLE WILSON,
Higher Education

FOOD   COST: $$$

Mixology encompasses both the intoxicating array of alcoholic cocktails and the intricate world of mocktails and nonalcoholic concoctions. Mixologists combine flavors, textures, and aesthetics to create drinks that both refresh and intrigue. Tracing back to the eighteenth century during the American Prohibition, bartenders were forced to mix juices and other flavors with poor-quality bootlegged spirits to make them palatable, inadvertently birthing the complex art of cocktail creation. For hobbyists who appreciate the subtleties of flavor, mixology can be both a source of personal enjoyment and social entertainment.

GET STARTED

1. **Research and learn.** Delve into the history and techniques behind classic cocktails and mocktails.

2. **Gather the equipment.** Invest in essential mixology tools such as a shaker, strainer, jigger, muddler, and bar spoon. These tools will be invaluable whether you're muddling fruit for a mocktail or stirring a sophisticated alcohol-free aperitif.

3. **Experiment and share.** Use a variety of ingredients from fresh herbs and spices to syrups, bitters, and fresh juices to create new concoctions. Whether it's a local class, online forum, or a group of friends, sharing your creations can enhance your skills and appreciation for the craft.

*   *https://www.cocktailsnobnyc.com/about*

Mixed Martial Arts (MMA)

"It seemed that it would be a great chance to work on my body and mental health while learning tools that could help me defend myself as a woman who travels a lot alone for work."

—JESSICA RÍOS VINER,
Union Campaigner

PHYSICAL FITNESS   COST: $$$

Mixed martial arts, commonly known by its acronym MMA, is a full-contact combat sport that melds a kaleidoscope of fighting techniques from various martial arts disciplines. It came into the modern limelight with the establishment of the Ultimate Fighting Championship (UFC) in the early 1990s in the United States. The appeal of MMA lies in its raw, unbridled nature and the level of skill and fitness it demands. It's not for the faint-hearted but rather for those who seek a rigorous physical challenge and the thrill of hand-to-hand competition. MMA stands apart from other martial arts activities in its free-form style. MMA is a melting pot of techniques and styles that can make it unpredictable and multifaceted. Engaging with MMA can be a transformative experience, blending intense physical exertion with strategic thinking. It's a sport that embodies the spirit of a warrior within the confines of a disciplined and respectful environment.

GET STARTED

1. **Find a gym.** Look for a gym that offers MMA training with experienced instructors. A good gym will provide a safe environment to learn and practice, and many offer trial lessons or periods to get acquainted with the sport.

2. **Equip yourself.** Purchase essential gear like MMA gloves, headgear, groin protectors, and mouthguards. Rash guards and other form-fitting clothes are typical attire worn in MMA training.

Model Figurine Building

*"I can put my idea into Gunpla and build it the way I imagined. It is a way to explore myself."**

—KATE AU YEUNG,
Human Resources Executive

TOYS   COST: $$

Building model figurines is the craft of assembling small-scale representations of characters, creatures, and machines. These models can range from robots and mechs (mechanized robots piloted by humans) to science fiction and anime characters. The modern hobby of model figurine building began to gain traction in the nineteenth century with the creation of model soldiers for military training, which later transitioned into a leisure activity. This hobby is often a unique expression of fandom for certain franchises and is a haven for the patient and precise. It is for those who revel in the quiet focus required to paint an eyelash on a miniature face or to ensure the accuracy of a uniform.

GET STARTED

1. **Choose your niche and set.** Start by selecting a genre or type that resonates with you, be it historical figures, pop culture icons, or creatures of myth. Most model figurines come as kits that include all the pieces you need to assemble your specific figurine.

2. **Gather the supplies.** You'll need a good set of small paintbrushes, modeling glue, and perhaps a set of fine-tipped markers or paints designed for models.

---

* *Sam Li, "'People Are Jealous of Me': Building Gundam Models Is His Job and His Hobby— and He Loves It," South China Morning Post, December 29, 2022, https://www.scmp.com /lifestyle/entertainment/article/3204800/people-are-jealous-me-building-gundam-models-his -job-and-his-hobby-and-he-loves-it.*

Model Trains

"I tell people all the time that this is my therapy. They think I'm joking, but my wife will tell me from time to time: 'You're getting pretty uptight, why don't you go out to the shop and build something.'" *

—SKIP HARPER,
Retired

TOYS   COST: $$

Model trains are a delightful intersection of engineering, artistry, and nostalgia. This hobby involves assembling, operating, and often constructing detailed scale models of trains and their environments, known as layouts. Model trains can be traced back to the 1840s in England, with the first miniature models made as promotional items for railway companies. It wasn't until the early twentieth century that they became popular as children's toys. However, the true artistry of model trains as we know it began to take shape when adult enthusiasts sought greater realism and detail, transforming these toys into precise scale replicas.

GET STARTED

1. **Select a scale.** Model train scales are categorized by their size relative to the real train that they model. For beginners, the HO (1:87) scale is often recommended, balancing between the ease of handling and the potential for detailed modeling.

2. **Acquire a starter kit.** Begin with a basic set that includes a locomotive, some track, and a few carriages. This lets you get a feel for assembly and operation without overwhelming investment.

---

* Andrew Mobley, "'Cheaper Than a Psychiatrist:' Central Arkansas Train and Hobby Show Gains Steam with Impressive Model Displays," KATV, August 27, 2023, https://katv.com /news/local/central-arkansas-train-and-hobby-show-gains-steam-with-impressive-model -displays-skip-harper-daryl-conner-rail-and-sprue-hobbies-conway-expo-center-arkansas-lego -users-group-arklug-convention-miniatures-red-river-valley-n-gineers-richard-glatter-august.

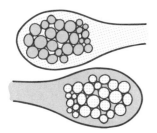

Molecular Gastronomy

*"Molecular gastronomy is just the application of science to produce certain flavor or textures in food. It's oh-so delectable."**

—ROY JENSEN,
Chemistry Teacher

FOOD   COST: $$$

Molecular gastronomy applies principles from chemistry, physics, and biology to culinary techniques and recipes to create dishes with novel tastes, textures, and presentations. Some of the methods that characterize molecular gastronomy include spherification (creating spheres that burst with liquid flavor), foams, gels, and using liquid nitrogen. This avant-garde culinary practice arose in the late twentieth century, but its mainstream breakthrough is often attributed to the work of chefs like Ferran Adrià and Heston Blumenthal as well as food scientists like Nicholas Kurti and Hervé This. Molecular gastronomy turns the kitchen into a food lab where experimentation reigns.

GET STARTED

1. **Educate yourself.** Start with some foundational reading. Dive into the literature of Hervé This or Harold McGee to understand the science behind your favorite dishes.

2. **Gather the tools and start simple.** Acquire a few basic tools of the trade: precision scales, syringes, and a selection of texturizing agents like agar-agar or sodium alginate. Begin with easy recipes like making fruit caviar or a spherified cocktail, before progressing to more complex techniques and ingredients like liquid nitrogen.

---

* *Kevin Ma, "Better Cooking through SCIENCE!" St. Albert Gazette, January 19, 2018, https://www.stalbertgazette.com/local-news/better-cooking-science-1297660.*

Mooing

"It all started when I was in 4-H camp when I was ten. I had a get-together with friends, and they started doing animal noises. I decided to try a cow, and I've been able to do it since then."*

—BRANDON ROGERS,
Student

COMPETITIVE   COST: $

Mooing is the artful and often humorous imitation of the vocalizations of cattle. Mooing as a recreational hobby grew particularly popular in rural regions, especially in the United States where agricultural fairs are a part of local culture. In places like Wisconsin, known as "America's Dairyland," mooing contests have garnered a following with participants of all ages. These contests not only celebrate the skill of accurately imitating a cow but also honor the dairy industry and its contributions to the community. Mooing offers a unique way to connect with the agricultural heart of society and engage in an activity that's sure to bring laughter and levity to any gathering.

GET STARTED

1. **Listen and learn.** Visit a local farm or search for recordings of cattle to understand the nuances of their calls. Begin by imitating the sounds you hear. Pay attention to the pitch, length, and emotion of the moos. Practice until you can produce a convincing replica.

2. **Perform and connect with others.** Share your newly honed talent with friends at social gatherings or look for a local fair that hosts mooing contests.

---

* *"Moo-la-palooza: The Moo Heard Around the World,"* Milwaukee Journal Sentinel, *August 11, 2011, https://www.youtube.com/watch?v=LPRHSYaEbe8.*

Mosaic

"I love junk and [inanimate] body parts. Mosaicking in my style covers both interests."

—JULIA LAUDERDALE ORZESKE,
Attorney

ART   COST: $$

Mosaic is an art form created by assembling a myriad of small pieces of material, like glass or stone, and setting them into a base with grout or mortar to produce an image or pattern. The result is a vibrant, tactile artwork that captures the essence of each individual piece in a harmonious, cohesive whole. Early examples of mosaic date to ancient Mesopotamia, but it was the Greeks who elevated it to an art form and the Romans who spread the practice across their empire. Mosaics allow for the recycling of materials, turning broken tiles, glass, and other nontraditional materials like doll parts or buttons, into stunning works of art.

GET STARTED

1. **Gather the supplies.** Basic supplies include tesserae (a small block of colored tiles, glass pieces, or stones used for mosaicking), adhesive, a base to apply your mosaic (such as a tabletop or a wall surface), and grout to fill the spaces between the pieces.

2. **Master the basics.** Familiarize yourself with mosaicking techniques, including cutting tesserae, arranging them, and applying grout. You can learn through online tutorials, books, or workshops.

3. **Start simple.** Begin with small, manageable projects like a coaster, wall pieces, or a small tabletop. You'll want to gain experience with using the traditional tesserae before branching into less conventional materials.

Mural Painting

"I began painting my favorite local businesses, which then blossomed into a passion for painting murals celebrating immigrant stories."

—SOPHIA FANG,
Grad Student

ART   COST: $$$

The practice of mural painting stretches back to the ancient times of cave dwellers, with some of the oldest examples found in the Paleolithic cave paintings in France and Spain. From the frescoes of ancient Egypt and Rome to the politically charged murals of the Mexican Muralism movement spearheaded by artists like Diego Rivera in the twentieth century, murals gradually evolved into a cornerstone of cultural expression. Distinguished by its scale and public placement, mural painting is often a communal effort. A mural can turn a nondescript wall into a landmark and a conversation starter, making it an art form that truly belongs to the people.

GET STARTED

1. **Study murals and their techniques.** Examine murals you admire and familiarize yourself with different mural techniques like gridding, projecting, and stenciling.

2. **Plan your design and space.** Choose a suitable wall if pursuing a private mural or propose it to local businesses or community centers that have space. Digital mock-ups are another way to help bring your vision to life. Remember to plan for the weather for outdoor murals!

3. **Gather the supplies.** Basic supplies include paints, brushes, and ladders. You may also consider recruiting others for support with larger murals. Prep the wall by cleaning or priming and outline your design before diving into painting.

Museums

"One of my favorite parts of going to museums is standing in front of a work by a famous artist, and really absorbing the idea that I'm standing where the artist stood and looking at strokes made by their hand."

—JENN CERULLY,
Stay-at-Home Mom

NATURE/OUTDOOR   COST: $

Museums encapsulate humanity's vast pool of knowledge and creativity within their walls. The Louvre, which opened as a public museum in 1793 in Paris, was a pivotal moment that democratized access that was once only available to the elite. Today, ethical considerations are increasingly at the forefront of the museum-going experience as the provenance of artifacts, often entwined with colonialism and improper acquisition, have come under scrutiny. Museumgoers can balance their thirst for knowledge with a conscious acknowledgment of the complex histories of how certain items came under museum ownership.

GET STARTED

1. **Choose a museum to visit.** Identify local museums or galleries and explore their collections. Many offer thematic tours or special exhibitions that can provide a focused experience.

2. **Keep ethical considerations in mind.** Research collections to understand their history and origins. Consider supporting institutions that have transparent policies on artifact acquisition or becoming an advocate for the ethical stewardship of cultural artifacts.

3. **Increase your participation.** Research museum memberships that often grant expanded access, invitations to events, or reciprocal benefits at other institutions. Attending museum-led workshops or lectures can also offer deeper insights.

Musical Looping

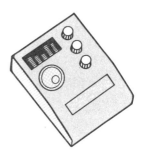

*"Just the way I put patterns and loops together, there's a certain style of music I make. I don't know, I just like the way it is."**

—OCHAI AGBAJI,
Professional Basketball Player

TECH   COST: $$$

Musical looping is when an artist records samples of music in real time and then replays them in a loop, over which they can layer more sounds. This creates a complex and harmonious composition that can include rhythms, melodies, and textures, all from a single musician. Musical looping can be traced to the early twentieth century with the advent of tape recording. Musicians would record tracks on tape and then manually loop them by splicing the ends together. This technique was refined over the decades with the introduction of digital technologies, allowing for instantaneous looping and a more intuitive creation process. Musical looping allows an artist to perform a solo act with the depth of a full band.

GET STARTED

1. **Equip yourself.** Start with a basic loop pedal like the Boss RC-1 Loop Station or TC Electronic Ditto Looper. Software applications like GarageBand or Ableton Live Intro allows for multiple tracks of looping.

2. **Learn the basics.** Understand how to record, loop, overdub, and undo layers. Start with simple loops, like a chord progression or a basic beat, and gradually add layers. There are many tutorials available online that can guide you through the process.

---

* *Swain, Michael, "KU Basketball's Ochai Agbaji Has Unique Hobby." 247 Sports, March 19, 2020, https://247sports.com/college/kansas/Article/ku-basketball-wing-ochai-agbaji-likes-to-create-music-dj-145159132/Amp/.*

Musical Theater

"I have been a singer all my life but only recently started getting involved in musical theater in my forties. It combines what I love to do most with developing new skills in dancing and acting."

—CLARA CHENG,
Professor

MUSIC   COST: $$

Musical theater combines acting, singing, and dancing to tell a story. It's characterized by the integration of music, often with catchy melodies and expressive lyrics, into theatrical performances. Unlike traditional theater, which relies primarily on dialogue, musical theater uses songs to advance the plot, develop characters, and convey emotions. The origins of musical theater can be traced back to the nineteenth century with roots in operetta and vaudeville. However, in the early twentieth century, particularly with shows on Broadway in New York City and the West End in London, musical theater evolved into the form most recognize today. This hobby is well-suited for those who enjoy the challenge of combining multiple disciplines, appreciate storytelling through song and dance, and are keen on exploring various aspects of stage performance.

GET STARTED

1. **Explore musicals.** Familiarize yourself with the musical theater repertoire. Listen to soundtracks, watch recordings of performances, and attend live shows to understand the genre's diversity.

2. **Take lessons or join a group.** Consider taking singing, acting, and dancing lessons. Otherwise, community theaters are great places to gain experience. Audition for roles in local productions to practice performing in front of an audience and to learn from others.

Mycology

"Mycology lends itself quite well to being secluded: you go out, collect, bring things back, do a lot of research. I really enjoy that very much."*

—**PAMELA CATCHESIDE,**
Retired Teacher

NATURE/OUTDOOR   **COST: $**

The term "mycology" stems from the Greek *mykes,* meaning "fungus," and *logia,* meaning "study." Mycology as a science began to take root between the sixteenth and eighteenth centuries with figures like Italian naturalist Pier Antonio Micheli (1679–1737) and Swedish botanist Elias Magnus Fries (1794–1878), who pioneered classifications. Mycology as a hobby encompasses a wide variety of activities from collecting and cultivating fungi to researching medicinal properties.

GET STARTED

1. **Educate yourself.** Knowledge is crucial, as fungi can range from delicious to deadly. Invest in a good field guide that details local fungi and familiarize yourself with the basics of fungal biology.

2. **Gather the supplies.** Prepare with a basket for your finds, a knife for harvesting, and a notebook for observations. Don't forget a camera to capture the ephemeral beauty of your discoveries.

3. **Start local.** Explore nearby woods, fields, or even urban areas after rain, when fungi are most likely to emerge. Never consume wild mushrooms without absolute identification. Many edible fungi have toxic look-alikes. Joining local mycological societies or online forums can provide experienced insight.

* Ribeiro, Celina, "Never Too Late: How a Retired Teacher's 'Fungi Hobby' Led to Her Finding 20 New Species," The Guardian, January 5, 2021, https://www.theguardian.com/lifeandstyle /2021/jan/06/never-too-late-how-a-retired-teachers-fungi-hobby-led-to-her-finding-20-new -species.

Nail Art

"As a digital artist in a male-dominated field by day, getting in touch with tactile art oft maligned as 'women's work' by night has been deeply grounding."

—MAXINE IGLICH,
Video Editor and Motion Graphics Specialist

ART   COST: $

Nail art is the creative expression of decorating and embellishing nails, transforming them into miniature canvases of personal style. This hobby extends beyond the simple application of nail polish, evolving into an art form where nails are adorned with intricate designs, vibrant colors, and an array of embellishments like gems, stickers, and even hand-painted artwork. The earliest records of nail art come from ancient China where nobles would color their nails with silver and gold. In ancient Egypt, nail color indicated social status with shades of red signifying the highest rank. Today, nail art is celebrated as a form of self-expression and an accessory as customizable as the clothes we wear or the hairstyles we choose.

GET STARTED

1. **Gather the supplies.** Invest in a foundational nail art kit that includes various polish colors, a top and base coat, and a set of tools for detailing like brushes and dotting instruments.

2. **Find inspiration.** Look to social media, fashion magazines, and even the world around you for design ideas. Nail art is a hobby where imitation often leads to innovation.

3. **Master the basics.** Begin with simple designs and, as your skill progresses, venture into more complex techniques like marbling, stamping, or applying decorative accents.

Noodling

"I've enjoyed using a rod and reel from time to time, but it's not like getting bit. Once you get bit that first time, if you're an adrenaline junkie, it's addictive." *

—TONY GIBSON,
Building Stone Industry

NATURE/OUTDOOR   **COST: $**

Noodling, also known as hand-fishing, requires a noodler to reach into known catfish holes in riverbeds and catch fish by making them bite down on their hand. Noodling is believed to have been practiced by various Native American tribes and later adopted by settlers as a means of survival before becoming a cultural pastime. Today, it is most popular in southern and midwestern United States, where it's passed down through generations and weaved into the cultural fabric of rural river communities. Noodling can be stressful and injurious to fish, particularly if they are nesting or guarding eggs. Keeping this and other ethical considerations in mind, many handle fish with care and practice catch-and-release methods.

GET STARTED

1. **Research local laws and regulations.** Noodling is not legal in all states or regions due to concerns about safety and conservation. It's essential to check local laws and obtain any necessary permits or licenses before you begin.

2. **Explore and respect the environment.** Familiarize yourself with local rivers and lakes. Be mindful of local wildlife regulations and practice catch-and-release where appropriate. Always noodle with a partner for safety.

---

* *Johnny Wilson, "When 'Noodling' Tony Gibson Gets a Bite, He Really Gets a Bite,"* Johnson City Press, *November 15, 2020, https://www.johnsoncitypress.com/living/when-noodling-tony -gibson-gets-a-bite-he-really-gets-a-bite/article_0297f118-236a-11eb-9a89-9b7aa9765e5d.html.*

Nude Modeling for Live Drawings

"As someone with broken eyes, I needed to see myself through [the] eyes of someone else." *

—BRIANNA,
Actor and Dancer

ART   COST: $

Demanding patience, confidence, and an understanding of the symbiotic relationship between artist and model, nude modeling within the context of live drawings explores the nuances of posture, anatomy, and the play of light and shadow on the human body. It requires the ability to hold poses for a few minutes to several hours. Nude modeling as a modern hobby emerged by the mid to late twentieth century, as the practice became more democratized and less stigmatized, making it accessible to a wider community of amateur artists and models. Models often describe the experience as empowering and a unique way to participate in the creation of art while embracing body positivity.

GET STARTED

1. **Find opportunities.** Contact local art classes and groups to inquire about modeling opportunities. Many communities have open sessions where models of all body types are welcomed. Consider attending life drawing sessions as an artist first to understand what is expected of models.

2. **Prioritize personal safety.** You should always have the option to decline poses that make you uncomfortable and to take breaks. Understand the policy on photography and ensure no images are taken of you without your consent. Consider bringing a friend or fellow model to your first few sessions until you feel comfortable.

* *Robin Eileen Bernstein, "The Naked Truth About Nude Art Modeling," Salon, June 29, 2018, https://www.salon.com/2018/06/29/the-naked-truth-about-nude-art-modeling/.*

Obstacle Course Racing (OCR)

"I had been training at the gym for a few months and decided to test my progress by signing up for a local OCR. I ended up loving it!"

—SYDNEY STEPHENSON,
Outpatient Mental Health Counselor

PHYSICAL FITNESS   COST: $$$

Obstacle Course Racing, or OCR, is a thrilling physical challenge that combines running with various obstacles that test strength, endurance, and agility. Participants navigate courses featuring barriers, such as walls to climb, weights to carry, and muddy trenches to cross. The courses are designed to push racers to their physical and mental limits. Influenced by obstacle courses used in military training, modern OCR started with events like the Tough Guy competition in 1987 in the United Kingdom and has since grown into a global phenomenon with other popular events like Spartan Race and Tough Mudder.

GET STARTED

1. **Strengthen your fitness.** Start with regular cardiovascular and strength training. Activities like running, swimming, and bodyweight exercises are good for building base levels of the endurance and strength needed for OCR.

2. **Explore specific training.** Search local gyms that offer OCR-specific training classes with mini obstacle courses. If none are available near you, incorporate exercises that mimic OCR challenges like climbing, lifting, and balancing activities.

3. **Start small.** Look for races that are tailored to beginners like Rugged Maniac. Mainly held in the United States and Canada, it features a 5K course with obstacles like trampolines, water slides, and mud pits that emphasize fun over difficulty.

Oenology

*"The fun is making it, deciding what to create and when it's ready."**

—LOU CAMILOTTO,
Retired Teacher

(FOOD) (COST: $$$)

Oenology, often spelled "enology" in other parts of the world, is the science and study of all aspects of wine and winemaking except for grape growing and harvesting, which is a field known as viticulture. The nuanced art of oenology delves into the chemistry and biology of turning grapes into wine, exploring fermentation processes, wine aging, and the complex interactions between the biochemistry of the fruit and the resulting taste profiles. The ancient Greeks and Romans refined winemaking into a science, documenting their methods and the variations in flavor, color, and aroma—practices that can be seen as the early foundations of today's oenological techniques.

GET STARTED

1. **Research the fundamentals.** Start with a foundational understanding of wine. Books, online courses, and workshops can introduce you to the key concepts of wine varieties, the winemaking process, and the chemistry behind the fermentation.

2. **Seek out experiences.** Attend guided tastings where you can learn from experts about the different aspects of assessing wine quality, flavor profiles, and terroir, which is the way a particular region's climate and soils affect the taste of wine. Look for opportunities to participate in the winemaking process. This could be through volunteering at a local winery or even trying to make your own wine at home with a winemaking kit.

* Eric Asimov, "The Agony and Ecstasy of Home Winemaking," The New York Times, October 19, 2023, https://www.nytimes.com/2023/10/19/dining/drinks/home-wine-making.html.

Off-Roading

"It's like going on a roller coaster except that someone you know is driving, and there's a chance that you could die. Which makes it more fun." *

—ELIJAH POLLACK,
Student

NATURE/OUTDOOR   COST: $$$

Off-roading is the adventurous hobby of driving or riding a vehicle on any surface that is not paved, such as sand, gravel, riverbeds, mud, snow, rocks, or any natural terrain. It can involve a variety of vehicles designed to handle these rough conditions, including four-wheel drives (4WD), all-wheel drives (AWD), ATVs, dirt bikes, and even specialized vehicles like dune buggies. Off-roading emerged during the twentieth century as a recreational activity with the Jeep during World War II, becoming an iconic vehicle that popularized the concept of driving "off-road."

GET STARTED

1. **Educate yourself.** Learn about the different types of off-roading and what each entail. From rock crawling to dune bashing, each has its own set of challenges and requires different vehicle specifications.

2. **Rent an experience.** Rent off-road vehicles for temporary excursions as an economical way to start. Many off-road parks and tourist destinations known for their trails offer rental services, which include the vehicle and sometimes even a guided tour.

---

* *Neal Pollack and Elijah Pollack, "On Loving Off-Roading, Even When You're Pulling for a Future That's All-Electric," The Observer, May 8, 2019, https://observer.com/2019/05/off-roading-4x4-history-future-electric-cars/.*

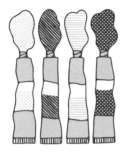

Oil Painting

"I paint to relax, to work through difficult periods of life, to stop time, to celebrate milestones, and to express fanciful delusions no matter how ridiculous they are."

—HANNAH PHILLIPS,
Chief Creative Officer

ART   COST: $$

Unlike watercolors or acrylics, oil paints have a unique texture and a slow drying time, allowing artists to work with the paint, blending and layering to achieve varying effects from translucent glazes to thick, textured strokes. The technique of oil painting dates to Europe in the Middle Ages, with its practice becoming widespread during the Renaissance when it became the principal medium for creating art due to its adaptability and durable finish. Its unparalleled depth and luminosity in addition to the ability to build layers over days or even months gives oil painting a dimensionality and a complexity that is difficult to replicate with other mediums.

GET STARTED

1. **Create a safe workspace.** Working with oil paints requires careful consideration of safety and cleaning measures, especially when using solvents like turpentine, which can be toxic and emit strong fumes. Set up a space with plenty of airflow and natural light. Follow local regulations for the disposal of hazardous materials. Never pour solvents down the drain.

2. **Gather the materials.** Start with a basic set of oil paints, a few brushes of different sizes, a palette, canvas or oil painting paper, and turpentine or a less toxic alternative like odorless mineral spirits for cleaning brushes.

Origami

"I started out just folding papers, wanting to keep busy and de-stress myself. It's kind of turned into something much bigger than that." *

—MICHAEL STONE,
Teacher

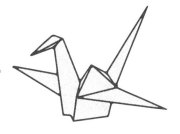

ART   COST: $

Origami is the Japanese art of paper folding that transforms a flat sheet of paper into a finished sculpture without the use of cutting or glue. From simple designs like paper planes and boats to the more complex and intricate representations of animals, flowers, and more, origami is as much a craft as it is a form of expression, mathematics, and a meditative practice. Origami is a unique combination of art, science, and dexterity that offers a rewarding challenge for the hands. All you need to start origami is a piece of paper and some patience. It's a hobby that appeals to those who enjoy precision and problem-solving, as well as those looking for a tranquil activity to calm the mind.

GET STARTED

1. **Get paper.** Origami paper is typically thinner and easier to fold than regular paper. It often comes in a square shape and in a variety of colors and patterns.

2. **Learn and practice.** Start with simple origami projects like the classic crane or paper box to become familiar with basic folds and techniques. There are numerous books and online tutorials available for beginners. Set aside time to fold regularly, gradually trying more complex designs as you progress.

---

* Max Sullivan, "York Teacher's Origami Hobby Turns into Something 'Much Bigger': Helping Abuse Survivors," Seacoastonline, February 3, 2023, https://www.seacoastonline.com/story/news/local/2023/02/03/brixham-montessori-school-teacher-hobby-helps-domestioc-abuse-survivors/69858066007/.

Outdoor Gardening

"I began gardening a year into my sobriety journey. I found that gardening was similar to sobriety in that you plant the seeds and then you get to watch them grow."

—TASHA LAMB,
Custodian

NATURE/OUTDOOR　　**COST: $$**

Outdoor gardening is a hobby that offers a hands-on connection with nature and rewards patience and persistence with verdant growth and blooms. It requires a keen awareness of local climate, soil conditions, and wildlife. Outdoor gardening includes a wide variety of horticultural activities from growing colorful flower beds to nurturing fruits, vegetables, and herbs. It can involve landscape design, a functional vegetable garden, or a mix of ornamental and edible plants. A hobby that can be both meditative and productive, outdoor gardening offers a unique blend of physical activity, creativity, and a deep connection to the rhythm of the seasons.

GET STARTED

1. **Assess your space.** Evaluate the space you have available, the amount of sunlight it receives, and the type of soil present. Consider joining a community garden if you don't have access to your own outdoor space.

2. **Gather the tools.** Equip yourself with basic gardening tools such as a spade, gloves, watering can, and pruning shears. Choose easy-to-grow plants that are suitable for your region to ensure early successes that will keep you encouraged on your gardening journey.

3. **Keep learning and connecting.** Read up on gardening basics, attend workshops, or join a local gardening club to extend your knowledge and gain support.

Outdoor Rock Climbing

"Being able to be out with nature is amazing. It's just you and the rock. Getting to the top and being able to look down to see how far you've come is why I keep coming back."

—NANCY TRAN,
Project Analyst

NATURE/OUTDOOR   COST: $$$

Outdoor rock climbing is an exhilarating and physically demanding hobby that involves ascending natural rock formations using one's hands, feet, and climbing equipment. Climbers navigate pathways that vary in distance and difficulty and are called "problems" in bouldering or "routes" in roped climbing. Rock climbing as a sport began around the late nineteenth century in Europe, particularly in Germany, Italy, and the United Kingdom, where what initially began as a necessary skill for mountaineering evolved into a recreational activity.

GET STARTED

1. **Learn the basics.** Enroll in a beginner's climbing course or join a climbing club to learn the fundamentals of climbing safety, techniques, and equipment use. You can build your skills and confidence at an indoor climbing gym before venturing outdoors.

2. **Gather the equipment.** Start with basic gear like climbing shoes, a helmet, and a harness. For bouldering, a crash pad is essential. For roped climbing, you need ropes, carabiners, and other safety equipment.

3. **Start small with others.** Begin with low-grade routes, which are less steep and have more frequent holds, making them ideal for a novice. Having a partner or group not only enhances safety but also makes the experience more enjoyable.

Outdoor Sketching

"About six years ago, I found a small group of urban sketchers. We meet to sketch what is happening in a different location every week."

—DIANE RABINOWITZ,
Artist

ART   COST: $

Outdoor sketching, also practiced as urban sketching, is the artistic pursuit of drawing scenes in real time within an urban or natural environment. This form of sketching captures life as it occurs, focusing on buildings, street scenes, parks, and other public places that offer a glimpse into the day-to-day. Distinct from studio work, it requires the artist to engage directly with the atmosphere and energy of a particular location, often leading to spontaneous and vibrant works that are infused with the immediacy of the moment. Outdoor sketching fosters a direct connection with one's surroundings and is particularly suited for those who have a love for observation and enjoy being outdoors.

GET STARTED

1. **Gather the supplies.** Assemble a small set of supplies that can be easily carried with you like pencils, markers, a sketchbook. You can also bring a portable set of paints, brushes, and a water container for mixing and cleaning to your destination.

2. **Choose a spot.** Start by selecting a comfortable location that interests you. Take the time to observe your surroundings before you begin. Start with loose, quick sketches to capture the primary shapes and composition, and then refine as you go.

3. **Join others.** There are many urban sketching groups and online communities where you can share your work, get feedback, and participate in sketching events.

Paintball

"It requires on-the-spot bravery, courage, quick decision-making, bold choices, and rapid creativity. It brings something alive in you that is pretty unique."*

—SARAH KITLOWSKI,
Healthcare Executive

GAMES/SOCIAL   COST: $$

Paintball is a sport where players use a paintball gun or marker and compete to eliminate opponents by tagging them with gelatin capsules containing water-soluble dye (paintballs). The game is played on an indoor or outdoor course, often designed with natural or artificial terrain and obstacles for players to hide behind and seek tactical advantage. Paintball originated in the 1980s with the first official game played in New Hampshire. A stock trader, writer, and ski shop owner—Hayes Noel, Charles Gaines, and Bob Gurnsey—first conceptualized the game by using a commercial paintball gun designed for marking trees and cattle. The game rapidly gained popularity and evolved into a sport with its own equipment and dedicated playing fields.

GET STARTED

1. **Find local paintball spots.** Look for paintball fields or arenas in your area, which will have equipment you can rent. This is a good way to try the sport without the initial investment in gear.

2. **Prioritize safety.** Understand the safety rules and always wear proper protection, which includes a vest and a mask designed specifically for paintball to protect your eyes and face. You'll want to wear comfortable, durable clothing.

---

* Grier Ferguson, "For Busy Health Care Executive, Paintball Provides Welcome Break." Business Observer, *January 8, 2021, https://www.businessobserverfl.com/news/2021/jan /08/executive-diversions-sarah-kitlowski-sarasota-omeza-paintball/.*

Palm Reading

"I've received some of the greatest insights of my life while reading the lines on other people's palms. It's an odd thing to say, but it's also true."*

—SHERALYN PRATT,
Author and Strategist

EDUCATIONAL   COST: $

Palm reading, also known as chiromancy or palmistry, is the art of interpreting a person's character or predicting their future by examining the lines, shapes, and patterns on their hand. Rooted in the belief that the hand is a map of our lives and personalities, the practice of palm reading can be traced back thousands of years across various cultures including Indian, Chinese, and Egyptian civilizations. Palm reading offers a unique blend of introspection, entertainment, and the opportunity to connect with others on a personal level. It appeals to those drawn to the esoteric and mystical aspects of life and enjoy storytelling and psychology. While palm reading is considered a pseudoscience by many, keeping an open mind and using it as a tool for reflection and entertainment can make it a fascinating hobby.

GET STARTED

1. **Study the fundamentals.** Learn about the major lines most palm readers focus on: the heart line, head line, life line, and fate line. Each has its traditional interpretations related to emotions, intelligence, life path, and destiny. Familiarize yourself with the shapes of hands, fingers, and the mounds of the palm. Each feature can be thought to contribute to an overall reading.

2. **Practice reading.** Start by reading your own palm to see how the lines and shapes correspond with your life experiences. Then practice with willing friends and family to hone your interpretation skills.

* *https://www.sheralynpratt.com/tag/palm-reading/*

Paper Quilling

"It looks amazing, really elegant." *

—HANNAH MILMAN,
Editorial Director

ART   COST: $

Paper quilling is an art that involves rolling, shaping, and gluing strips of paper to create decorative designs. Paper quilling originates from the Renaissance period when French and Italian nuns and monks used quilling to decorate book covers and religious items. Over time, quilling became a pastime particularly enjoyed by young women in England during the eighteenth century who would decorate tea caddies and pieces of furniture with their intricate designs. Often arranged into flowers, leaves, and various ornamental patterns, paper quilling can be used to adorn greetings cards, pictures, boxes, and more. It's a hobby that requires minimal tools and materials but yields highly satisfying and visually stunning outcomes. It is most suited for those who enjoy meticulous, hands-on craftwork and have a love for detailed artistic expression.

GET STARTED

1. **Gather the materials.** You'll need a quilling tool (or a toothpick), paper strips, glue, and a workboard to pin your designs in place as you work.

2. **Learn basic shapes and experiment.** Start by learning to make basic quilling shapes such as loose coils, tight coils, teardrops, and squares. Once you're comfortable with making basic shapes, you can start to combine them to make intricate designs and patterns.

---

* *Jennifer Forker. "Quilling Is Easy and Elegant." Telegram & Gazette, February 12, 2017, https://www.telegram.com/story/entertainment/fashion/2017/02/12/quilling-is-ancient-paper -craft-that-is-easy-to-learn-and-can-add-panache-to-valentines-day-cards/22479868007/.*

Papercutting

"New Year paper cuttings helped me make friends, especially within the American-Chinese community. It made me realize how much [they] appeal to people on a cultural level." *

—NICK TSAO,
Architect

ART   COST: $

Papercutting is an art form where an artist folds the paper, cuts away with scissors or a craft knife, then unfolds it to reveal an impressive design that is usually symmetrical and can range from simple silhouettes to mesmerizingly complex scenes and detailed floral patterns. Papercutting is a cultural practice steeped in history, varying in style and technique across different regions that reflect the traditions and values of the societies from which they emerge. Its earliest origins trace to sixth-century China, where it is known as *jianzhi,* and recognized as an Intangible Cultural Heritage by UNESCO. In Poland, it emerged in the 1800s as a folk craft called *wycinanki* and often reflects rural themes like roosters and flower patterns.

GET STARTED

1. **Gather the materials.** Begin with quality, medium-weight paper and invest in a sharp pair of scissors or a craft knife. A self-healing cutting mat is also a useful tool to protect your surfaces.

2. **Master the basics.** Learn to fold paper symmetrically and practice making straight cuts and curved lines. Start with simple patterns before attempting more complex designs.

---

* Kate Whitehead, *"Architect at the Cutting Edge: How Making Chinese Paper Decorations Became Nick Tsao's Second Career,"* South China Morning Post, *February 7, 2024, https:// www.scmp.com/magazines/post-magazine/arts-music/article/3251061/architect-cutting -edge-how-making-chinese-paper-decorations-became-nick-tsaos-second-career.*

Papermaking

"It's messy and colorful and fun, and while there's a steep learning curve, it's super-satisfying."*

—DENA OGDEN,
Writer

ART   COST: $

Paper was invented in China around 105 CE when Cai Lun, a Han Dynasty court official, devised the first papermaking process. He soaked materials like mulberry bark, hemp waste, old rags, and fishnets, and then beat them into a pulp. The pulp was then diluted with water and poured over a flat, porous frame made of bamboo strips or reeds. When dried, the mat of interwoven fibers became a sheet of paper. Papermaking as a modern hobby still emulates Cai Lun's method except with the addition of new tools and materials that make the process faster and more efficient. It appeals to those who value sustainability and enjoy its tactile and meditative nature, which can feel both therapeutic and deeply rewarding.

GET STARTED

1. **Gather the supplies.** You'll need a mold and deckle (which work together as a frame) to shape the paper, a vat to hold the pulp slurry, and absorbent cloths or felts. For the pulp, recycled paper or natural fibers can be used.

2. **Master the process.** Familiarize yourself with the steps of traditional papermaking, which include pulping, sheet forming, couching, pressing, and drying. Resources can be found in craft books or online tutorials.

*   *https://medium.com/yesandnostalgia/papermaking-is-the-niche-hobby-that-got-me-through-quarantine-92b27e4602be*

Paragliding

"For anyone like me who is drawn to the mountains and the air around them, paragliding is the most beautiful and intimate form of human flight."

—BRYAN FRIEDRICHS,
Property Manager

NATURE/OUTDOOR   COST: $$$

Picture yourself suspended high above the ground, a panoramic view of the landscape unfolding beneath you as you glide through the air with the grace of a bird—this is the essence of paragliding. The pilot sits in a harness, connected to a wing made of lightweight, resilient fabric, catching thermals and wind currents to ascend, travel, and descend. Paragliding evolved from the activities of early parachutists and mountaineers in the 1940s and became a popular recreational activity and competitive sport by the 1980s. Paragliding offers both a thrilling and serene way of witnessing the world from new heights and perspectives. It's a hobby for those with an adventurous spirit, are captivated by the beauty of nature, and find joy in flight.

GET STARTED

1. **Try tandem flights first.** Acquaint yourself with paragliding by booking tandem flights with an instructor.

2. **Become certified.** Most regions have some form of regulation for paragliding that often requires proper training and certification. Enroll in a certified paragliding course to learn about aerodynamics, meteorology, and safety protocols.

3. **Gather your gear.** Invest in quality gear, which includes a wing, harness, helmet, and reserve parachute.

Parkour

"Parkour taught me to overcome my fear and even work on it. If there is something that scares me, I know exactly what steps I need to take to get over those thoughts."*

—ALEX LINEIKIN,
Student

NATURE/OUTDOOR   COST: $

Parkour is about getting from one point to another in the quickest and most efficient way possible using only the human body. It emphasizes utility and functional strength, showcasing movements like running, jumping, climbing, and rolling. Parkour practitioners, known as *traceurs,* traverse cityscapes with the fluidity of a stream of water, finding the path of least resistance. The term itself was coined by David Belle in the late 1980s, influenced by his father Raymond Belle who used his training in the French military to develop the foundational principles of efficiency and speed that underpin the discipline. Parkour gained global attention in the early 2000s, quickly progressing from a niche activity to a world-recognized movement, often showcased in films, advertisements, and documentaries. Freerunning, a closely related discipline of parkour, centers more in self-expression by adding acrobatics and flair like flips, spins, and tricks.

GET STARTED

1. **Train your body.** Parkour is a physically demanding activity. Begin by conditioning your body with simple exercises like running, jumping, and climbing to build strength, flexibility, and endurance.

2. **Start small.** Practice the basics in a safe environment, like a parkour park or gym, before attempting more complex movements in urban settings.

---

* Mor Goren and Yuval Gamliel, "Israeli Teen Who Took Up Parkour to Cope with COVID-19 Blues," Ynetnews, September 3, 2022, https://www.ynetnews.com/culture/article/bjdwhmsyj.

Pet Sports

"My dogs are very active, and I needed to find them an outlet for their energy, so I started playing Frisbee in the backyard with them and it snowballed from there."

—JOHNNA ZONA,
Environmental Scientist

COMPETITIVE   COST: $

Pet sports encompass a wide array of competitive activities that involve animals showcasing their agility, intelligence, and natural abilities. From the precision and grace of a horse clearing show jumps to the deft maneuvers of a cat on an agility course, pet sports celebrate the varied talents of our animal companions. Pet sports, when approached with a spirit of stewardship and care, can strengthen the bond between humans and animals. It's a hobby that celebrates the physical and mental agility of our pets and the unique bond we share with them. Engaging in pet sports can enrich the lives of both the pet and the handler, offering a fulfilling pastime that builds trust, respect, and an unbreakable bond.

GET STARTED

1. **Explore the options.** Start by researching the various pet sports available to find one that aligns with your pet's breed, temperament, and interests, as well as your own.

2. **Prioritize safety.** The well-being of your pet needs to be the top priority. It is essential that any sport or training activity with animals is conducted humanely.

3. **Start with basic training.** Ensure your pet has a solid foundation in basic obedience and socialization. Embrace training methods that use positive reinforcement, rewarding desired behaviors with treats, praise, or play to foster a positive association with the activity.

Pet Therapy

"Coming to help people helps me." *

—ALAN PRESTON,
IT Company Owner

VOLUNTEERING   COST: $$$

Pet therapy, also known as animal-assisted therapy, is a heartfelt endeavor where animal lovers share their pet's warmth and companionship with those in need of comfort. Psychologist Dr. Boris Levinson is often credited with pioneering the modern use of pet therapy in the 1960s when he noticed the positive effect his dog had on patients during therapy sessions. Since then, the growth of pet therapy as a volunteer activity has grown exponentially. For the recipients of pet therapy, the presence of an animal can reduce stress, encourage communication, and provide a sense of comfort. For the handlers, it offers the reward of witnessing improvements in the lives of others, facilitated by the bond with their animal.

GET STARTED

1. **Prepare for the commitment.** Recognize the responsibility of working with vulnerable populations and ensure you have the time and emotional capacity to commit.

2. **Train and certify your pet.** Your pet must be well-trained, sociable, and able to pass a therapy animal certification, which assesses temperament and behavior in various situations.

3. **Volunteer and continue education.** You can start volunteering with established pet therapy organizations to gain experience and understand best practices. Stay informed about the latest research in animal-assisted therapy to ensure your practices are beneficial and up-to-date.

* Maddy Franklin, "At Moffitt Cancer Centers, Therapy Dogs Offer Joy and Support," Tampa Bay Times, August 5, 2023, https://www.tampabay.com/life-culture/pets/2023/08/05/moffitt-cancer-center-therapy-dogs-tampa/.

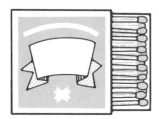

Phillumeny

"Ever since I was little, I loved collecting, so it felt natural to pick up a small pack of matches (or two) from places I've been to. If I didn't like the place, I won't take the matches."

—ALEX BASS,
Fine Art Studio Founder

COLLECTING   COST: $

Phillumeny, while not commonly known by its formal name, is the hobby of collecting match-related items like matchbox labels, matchbooks, match covers, and other matchbox paraphernalia. Unlike stamp collecting (philately) or coin collecting (numismatics), which often emphasize rarity or monetary value, phillumeny is as much about the artistry and design of the items as it is about their cultural and historical significance. John Walker, a pharmacist from England, is credited with inventing the first friction matches in 1826. These early matches were often called "Lucifers," its etymology meaning "light-bringing." Matchbox designs can reflect social history, advertising trends, political movements, and artistic movements, offering a unique lens through which to view the past.

GET STARTED

1. **Focus your collection.** Whether it's vintage labels, exotic locales, or a particular color or design, a focus can make your collecting more meaningful and manageable.

2. **Start local.** Begin by collecting matchboxes from local establishments you visit, such as restaurants, bars, and hotels. You can join online forums and local collector groups to learn from experienced phillumenists and gradually expand your collection.

---

* Camille Freestone, "Did You Really Go to That Restaurant If You Don't Have the Branded Matches to Prove It?" Coveteur, August 17, 2023, https://coveteur.com/match-cover-collecting-trend.

Photography

"I got started with this hobby to cast an intentional glance at the world—a way to find focus and beauty in the settings we inhabit every day."

—S. BENJAMIN ELKO JR.,
Pie Baker

ART   COST: $$$

The earliest known photograph was produced by French inventor Joseph Nicéphore Niépce in 1826. He created a process called heliography, which captured images on a chemically coated metal plate after long exposure to light. Photography has become more instant and accessible with the proliferation of smartphones and digital cameras, but analog photography remains popular for its hands-on nature and nostalgic aesthetic.

GET STARTED

1. **Choose a subject.** If you feel drawn toward connecting with others, portraiture might be the avenue to explore. If you enjoy immersing yourself in nature, take your camera with you on hikes.

2. **Choose analog or digital.** If you own a smartphone with a camera, you can immediately start with digital photography and use the embedded tools on your phone to edit your photos. For analog photography, you'll need to acquire a film camera and all required accessories (lenses, film, and so on). Though the learning curve is higher, analog photography can feel highly rewarding for those who enjoy its unique aesthetic and tactile experience.

3. **Learn basic photography principles.** Understand principles like the rule of thirds (a composition guideline), leading lines, framing, negative space, and depth of field.

Pickleball

"It's something that keeps you active, but is low-impact and beginner-friendly. What I love most is getting to be competitive while still having fun!"

—MADISON SHAFFER,
Corporate Insurance Communications

PHYSICAL FITNESS   COST: $

Pickleball is a paddle sport that combines elements of tennis, badminton, and table tennis. Players use solid paddles made of wood or composite materials to hit a perforated polymer ball, similar to a Wiffle ball, over a net. Invented by three fathers from Bainbridge Island, Washington, in 1965—Joel Pritchard, Bill Bell, and Barney McCallum—the name is allegedly attributed to Pritchard's dog, Pickles, who would chase stray balls during the game. The sport can be played both indoors and outdoors on a badminton-sized court with a slightly modified tennis net. The game is low-impact and easy to learn, making it accessible to a wide range of ages and skill levels. It's particularly suited for those who enjoy racket sports, social interaction, and a blend of strategic play and physical activity.

GET STARTED

1. **Learn the rules.** Familiarize yourself with the official rule book or watch instructional videos to understand the scoring system and rules of the game. Basics include two or four players, serving underhand, and typically playing to eleven points.

2. **Buy your gear and find a court.** Purchase a basic pickleball paddle, which can be relatively inexpensive, and a few pickleballs. Locate a community center, local gym, or outdoor park with a pickleball court to start playing.

Pickling

"I love how easy pickling is to start, and how forgiving it is—you can pickle practically anything, and it will almost always taste fantastic."

—EMILY CATALANO,
Owner of Digital Content Agency

FOOD   COST: $$

Pickling is the culinary art of preserving food by fermentation in brine or immersion in vinegar. The earliest records of pickling date to 2030 BCE in the Tigris Valley where cucumbers native to India were pickled. However, the tradition likely evolved independently across various cultures as a method to preserve food, especially in regions with long winters. Pickling not only extends the shelf life of foods but imparts a unique, tangy flavor and provides beneficial bacteria that contribute to gut health. Pickling is a year-round hobby for many culinary enthusiasts who enjoy the blend of science and creativity, and take pleasure in the transformative process of fermentation.

GET STARTED

1. **Understand the basics.** Learn the difference between vinegar-based pickling (quick pickles) and fermentation-based pickling (which creates a brine over time).

2. **Gather the supplies.** You'll need fresh produce like cucumbers, carrots, or cabbage; salt; water; vinegar; and a selection of spices and herbs. Glass jars with airtight lids are also essential for storing your pickled creations.

3. **Prioritize food safety.** Ensure cleanliness in your preparation, including sterilizing the jars to avoid contamination. Follow guidelines for proper storage to ensure that your pickled foods are safe to eat.

Pigeon Racing

*"My first fight was about pigeons, and that led me here. I'm gonna be an old man and die by my pigeons."**

—MIKE TYSON,
Retired Professional Boxer

COMPETITIVE   COST: $$$

Pigeon racing is a competitive sport in which specially bred and trained pigeons are released from specific locations and race back to their home lofts over a measured distance. The pigeon with the highest calculated velocity over the course is declared the winner. Belgian fanciers, or trainers, first formalized the sport in the 1800s after breeding the homing pigeon, a breed with refined navigation skills and swift flight. The hobby remains popular in Belgium with significant followings in the Netherlands, the United Kingdom, the United States, Australia, and China.

GET STARTED

1. **Research and learn.** Learn the ins and outs of pigeon care, including ethical practices, feeding, health maintenance, and training.

2. **Build or buy a loft.** A safe and comfortable loft is essential for housing your pigeons. Whether you build it yourself or purchase a premade one, ensure it meets the space and safety needs of racing pigeons.

3. **Acquire racing pigeons.** Obtain pigeons from reputable breeders with a track record of racing success.

---

* *Tanya Tewari, "Weeks After Predicting He'd Die Beside His Loving Pigeons, Emotional Mike Tyson Gets Teary-Eyed While Talking About His 'Power Animal' in Recently Surfaced Video,"* Essentially Sports, *September 13, 2023, https://www.essentiallysports.com/boxing-news-weeks-after-predicting-he-d-die-beside-his-loving-pigeons-emotional-mike-tyson-gets-teary-eyed-while-talking-about-his-power-animal-in-recently-surfaced-video/.*

Pilates

*"I fell hard for the exercise, which fatigued my muscles in all the right ways."**

—JAYME CYK,
Editor

PHYSICAL FITNESS   COST: $

Pilates, named after its creator Joseph Pilates, is a low-impact exercise that emphasizes the balanced development of the body through core strength and flexibility. Developed with his wife Clara in the 1920s, the practice is known for its focus on the center of the body, which when strengthened offers a solid foundation for any movement. The major draws of Pilates include its adaptability to many fitness levels and needs, its enhancement of muscle tone without adding bulk, and its ability to improve posture, flexibility, and mobility. It's particularly suited to those who are looking for a gentle but challenging workout, individuals rehabilitating from injuries, or anyone seeking a disciplined practice that unites body and mind. It offers a distinct approach to physical fitness with mindfulness of breath and alignment at its core.

GET STARTED

1. **Find a class.** It can be helpful to attend at least a few classes with a certified instructor at first to master the correct form for Pilates exercises. Look for a beginner's class at a local gym, community center, or Pilates studio. Mat Pilates is a form well-suited for home practice and can be learned by following online classes.

2. **Dress appropriately.** Wear comfortable, form-fitting clothing that allows for fluid movement and enables the instructor to see your form.

* *https://www.vogue.com/article/amanda-kassar-pilates-by-amanda-private-studio-los-angeles-full-body-workout*

Piloting

"There's nothing like leaving the ground in low clouds and rain climbing up and popping out above the clouds to a clear blue sky . . . so peaceful."

—GARRET T. HOOPER,
Engineering Manager

EDUCATIONAL   COST: $$$

Piloting is a hobby that encompasses everything from flying small planes to operating gliders and helicopters. For many, it's an exhilarating blend of freedom, precision, and exploration. While Orville and Wilbur Wright are renowned for their pioneering achievements in aviation during the early twentieth century, the field of recreational flying was popularized by numerous aviation enthusiasts worldwide. After World War I, a surplus of military aircrafts became available and former military pilots sought to continue flying in peacetime. Flying clubs began to emerge in the 1920s and 1930s, making aviation more accessible to the public.

GET STARTED

1. **Complete medical and legal requirements.** Before you can begin training, you must obtain a medical certificate and ensure you meet the legal requirements for flying in your region.

2. **Join a flying club.** Research flying schools or clubs in your area. Many offer introductory sessions or discovery flights, which are great opportunities to experience flying firsthand.

3. **Train toward certification.** Enroll in a certified flight training program. Training typically involves both ground school for theoretical knowledge and forty to sixty hours of flight training for practical skills. After obtaining your pilot's license, continuous learning and regular practice are key to maintaining and enhancing your skills.

Pinball Gaming

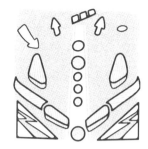

"I was hooked by the bells and chimes, the rhythmic flippers, and the spinning silver ball. Soon, I was regularly trading in dollar bills for pockets full of quarters, looking for my next game." *

—JUANA SUMMERS,
Public Radio Co-Host

COMPETITIVE   COST: $$

Pinball games are based in coin-operated arcade machines where players score points by manipulating one or more metallic balls on a playfield enclosed by glass. The goal is to keep the ball in play for as long as possible while navigating a maze of obstacles, bumpers, and targets. Inspired by a French game known as bagatelle from the 1700s, early pioneers like Steve Kordek and Harry Williams in the United States are credited for influencing the design and overall evolution of pinball machines during the 1930s and 1940s. Pinball gaming offers a unique combination of physical skill, strategy, and nostalgia. It's a hobby that transcends generations, inviting players into a world of flashing lights, intricate artwork, and the timeless challenge of beating the high score.

GET STARTED

1. **Find machines.** Begin by visiting local arcades or bars that house pinball machines. This allows you to play on different machines and understand the nuances of the game.

2. **Learn the game and join others.** Understand the basic techniques like flipping, nudging, and ball control. There are plenty of online resources, tutorials, and player communities that can offer tips and strategies. Many cities have pinball leagues or tournaments, which can be a fun way to improve your skills.

* *https://www.npr.org/2022/06/28/1091211119/juana-summers-pinball*

Plogging

"Plogging is a great opportunity for people to get together and be with like-minded volunteers—folks that also care about the environment—to preserve the good land that we have." *

—NATALIE UNRUH,
Water Quality Planner

NATURE/OUTDOOR   COST: $

Plogging, a portmanteau of "jogging" and the Swedish phrase *plocka upp*, meaning "pick up," is the unique hobby of jogging while stopping to collect litter along a route. Plogging was started around 2016 by Swedish environmental enthusiast Erik Ahlström. It quickly gained traction as a global movement, propelled by an increasing awareness and emphasis on sustainability and personal wellness. Plogging is a simple yet powerful way to make a difference, one run and one piece of trash at a time. As it continues to grow in popularity, plogging represents a movement toward a cleaner, healthier world, and a more eco-conscious approach to exercise.

GET STARTED

1. **Equip yourself.** In addition to a pair of comfortable running shoes, basic supplies you'll need include gloves or a grabber for handling trash and a bag to collect litter.

2. **Plan your route.** Choose a familiar area to start, like your neighborhood or a local park. As you jog, keep an eye out for litter along the way. Always prioritize safety. Be aware of your surroundings and keep cautious of sharp objects and potentially hazardous materials.

---

* *Valerie Verkamp, "'Plogging' Is a Way to Clean Trails, Neighborhoods,"* The Landmark, *October 9, 2023, https://plattecountylandmark.com/2023/10/09/plogging-is-a-way-to-clean-trails-neighborhoods/.*

Podcasting

"I felt the need to connect with folks and connect folks to each other in a new way. This need evolved into a podcast that shares the good news that's going on out there."

—TRESSA GLOVER,
Actor and Content Creator

TECH   COST: $$

A podcast is a series of spoken word audio episodes centered around a specific topic or theme, ranging from news and education to storytelling and comedy. Podcasts give creators complete control over content, format, and release schedule, while listeners can tune in on streaming services at their convenience. The term "podcasting" blends "iPod" (the iconic Apple media player) and "broadcasting," and its roots can be traced back to the early 2000s. Figures like Dave Winer, a software developer, and Adam Curry, a former MTV video DJ, played crucial roles in the development and popularization of the format. Podcasting is a medium that can be highly personalized, allowing you to discuss topics that you're most passionate about with a global audience.

GET STARTED

1. **Identify your niche.** This could range from genres like true crime or sports, sharing your professional expertise, or discussing nuances of identity from gender to ethnicity.

2. **Select your equipment.** Invest in a good-quality microphone and headphones. You'll also need recording and editing software, which can often be found for free or at a low cost. Many people begin by using their own smartphone.

3. **Plan and publish your content.** Outline your episodes, decide on a format (interview, storytelling, etc.), and develop a content schedule. Choose a podcast hosting service such as Spotify for Podcasters or Buzzsprout.

Poetry

*"Journaling turned into poetry.
Our words have power."*

—ISABELLA ST. KIM,
Retired Construction Worker

ART   COST: $

Poetry stands as one of the oldest and most enduring forms of creative expression. Using written language to express emotions, ideas, and stories, poetry is known for its rhythmic and aesthetic qualities, often employing rhyme and meter to evoke a deeper resonance with readers. However, poetry is far from confined to any single form or structure. From the love-themed Italian sonnets of the thirteenth century to the three-line haikus of Japan that often honor nature and the present moment, poetry is an incredibly versatile and personal mode of expression. Subjects can range just as widely from the profoundly personal to the universally relatable. Poetry appeals to those who are introspective and find solace in words. It is a hobby that offers a unique way to capture the intricacies of human emotion and experience.

GET STARTED

1. **Start writing.** Don't worry about adhering to specific structures or styles at first. The key is to express yourself and find your voice.

2. **Read widely.** Read works from different time periods, cultures, and styles to understand the breadth and diversity of the form.

3. **Experiment and explore.** Experiment with different poetic forms like free verse or limericks. Explore techniques like imagery, metaphor, and alliteration to enhance your work. Consider sharing your work through local poetry readings or online forums.

Pokémon GO

"I needed something to keep myself motivated to get out and go on walks and connect with people. I jokingly started playing three years ago and haven't stopped yet!"

—JILLIAN WILSON,
Warehouse Area Manager

TECH   COST: $

Pokémon GO is a mobile game that was developed and released by Niantic, Inc. in collaboration with Nintendo and The Pokémon Company in 2016. The game was one of the first to successfully integrate augmented reality (AR) technology on a large scale. It quickly became a global phenomenon, tapping into the nostalgia of the Pokémon franchise that originated in the 1990s with video games, a television series, and a trading card game. Players, or "trainers," use their smartphones to locate, capture, and train virtual creatures known as Pokémon, which appear as if they are in the player's real-world location. Trainers often meet and connect with others during their adventures, participating in group events like "raids" to capture rare Pokémon. Whether you're a long-time fan of Pokémon or new to the franchise, Pokémon GO offers a fun and active way to engage with the world.

GET STARTED

1. **Download the app.** Available on iOS and Android, you can download Pokémon GO from the app store on your phone. It is free to play with optional in-app purchases available for certain items or features.

2. **Start exploring and join community events.** Begin by exploring your local area. Pokémon will appear on your map, and you can attempt to catch them by using Poké Balls. Participate in local and global events to meet other players, capture rare Pokémon, and experience the full joy of the Pokémon GO community.

Pole Dancing

"For me, pole dancing is my form of meditation. It grounds me and allows me to feel sexy, strong, and empowered."

—JESSIE ZAK,
E-commerce and Experience Director

PHYSICAL FITNESS   COST: $$

Pole dancing has historical roots in Indian acrobatics and Chinese circus arts, where wooden poles were used to showcase incredible feats of strength and agility. The modern growth of pole dancing in mainstream fitness classes attests to its popularity as a comprehensive physical workout, shedding its stigma of being associated with the adult entertainment industry. Requiring a mastery of gripping, climbing, and maneuvering around a pole, pole dancing helps improve muscle strength, flexibility, and endurance. It's a hobby that offers a unique way for individuals to stay fit, boost their confidence, and enjoy the camaraderie of an inclusive community.

GET STARTED

1. **Join a class.** Look for beginner classes at local studios or gyms. Professional instruction is important to learn the correct techniques and avoid injuries.

2. **Buy the proper attire.** Find comfortable and form-fitting clothing to wear that allows for a wide range of motion. Grip aids can also be helpful for beginners.

3. **Invest in your own pole.** If you want to practice at home, most poles are 8 to 9 feet (2.4 to 2.7 meters) in height and require ample clearance around the diameter. Research professional installment to ensure your home space is adequate and safe for a personal pole. You'll also want full-length mirrors to help you observe and correct your form as you progress.

Polymer Clay

"What I cherish most is the intricate work, crafting the tiniest details in a quarter-inch space or smaller. It's my escape—working with headphones on, focused, where racing thoughts fade away."

—KELLI BOOHER,
Speech and Language Pathologist

ART   COST: $

Polymer clay is a malleable type of plastic-based clay that comes in a wide range of colors and is particularly ideal for shaping into intricately detailed forms like jewelry and small sculptures. Unlike earthen clays that require a kiln for firing, polymer clay hardens and sets when baked in a regular home oven, making it an accessible medium for hobbyists. Polymer clay was first developed in the 1930s and 1940s by the German dollmaker Kathe Kruse and her daughter Sofie "Fifi" Kruse, who sought a safer, more versatile material for her dolls. Polymer clay remains an attractive and popular medium for its ease of use, affordability, and the limitless creative possibilities it offers. It is less messy than traditional clay and stays malleable until baked, allowing you to start and stop projects at your own pace. Creating polymer clay art is a great hobby for anyone who enjoys detailed, hands-on crafting and seeks a creative outlet that is both flexible and relaxing.

GET STARTED

1. **Gather the materials.** Start with a selection of polymer clay colors. Choose a work surface like a ceramic tile or glass board, and a few shaping tools. A home oven is sufficient for baking the clay.

2. **Start simple.** Check out online tutorials and books to familiarize yourself with fundamental techniques like conditioning the clay and blending colors. Begin with small projects like beads, pendants, or simple figurines.

Pony Sweat

"Pony Sweat really gives me the opportunity to unplug my overthinking mind and not only get into my body but tap into my core self."

—ADRIANA S.,
Literary Agent

PHYSICAL FITNESS   COST: $

Pony Sweat is a unique and inclusive form of dance aerobics characterized by its emphasis on self-expression and body positivity. Unlike traditional aerobics where the focus is often on intensity and uniformity, Pony Sweat encourages individuality and the joy of movement. Participants are invited to move in ways that feel good to them, embracing their own rhythm and style. The concept of Pony Sweat was created in Los Angeles during the mid-2010s by actress Emilia Richeson-Valiente, who sought to develop an exercise class without the pressures of conforming to traditional fitness norms. Her vision was to create a space where everyone, regardless of their body type or dance experience, could enjoy the benefits of aerobic exercise in a supportive and judgment-free environment. Pony Sweat's appeal lies in its accessibility and celebratory nature. It's a hobby for individuals who are looking for a fun and liberating way to exercise and seek an alternative to conventional fitness culture.

GET STARTED

1. **Find a class.** Look for Pony Sweat classes in your area. Many classes are offered in dance studios or community centers. There are also online options available, including recorded sessions and live-streamed classes.

2. **Join the community.** Pony Sweat is as much about community as it is about exercise. Engage with fellow participants and embrace the supportive atmosphere.

Pop-Up Art

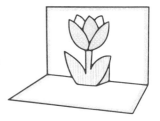

"We normally think of paper as flat, quiet, and obedient. With pop-ups, I love that even humble everyday paper can jump, sing, and surprise us."

—MARC,
Human-Centered Designer

ART   COST: $

Pop-up art is a form of paper engineering that breathes life into a flat page by transforming it into a three-dimensional story. Imagine turning over a sheet of paper and witnessing moving pieces of art that rise from the page! Pop-up art began to flourish in the nineteenth century with the work of Lothar Meggendorfer (1847–1925), a German illustrator who created complex and delightful moving books for children. Paper mechanics became a storytelling device, making books come alive in readers' hands. In the world of pop-up art, every crease tells a story, and every cut can lead to a delightful surprise. It's a hobby that invites you to not only tell a story but to make it leap into the real world. Pop-up art draws in those with a love for paper crafts and an appreciation for tactile experiences that the digital world often lacks.

GET STARTED

1. **Learn the basics.** Start by learning the foundational techniques of paper folding and cutting. Books and online tutorials can guide you through simple forms like the V-fold and layering.

2. **Gather the tools.** Precision is key, so arm yourself with the essentials: quality paper, a craft knife, a cutting mat, and a bone folder for creasing.

3. **Start simple.** Craft your first pop-ups using basic shapes and mechanisms. A great beginner project is making pop-up cards. As you grow more comfortable, you can begin introducing more intricate designs and movements.

Pottery

"Centering the clay is tremendously relaxing. I've been doing pottery since the COVID-19 pandemic started and continue to learn and find my relaxing place in the world."

—AMY S. REED,
Financial Business Analyst

ART   COST: $$

Pottery is the art of transforming clay into functional and decorative items like bowls, vases, and sculptures. The multistep process includes preparing the clay, molding it into desired shapes, and finally firing it in a kiln to achieve durability and strength. The oldest known pieces of pottery are ceramic fragments discovered in Xianrendong Cave in southern China. These fragments date back to eighteen to twenty thousand years ago, during the late Paleolithic period, suggesting that our ancestors engaged in pottery making thousands of years before the advent of agriculture and permanent settlements. Pottery offers a therapeutic, almost meditative experience, as the potter becomes deeply engaged in the act of creation.

GET STARTED

1. **Enroll in a class.** Beginner classes are a great way to introduce yourself to foundational pottery skills like clay handling, wheel-throwing techniques, and basic sculpting. Look for classes at community centers, art schools, or specialized pottery studios.

2. **Gather your own tools.** Pottery usually requires ample space to accommodate a wheel, kiln, sink, and storage for your creations. However, it can still be helpful to have your own set of basics, like an apron and various hand tools like a rib (a shaping tool), wire cutter, sponge, and needles.

Puppetry

"Through my puppets, I can reimagine my past, respond to present circumstances and situations, and consider how to head into the future."

—SHERRI ROBERTS,
Retired Health Educator

ART   COST: $

Puppetry is the art of bringing to life inanimate objects to tell a story. From shadow puppets in Asia to marionettes in Europe, puppetry is an ancient performance art that developed independently in different regions around the world. Puppetry can be used for both entertainment and education within a diverse range of contexts from cultural traditions to avant-garde theater performances. In building unique puppets and performing with your creations, puppetry as a hobby can offer an outlet for creative expression, therapeutic storytelling, and a social platform.

1. **Choose your style and materials.** Consider the scale you enjoy working with and what kind of stories you want to express through your art. You can create finger puppets for something small and intimate or life-size puppets for more gravitas. Common beginner's puppets include sock puppets, paper bag puppets, and craft-stick puppets, but you can use any material to create your puppets.

2. **Learn puppetry techniques.** The basic hand technique for animating a sock puppet is to open and close your hand between your thumb and other four fingers, while marionette puppetry requires delicately manipulating strings and wires from a height that control the puppet below you.

Pyrography

"I love the start when I'm starting to draw the piece out. I'll go from a deer looking like some sort of dog-horse to actually looking like a deer." *

—ISABELLA ROBBINS,
Student

ART   COST: $

Pyrography, commonly known as wood burning, is the art of decorating wood or other natural materials by burning designs, patterns, and pictures into their surface with the controlled application of a heated object. The practice of pyrography dates to ancient times but started gaining popularity as a modern recreational hobby during the Victorian era when new tools allowed for more detailed and refined work. Pyrography requires a steady hand and a focused mind, making it a meditative and satisfying experience. It is a rewarding hobby that combines artistic skill with a love for natural materials.

GET STARTED

1. **Gather the tools.** Invest in a basic pyrography kit, which typically includes a wood-burning pen, various interchangeable tips for different techniques, and safety gear like gloves and a mask.

2. **Gather the materials.** Start with soft woods like basswood or pine, which are ideal for novices because they're easier to burn. Though wood is the primary material used in pyrography, you can also use the technique on leather, gourds, cork, or bamboo.

---

* Patrick Davies, "Student Discovers a Passion for Pyrography," 100 Mile Free Press, June 18, 2023, https://www.100milefreepress.net/entertainment/student-discovers-a-passion-for-pyrography-5462404.

Pysanky

"There's just something about the shapes and the colors and the patterns. They stick in my head. I can see a pattern on a piece of Christmas wrapping and think about it all day." *

—BOB DEATON,
Retired Army Colonel

ART   COST: $

Pysanky is the intricate practice of egg decorating using a wax-resist method. The name comes from the Ukrainian verb *pysaty*, meaning "to write," as the designs are not painted on but applied with beeswax. Its exact origins are unclear, but the art form has been an integral part of Ukrainian culture for thousands of years. Each region in Ukraine developed its own distinct style of pysanky, where every pattern, color, and motif hold specific meanings that often tell a story or impart a blessing. Pysanky is a way to connect with a rich cultural history and participate in a centuries-old tradition.

GET STARTED

1. **Gather the supplies.** Essential supplies include a special tool for applying the wax called a *kistka*, beeswax, dyes in various colors, and, of course, eggs. Use raw, room-temperature white eggs that have been washed with dish soap and wiped with vinegar.

2. **Learn the basics.** Familiarize yourself with the wax-resist process, which involves applying wax to the egg in the areas that you want to remain white, then dyeing the egg.

3. **Understand the symbols.** Each symbol and color has its own meaning and significance. This understanding will enrich your practice and help you create more authentic designs.

* *Joanne Kimberlin, "He's a 'Man's Man' with a Delicate Hobby: Painting Eggs,"* The Virginian Pilot, *January 1, 2021, https://www.pilotonline.com/2021/01/01/hes-a-mans-man-with-a-delicate-hobby-painting-eggs/.*

Quidditch

*"Not being a big Harry Potter fan I couldn't have ever imagined it would be something of interest. But when I saw it was full contact, my friends persuaded me to give it a try, and next thing I knew I was hooked."**

—KEDZIE TELLER,
Social Content Specialist

GAMES/SOCIAL   COST: $$

Quidditch is a sport inspired by the fictional game, played on flying broomsticks, featured in J.K. Rowling's fantasy series, *Harry Potter.* In 2005, students Xander Manshel and Alex Benepe at Middlebury College created the real-life, grounded adaptation, which quickly gained popularity and evolved into an organized sport with international tournaments and a governing body—the International Quidditch Association. Quidditch is a mixed-gender sport that blends elements of rugby, dodgeball, and tag. Regardless of whether you're a *Harry Potter* enthusiast, you can enjoy quidditch as an unconventional team sport that promotes equality, inclusivity, and sportsmanship.

GET STARTED

1. **Learn the rules and equip yourself.** Familiarize yourself with the official rule book of Quidditch to understand the gameplay, positions, and equipment. Basic equipment includes a broom or a PVC pipe as a broom substitute, a Quaffle, Bludgers, hoops, and comfortable athletic wear.

2. **Find a local team or league.** Search for Quidditch clubs or teams in your area. Many universities and communities have teams, and they often welcome new members of all skill levels with practice games.

---

* Colin Morris, *"Austin After Hours: 7 Hobbies That Keep Tech Workers Sane,"* The Virginian Pilot, *March 18, 2016, https://www.builtinaustin.com/2016/03/18/best-hobbies-austin-tech.*

Quilting

"There is something magical about exploring the myriad possibilities of combining pieces of fabric into functional pieces of art."

—KIRA,
Feldenkrais Practitioner

FIBER ARTS   **COST: $**

The origins of quilting can be traced back thousands of years to ancient civilizations across Asia, the Middle East, and Europe. It gained significant popularity in the United States during the eighteenth and nineteenth centuries, as quilting was not only a practical way to create warm bedding but also became a communal activity, especially among women. In contrast to other fiber arts, quilting's hallmark is its layered construction and the specific technique of stitching through these layers. A quilt typically consists of three layers: a quilt top (decoratively pieced or appliquéd fabric), a layer of insulation (the batting), and a back piece. This provides quilting its unique texture and depth, setting it apart as both a craft and a form of artistic expression.

GET STARTED

1. **Learn the basics.** Familiarize yourself with the basic techniques of quilting, such as cutting, piecing, and stitching. There are numerous online resources, books, and classes available for beginners.

2. **Gather the supplies.** Essential supplies include fabric, batting, a good-quality sewing machine (though hand-stitching is also an option), thread, needles, a rotary cutter, cutting mat, and a quilting ruler.

3. **Start simple and join others.** Start with a simple project like a small lap quilt or a quilted pillow cover. Consider joining a local quilting group or taking a class to enjoy the camaraderie of fellow enthusiasts.

Rafting

"You're hard-pressed to have a bad day on the water, and I think that's just what makes it so special. So I think that's why I love it." *

—CHLOE ROSIN,
Physical Therapist

NATURE/OUTDOOR   COST: $$$

Rafting is an exhilarating outdoor group activity that involves navigating a river or another body of water in an inflatable raft. Rafts typically accommodate four to eight people and requires both teamwork and strategy to traverse varying water conditions that range from calm to tumultuous. Rafts were birthed from necessity as a means of transportation. Rafting as a hobby grew around the mid-twentieth century, especially in the United States. It appeals to adventure seekers, nature enthusiasts, and those who enjoy collaborative and physically active pursuits.

GET STARTED

1. **Take a guided tour.** Joining guided rafting tours is a great way to introduce yourself to this activity. Professional guides can provide instruction, safety briefings, and a secure environment for your first few experiences.

2. **Gather gear.** Essential gear includes a life jacket, helmet, and proper clothing for the conditions. Most guided tours offer the necessary equipment for rent.

3. **Choose a level.** Rafting experiences are distinguished by class according to their level of difficulty. Start with calmer rivers, noted as Class I or II rapids, before gradually progressing to more challenging waters.

* *"Whitewater Rafting Company Celebrates Return of Visitors to Stillwater River,"* KTVQ, *July 25, 2023, https://www.ktvq.com/news/local-news/whitewater-rafting-company -celebrates-return-of-visitors-to-stillwater-river.*

Raising Chickens

"Chickens may not be all that smart, but they are actually affectionate, always happy to greet people, and make the funniest little noises . . . the eggs are a plus too!"

—DEBORAH,
Production Artist

NATURE/OUTDOOR   COST: $$$

The domestication of chickens dates back thousands of years, with archaeological evidence suggesting it began in Southeast Asia. As a modern hobby, raising chickens has seen a particular resurgence in urban and suburban areas, fueled by a growing interest in organic and locally sourced food. Chickens are natural foragers and can help control pests in your yard. They have distinct personalities, and their behaviors can be surprisingly entertaining. Watching them interact, forage, and explore is often amusing and a delightful part of this hobby.

GET STARTED

1. **Observe local regulations.** Check your local laws and regulations about keeping chickens. Some areas have specific rules about coops, the number of chickens allowed, and whether roosters are permitted.

2. **Set up a coop.** A coop provides shelter from weather and predators. It should include nesting boxes for laying eggs and a roosting area for sleeping. Generally, each chicken should have at least 1 to 3 square feet (0.09 to 0.32 square meters) of space.

3. **Choose your chickens.** There are many breeds, each with its characteristics, such as egg production, temperament, and adaptability to climates. Research breeds to find the ones that best fit your environment and needs.

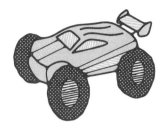

RC Driving

"Everybody says the same thing, 'Oh, you're playing with toy cars,' but really it's an amazing sport."*

—HEATHER NORRIE,
Veterinary Technician

TECH   COST: $$

The world of RC driving, or remote-controlled driving, combines engineering, speed, and community with the thrill of racing on a small scale. Hobbyists "drive" their miniature vehicles—from race cars to trucks and buggies—at a distance by controlling them with a handheld transmitter. These vehicles usually come in kits that require assembly, offering the additional enjoyment of getting to build and customize the cars. RC driving began in the 1960s when advances in electronics made remote-controlled toys more accessible. Today, RC driving has evolved into a highly competitive sport with races and events held worldwide.

GET STARTED

1. **Choose a vehicle.** Start with a ready-to-run (RTR) model suited to your interests. Electric vehicles are generally recommended for beginners due to their ease of use and maintenance. Familiarize yourself with your vehicle's components and how they work.

2. **Find a driving space.** Identify a safe area to practice, such as a local park, an RC track, or even your backyard. Different terrains offer different challenges and learning opportunities.

3. **Connect with others.** Join local RC clubs or online forums that can help you improve your driving skills and inform you about local events and competitions.

* *Angelo Bavaro, "R/C Racing Is Both a Hobby and 'an Amazing Sport' in Enfield," FOX61, September 21, 2023, https://www.fox61.com/article/news/local/hartford-county/rc-racing-madness-enfield-connecticut/520-01511458-bfc8-4bf3-b7a0-167a0c436f2f.*

Reading

"I'm a quadruplet and also have siblings who are twins; growing up in such a loud, chaotic household, reading was the only way for me to escape into my own world."

—JENNA LEFKOWITZ,
College Admissions Reviewer

EDUCATIONAL   COST: $

The allure of reading lies in its boundless capacity to educate, entertain, and enlighten. It's a hobby that transcends age, culture, and background, appealing to anyone with a curiosity for the unknown and a thirst for learning. The advent of written language began in Mesopotamia around 3200 BCE, but it wasn't until the invention of the printing press by Johannes Gutenberg in the fifteenth century when access to books became more democratized and led to the growth of reading as an activity for leisure and personal growth. Reading nurtures empathy, broadens perspectives, and enhances critical thinking. It is especially suited for those who seek mental stimulation and emotional enrichment.

GET STARTED

1. **Choose your book.** First identify topics or genres that intrigue you. Whether it's history, science fiction, mystery, or self-help, choosing subjects that pique your curiosity is key to an enjoyable reading experience. Visit local libraries or bookstores or explore digital platforms for e-books and audiobooks to access your selected reading material.

2. **Set a routine.** Carve out a dedicated time and space for reading. Whether it's a quiet morning ritual or a wind-down activity before bed, a regular routine can help you maintain this hobby.

Refurbishing and Restoring Furniture

"Rediscovering my love for refinishing furniture has been a true gift to me. The fact that it can also benefit the environment and a local charity make it even more rewarding."

—AIMEE TAYLOR,
Marketing Consultant

HOME   COST: $$

Refurbishing and restoring furniture are twin arts of breathing new life into older or worn furniture pieces. Refurbishing involves revamping and updating a piece to suit current tastes or functional needs, often through painting, reupholstering, or creative redesign. Restoration, on the other hand, is the meticulous process of returning furniture to its original state, preserving its historical essence and craftsmanship. The charm of refurbishing and restoring furniture lies in its blend of creativity, history, and sustainability. It appeals to those who appreciate the stories embedded in old furniture and enjoy the process of transformation or preservation.

GET STARTED

1. **Learn basic skills.** Gain knowledge in basic carpentry, upholstery, and refinishing skills. Online tutorials, community college courses, or local workshops can be excellent starting points.

2. **Gather the materials.** Assemble a toolkit that includes items like sandpaper, paint, brushes, and upholstery materials. Over time, you can expand your toolkit as you develop more advanced skills. You can start with pieces of furniture you already own or seek out thrift stores, flea markets, garage sales, or online marketplaces to find used furniture items that can be refurbished or restored.

* Kristen Wolfe, "An Experiment in Rescuing Furniture by Aimee Taylor (Finished for Good)," ReStore, *March 2, 2022, https://www.loudounrestore.org/blog/2022/3/2/an-experiment-in-rescuing-furniture-by-aimee-taylor-finished-for-good.*

Resin Casting

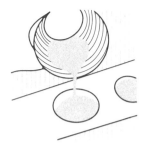

*"It's exciting, it's seductive, you can embed
things in it, you can work with colors."**

—GINA WESTERGARD,
Professor

ART   COST: $$

Resin casting is a creative process where liquid synthetic resin is poured into molds to create detailed and durable plastic-like objects. This versatile craft allows for the encapsulation of various items like flowers, glitter, or even small keepsakes within the resin, creating strikingly beautiful pieces that are often translucent. The resin, once hardened, can also be shaped, polished, and transformed into a multitude of decorative or functional items from jewelry to paperweights or intricate works of art. The roots of resin casting can be traced back to the early twentieth century with the development of synthetic resins like Bakelite, which allowed for the mass production of decorative objects.

GET STARTED

1. **Choose your resin and supplies.** Start by researching the different types of resins available and their specific properties. Epoxy resin is a great one to start with due to its clarity and ease of use. Other supplies you'll need include a hardener, molds, colorants, and any items you wish to encapsulate. Invest in safety equipment like gloves and goggles as well to protect against spills and fumes.

2. **Create a workspace.** Designate a clean, dust-free area to work in. Resin is sticky and can be messy, so a well-prepared space is crucial.

---

* Alicia Marksberry, *"A Resin Jewelry: A New Trend with Dangerous Drawbacks,"* Chalk Magazine, *April 7, 2021, https://www.kansan.com/chalkmagazine/resin-jewelry-a-new-trend -with-dangerous-drawbacks/article_c76f4248-97d2-11eb-8a6c-073e2e8b75c8.html.*

Retro Gaming

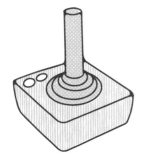

*"My wife and I have easily spent several hundred dollars on our gaming collection. When we have kids, we want them to be able to see the kind of games we played growing up. That alone makes the search, and price, worth it."**

—DANIEL HOWLEY,
Technology Editor

TECH   COST: $$

Retro gaming is a nostalgic and immersive journey back in time that celebrates the history and evolution of video games. Focusing on playing and collecting titles and systems that defined the childhoods of many, retro gamers revel in the charm and simplicity of old-school games, which often feature pixelated graphics and simpler gaming mechanics. The video game industry started in the 1970s with the introduction of home consoles like the Atari 2600 and arcade classics like *Pac-Man* and *Space Invaders*. By the early 2000s, video gaming advanced so rapidly that gamers started to look back fondly at earlier generations of gaming, marking the beginning of retro gaming as a distinct hobby.

GET STARTED

1. **Acquire the gaming systems.** Look for gaming consoles online, in second-hand stores, or at gaming conventions. You can also consider modern replicas or emulation software like RetroArch that allows you to play games from different systems within one interface.

2. **Build your collection.** Begin collecting games that hold personal significance or are considered classics. Flea markets, online marketplaces, and retro-gaming stores are great places to look.

---

*   https://finance.yahoo.com/news/retro-gaming-is-a-pricier-hobby-than-youd-think-214213571.html

Rice Toss Art

*"Art comes in so many different shapes and forms, and it is the artist that gives it life. Who would have thought using something such as rice could create such beautiful art?"** *

—ALISSA TEO,
Mother and Creative Director

ART   COST: $

Rice toss art, also called tossed rice art or aerial rice art, involves laying out a design onto a flat surface using uncooked, colored rice grains and then throwing them into the air. The action is often filmed in slow motion, showing the grains momentarily suspended in the air and revealing the artist's intricate images and patterns. Tossing rice and creating art with dyed rice grains have roots in several Asian cultural traditions. However, the modern iteration of rice toss art came from social media platforms like TikTok where creators started to document and share it as a novel way of creating a visual spectacle.

GET STARTED

1. **Gather the materials and create a workspace.** Buy rice and food coloring (liquid or gel). You'll need a flat surface like a piece of cardboard to lay out your design and a backdrop that makes the rice art stand out when you toss it. Designate a space to work in and consider how to store and protect your art from pests or rodents.

2. **Practice and capture your toss.** Practice tossing rice in different ways to understand how it behaves in the air and falls back down. Set up a camera or smartphone to record or photograph your process, especially the moment of the reveal when the rice is mid-air.

---

* Siphokazi Zama, "Alissa's Tossed Rice Art Is Super Impressive—But Watch Closely or You May Just Miss It!" News24, July 18, 2022, https://www.news24.com/you/news/international /alissas-tossed-rice-art-is-super-impressive-but-watch-closely-or-you-may-just-miss-it-20220718.

Robotics

"I love technology, it's one of my favorite hobbies. My favorite part about tech is something people from the past thought was only the imagination of a child—robots!" *

—ZACHARY CORALLO,
Student

TECH   COST: $$$

Robotics involves the design, construction, operation, and application of machines that can perform tasks that range from the simple and mundane to the highly complex and interactive. The term "robot" was first introduced in 1920 by Czech writer Karel Čapek in his play *R.U.R.* (or *Rossum's Universal Robots*). The field of robotics as distinct area of study was established throughout the mid-twentieth century, greatly advanced by inventors and scientists like George Charles Devol Jr. (1912–2011). Robotics as a hobby offers an exciting way to develop technical skills, foster creative thinking, and participate in the rapidly evolving field of automation and artificial intelligence (AI).

GET STARTED

1. **Research and learn.** Begin by exploring online courses, tutorials, and books on the basics of robotics. Resources that cover fundamental electronics, programming, and mechanical design are particularly useful. Engaging with a community of robotics enthusiasts is also a great way to gain support and inspiration.

2. **Start with a kit.** For beginners, starting with a robotics kit can be a great way to learn. These kits usually have all the necessary parts and instructions to build a simple robot.

* *https://www.newsday.com/lifestyle/family/robotics-twsu-microbot-kidsday-i95948*

Rock Balancing

*"I used to do sand sculptures, then about nine years ago, I started seeing people do rock balancing, and I started doing that, and it progressed from there. It just became an obsession."**

—STEVE WARZEL,
Artist

NATURE/OUTDOOR   COST: $

Rock balancing is a serene and captivating hobby that involves carefully positioning rocks in various arrangements to create structures that appear to defy gravity. Often bearing spiritual or ritualistic significance, the practice stretches back to ancient times across various cultures. Requiring patience and a gentle touch, each stone is meticulously balanced upon another without any adhesive substances, relying solely on gravity and precise positioning to maintain the structure. The formations can range from simple stacks to intricate and seemingly impossible assemblies.

GET STARTED

1. **Collect rocks.** Begin by checking local regulations and familiarizing yourself with public areas where collecting rocks is allowed. Find a variety of rocks with different sizes, shapes, and weights. Look for rocks with flat surfaces that will make balancing easier.

2. **Find a location.** Choose a calm, quiet spot where you can practice balancing your rocks without distractions. This could be a riverside, a beach, or your backyard. You may need to dismantle your balanced rock creation according to the guidelines of certain spaces (like national parks).

---

* Saul Flores, "Milford Man's Rock Sculptures on Brief Display at Beaches, Then Gone Forever," The Milford Mirror, January 3, 2023, https://www.milfordmirror.com/living/article /Milford-resident-rock-sculptures-17681485.php.

Rockhounding

"As a kid, I'd collect the prettiest rocks from our driveway and put them on display. Fast forward twenty-five years, and now you'll find me in abandoned gem mines still looking for the prettiest rocks to put on display on my 'Rock Wall.'"

—NICOLETTE ASH,
Technical Account Manager

NATURE/OUTDOOR   COST: $

Rockhounding, sometimes called rock hunting, is a delightful hobby for outdoor enthusiasts attracted to the idea of finding natural treasures in the Earth's soil. An activity that often leads to picturesque landscapes, rock-hounders search for and collect rocks, minerals, and sometimes fossils from sparkling quartz to colorful agates. This hobby began to grow noticeably as geology became a recognized field of science during the eighteenth and nineteenth centuries. Offering the excitement of a hunt and the opportunity to connect with nature, rockhounding is especially appealing to those with a keen interest in science and the natural world.

GET STARTED

1. **Educate yourself.** Learn the basics of geology and familiarize yourself with the types of rocks and minerals commonly found in your area. Books, online resources, and local geology clubs can be great sources of information.

2. **Gather the tools.** Start with a few essential tools like a rock hammer, chisel, and a sturdy bag or backpack to carry your finds. Don't forget safety gear like gloves and protective eyewear.

3. **Plan your excursion.** Research locations known for rockhounding. Many areas have public lands where you can legally collect rocks. Always ensure you have the necessary permissions and are aware of the local regulations.

Rock Painting

*"It's been my positive outlet. Painting and hiding rocks makes my day when people post pictures of the rocks that I had painted."**

—**CRYSTAL OLNEY,**
Mother

ART   COST: $

Painting on rocks offers a uniquely grounding and therapeutic experience by combining the handling of a weighted natural element and the meditative process of creating artwork on a small surface. It is usually practiced as a solitary activity but carries with it a deep sense of community, as it often involves placing painted rocks in public spaces for others to find. Rock painting requires minimal supplies and can be enjoyed by people of all artistic skill levels. It's a great hobby if you're looking for a low-cost creative outlet and enjoy the idea of spreading happiness and positivity in unexpected places.

GET STARTED

1. **Gather the supplies.** Start with a collection of smooth, flat rocks. Next, purchase some acrylic paints, brushes of various sizes, and a sealant like Mod Podge to protect your designs from the elements.

2. **Prepare and paint your rocks.** Clean yours rocks to remove any dirt or debris before painting. You can paint anything from simple designs or messages to miniature landscapes.

3. **Consider sharing.** You can keep your painted rocks to yourself or place them in random public locations (where allowed) for others to find.

---

* Ashley Ludwig, *"Rock Painting Hobby Becomes Therapy For SoCal Mom,"* Patch, February 23, 2018. https://patch.com/california/losalamitos/los-alamitos-mom-rocks-hand-painted -treasures.

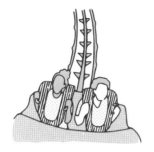

Roller Coaster Riding

"Roller coasters are the ultimate form of controlled chaos! Think about it—their sole purpose as an engineering work of art is that they are designed to scare and thrill."

—ANDY KELEMEN,
Commercial Director

NATURE/OUTDOOR **COST: $$$**

Roller coasters, usually found in amusement parks and theme parks, offer a unique blend of excitement, adrenaline, and entertainment. Enthusiasts often travel to different parks to experience a variety of roller coaster designs from classic wooden coasters to modern steel giants with cutting-edge technology. The earliest roller coasters originated in Russia during the seventeenth century as ice-covered slides known as "Russian Mountains." American inventor LaMarcus Adna Thompson (1848–1919) is credited with developing the designs of modern roller coasters that so many enjoy today. Experiencing the speed, the twists, the drops, and sometimes the feeling of weightlessness of roller coaster rides provide a break from the mundanity of everyday life. It's an exhilarating hobby well-suited for thrill-seekers and those who appreciate engineering marvels.

GET STARTED

1. **Research the options.** Start by researching different amusement parks and their roller coasters. Websites, forums, and guidebooks dedicated to theme parks can provide valuable insights into which coasters are must-rides and what experiences they offer.

2. **Visit different parks.** Begin your roller coaster journey by visiting nearby amusement parks. As you become more immersed in the hobby, consider planning trips to famous amusement parks—both nationally and internationally—to experience world-renowned roller coasters.

Roller Derby

"The thing I love most about roller derby is perseverance; the entire sport is literally getting knocked down and getting back up again."

—CHRISTA K.,
Digital Marketplace Specialist

GAMES/SOCIAL   COST: $$$

Roller derby is a high-energy, contact team sport played on roller skates that combines speed, strategy, and athleticism. It typically involves two teams with no more than five members from each team skating around a track at any given time. Points are scored when a designated scorer, known as the "jammer," laps members of the opposing team. Roller derby originated in the United States during the Great Depression. Leo Seltzer, an event promoter, is often credited with conceiving the sport during this time, while its more current revival owes much to grassroots and feminist movements in addition to its popular portrayals in media. Roller derby appeals to those looking for an intense, full-body workout and an adrenaline rush. The sport is renowned for its inclusive and empowering community, making it appealing to individuals seeking a strong sense of camaraderie and teamwork.

GET STARTED

1. **Join a local team or league.** Familiarize yourself with the rules of the game and look for a local roller derby team or league to join. Many offer "fresh meat" programs for beginners to learn the basics of skating and gameplay.

2. **Acquire the gear.** Purchase or rent the necessary equipment which includes roller skates, a helmet, mouthguard, elbow and knee pads, and wrist guards.

3. **Commit to practice.** Roller derby requires a good level of physical fitness and skill on skates. Regular practice is essential to developing your abilities and understanding of the sport.

Roller Skating

"Not only is it a release, I've become part of a community that's so supportive and welcoming that members ubiquitously refer to it as a family."

—JEFF GUERRERO,
Marketing Manager

PHYSICAL FITNESS   COST: $

Roller skates feature four wheels arranged in two parallel pairs with brakes at the tops of the skates called a toe stop. Roller skating is a versatile hobby that combines the joy of movement with the rhythm of skating, yielding various styles from jam skating to artistic skating and sports skating like in roller derby. Belgian inventor John Joseph Merlin is credited with creating the first roller skates in 1760. With their rudimentary design that lacked the ability to maneuver or brake, Merlin famously crashed into a large mirror while demonstrating his skates at a masquerade party in London. Despite this initial mishap, Merlin's design laid the groundwork for modern roller skating, gaining widespread popularity by the late nineteenth and early twentieth centuries, particularly in the United States where roller rinks were a fixture of social life for many.

GET STARTED

1. **Find a spot to skate.** Identify safe and suitable places to skate. Search for local roller rinks, smooth outdoor surfaces, or community parks.

2. **Choose your gear.** Select a pair of roller skates that fit well and provide good ankle support. Newbies might opt for skates with softer wheels for better grip and stability. Invest in protective gear such as a helmet, knee pads, elbow pads, and wrist guards. When starting out, you can also rent skates and equipment at roller rinks.

Rollerblading

"I love the feeling of freedom, the movement, the speed, the wind at my face. Learning how to skate is like learning to walk all over again, but really, you're learning to fly."

—BRUCE NMEZI,
Research Scientist

`PHYSICAL FITNESS`   `COST: $$`

Rollerblading, also known as inline skating, is a dynamic hobby that involves gliding on skates that have a single line of wheels arranged in the middle. This design allows for smooth, agile movement, closely mimicking the experience of ice skating. The origins of rollerblading trace back to the early 1980s when Scott and Brennan Olson, two Minnesota brothers, discovered an inline skate while looking for offseason hockey training options. The single-row design of rollerblades demands more precision in balance than roller skating but allows for faster, smoother movement, making it ideal for street and speed skating. Unlike roller skates with a toe stop, rollerblades feature a heel brake. Rollerblading offers a full-body workout that enhances your cardiovascular health, balance, and muscular strength.

GET STARTED

1. **Find a rollerblading location.** Find a safe area to practice, like a roller rink, skate park, or park path. Boardwalks are common areas for rollerblading, but be mindful of pedestrians in public spaces and check local regulations.

2. **Select your skates and gear.** Choose a pair of rollerblades suited for beginners, which usually provides more stability and control. Safety is crucial when learning to rollerblade; invest in protective gear like a helmet, knee pads, elbow pads, and wrist guards.

Rowing

"I had to give up my favorite sports due to a serious head injury. I loved being on the water and I loved intensity but didn't know what to substitute. Thankfully, an acquaintance who was a serious rowing coach and I reconnected."

—CHERYL TOWERS,
Artist

PHYSICAL FITNESS   COST: $$$

Rowing is an engaging water sport that blends physical endurance with the rhythm and grace of moving in unison within the water. It broadly divides into two primary styles: sweeping and sculling. When people refer to rowing in a more specific sense, they are often talking about sweeping or sweep rowing. Sweep rowing is a team activity—ranging from two to eight people per boat—where each rower maneuvers a single oar with both hands. Rowers must work in harmony, synchronizing their strokes to maximize efficiency and speed. In sculling, individual rowers use two oars, one in each hand. It can be practiced solo in smaller boats known as single sculls, or in larger team boats. Rowing as a competitive sport began in England during the eighteenth century and has been a part of the Olympic Games since 1900.

GET STARTED

1. **Choose a style.** Decide whether you are drawn to the individual challenge and technique of sculling or the teamwork and synchronization of sweep rowing.

2. **Join a club.** Enroll in a rowing program at a local club. Clubs provide access to boats, coaching, and a community of rowers. They cater to various skill levels and often have beginner courses to teach fundamental techniques, safety, and boat handling for both sculling and sweep rowing.

Rube Goldberg Machines

"Creativity is not limited to artists and writers. It's the ability to solve problems in new and unexpected ways."

—RUBE GOLDBERG,
Cartoonist, Author, and Inventor

EDUCATIONAL **COST: $**

A Rube Goldberg machine is like a chain reaction; each part triggers the next, leading to an often humorous and unexpected conclusion. Rube Goldberg was an American cartoonist who gained fame during the 1920s and 1930s for his depictions of comically intricate and overly complicated machines. For example, the objective might be a simple task like cracking an egg. In a Rube Goldberg comic, you would see a series of interconnected, whimsical steps: a candle burns a string, releasing a pendulum that swings to push a boot, which then kicks a bucket and causes a ball to roll down a ramp and finally hit a hammer, which then cracks the egg. Building Rube Goldberg machines is a creative exercise that works against the adage, "Work smarter, not harder."

GET STARTED

1. **Gather the materials.** Start by collecting various household items like dominoes, marbles, old toys, string, or anything that can be used to create a chain reaction.

2. **Plan your design.** Decide on a simple end goal for your machine like popping a balloon or ringing a bell. Plan how each element can lead to the next. Aim to start with at least five steps. It can be helpful to sketch out your machine on paper.

3. **Build, test, and share.** Start building your machine based on your design. This will likely involve a lot of trial and error, so patience is key.

Running

"I saw a film about the Barkley Marathons and was struck by the commitment to running all the roads of Tennessee. I started to cover the 4,300 streets of the city of Pittsburgh, taking pics and blogging along the way."

—EDWARD MAY,
IT Manager

PHYSICAL FITNESS   COST: $

Running is as simple as it is profound. The speed and rhythm involved offers a unique sense of calm, empowerment, and liberation for those who enjoy running as a hobby. Running became a competitive sport in the first Olympic Games in 776 BCE. As a recreational activity, it particularly boomed in the United States during the 1970s. In addition to a growing public awareness around the importance of physical fitness and health, Frank Shorter's marathon victory in the 1972 Munich Olympics inspired many Americans to take up the sport. This is also when the term "runner's high" originated, referring to the sense of painlessness and euphoria felt after a long run.

GET STARTED

1. **Select your shoes.** Consider what surface you'll primarily be running on and invest in a quality pair that provides a good fit and support for your feet.

2. **Start slow and set goals.** Begin with short distances or intervals of running and walking before gradually increasing the duration and intensity of your runs. Setting goals, whether it's running a certain distance or participating in a local race, can provide motivation and a sense of accomplishment.

3. **Listen to your body.** Pay attention to your body's signals. Rest when necessary and stay hydrated to support a long-time running journey.

Sailing

"I love sailing because it's so relaxing and there's something amazing about going to beautiful places using the power of Mother Nature."

—JOHN CASSANO,
Auto Repair Shop Owner

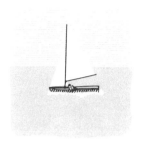

NATURE/OUTDOOR   COST: $$$

Sailing involves controlling a sailing vessel by adjusting its rigging and rudder in response to wind and water conditions. From small dinghies to larger yachts, sailing offers a range of experiences from the solitary to the social. Sailing is distinguished from other water sports and activities by the unique set of skills it requires—understanding wind directions, sail management, navigation, and often a deeper knowledge of weather patterns. Sailing is a pursuit that rewards patience, skill, and respect for the elements while providing a unique way to experience the natural world.

GET STARTED

1. **Learn the basics.** Enroll in a sailing course. Many yacht clubs and sailing schools offer beginner courses that cover fundamental skills, safety procedures, and basic navigation. You'll also want to familiarize yourself with reading weather patterns, which is critical for safe sailing.

2. **Start small.** Start with a small, manageable boat. Dinghies are often recommended for beginners due to their simplicity and responsiveness. Spend time on the water to develop your abilities; start sailing in calm, protected waters before venturing into more challenging conditions.

Salsa Dancing

"The social dimension of partner dancing is built into the hobby, making it an easy way to meet people for introverts and extroverts alike."

—SARAH K. SLEVINSKI,
Library Services Associate

DANCE   COST: $

Salsa combines elements of Afro-Cuban and Caribbean dances with the beats of salsa music. The name "salsa," meaning "sauce" in Spanish, aptly describes the rich and spicy blend of influences that make up this dance. Originating from a melting pot of Latin American cultures, its roots can be traced back to the 1960s and 1970s in Cuba and Puerto Rico. As Latin American musicians and immigrants brought their cultural rhythms to cities like New York, salsa evolved into a distinct dance style characterized by its energetic movements, spinning, and vibrant music. Salsa is a partner dance, typically involving a leader and a follower, with intricate footwork and fluid body movements. The dance is both a social activity and a form of artistic expression, making it appealing to a wide range of people.

GET STARTED

1. **Join a class.** Look for beginner salsa classes in your area. Group classes are a great way to learn the basic steps and rhythms in a fun and supportive environment.

2. **Prepare your attire.** Wear breathable fabrics that allow you to move freely. Though there are shoes specifically for salsa that feature suede soles for smooth turning, you can choose any pair of low-heeled, closed-toe shoes to start.

3. **Recognize the music.** Listen to salsa music regularly to get a feel for its unique rhythm and timing.

Samba

"Samba became a way to challenge and express myself, but what I love most is being able to celebrate my body's abilities through the power and energy of this dance."

—ALEX R.,
Relationship Manager Assistant

DANCE   COST: $$

Samba's roots are found in the musical traditions brought over by enslaved Africans to Brazil during the sixteenth through nineteenth centuries. The word "samba" is believed to originate from the Bantu languages of West Africa, particularly the term *semba,* or *masemba,* which refers to a pelvic thrust dance move. Samba stands out from other dance forms with its solo performance style. Equally integral to samba are its dazzling costumes, characterized by sequins, feathers, and headpieces. Samba offers a gateway into the rich tapestry of Brazilian culture and appeals to individuals who love expressive, high-energy dance forms.

1. **Join a class.** Look for dance schools or studios that offer classes to learn the basic steps and rhythms of samba.

2. **Immerse yourself in the culture.** Familiarize yourself with samba music and attend cultural events or carnivals. Observing and joining these events can provide a deeper understanding and appreciation of the dance.

3. **Explore costume design.** Joining a cultural event can also offer insight into samba's costumes. Learn about traditional costume designs through workshops or by joining a local samba troupe.

Sandcastle Building

*"Some people like to sit in the sun and read a book, I'd rather build a sandcastle."**

—CHUCK POLLARD,
Tech Company Executive

NATURE/OUTDOOR   COST: $

Sandcastle building, a quintessential beach pastime, transforms humble grains of sand into majestic and imaginative structures. The growth of this hobby was spurred by sandcastle competitions that started gaining traction around various coastal regions throughout the world during the twentieth century. The competitions provided an opportunity for the public to enjoy impressive visual spectacles but also inspired hobbyists to push the boundaries of what could be achieved with sand and water. Sandcastle building encompasses a wide range of sculptures and forms from mythical beasts to narrative scenes.

GET STARTED

1. **Choose a space.** If you live near a beach, find a spot where the sand is wet but not submerged. Proximity to water is key for easy access to wet sand. If you don't live near a beach, consider purchasing or creating a sandbox that can be placed in your yard or a large space within your home.

2. **Gather the tools.** Standard tools include buckets, shovels, and simple sculpting tools. You can also use everyday items like spoons, straws, or even a melon baller for detailed shaping.

---

* *Andrew Ramspacher, "The Lawn By the Sea: UVA Dad Creates Sandy Version of Jefferson's Academical Village," UVA Today, July 31, 2023, https://news.virginia.edu/content/lawn-sea -uva-dad-creates-sandy-version-jeffersons-academical-village.*

Scrapbooking

*"Scrapbooking is a fun and relaxing
outlet for my creativity, and I get to preserve
special memories in the process!"*

—KATHRYN HOOPER,
Psychologist

ART   COST: $

Scrapbooking is a creative way to preserve memories and tell stories using photographs, artwork, and memorabilia. The term "scrapbooking" can be traced back to the fifteenth century in England with commonplace books, which were similar to personal journals and used to keep scraps of paper, quotes, and other keepsakes. Each page in a scrapbook is a canvas where memories are not only stored but brought to life with decorative papers, texts, and various embellishments. Scrapbooking allows individuals to craft a visual narrative of their life's special moments from everyday joys to landmark events. It's a hobby that offers a creative outlet that is both fulfilling and deeply personal.

GET STARTED

1. **Gather the supplies.** Introductory supplies include an album, archival paper, adhesive, scissors, and pens. You can also incorporate a variety of embellishments like stickers, ribbons, stamps, and other ephemera.

2. **Organize your materials.** Sort through your photos and memorabilia, selecting items that best represent the story you want to tell. Arrange them chronologically, thematically, or in any order that makes sense to your narrative.

3. **Design your pages.** Start by laying out your designs, combining photos with text and embellishments, before affixing them down onto each page.

Screen Printing

"There are no mistakes when I'm dyeing fabric. If I do something unexpected, it could be a really great discovery or it could be really bad. But I can always dye it again." *

—MELISSA MATSON,
Violist

ART   COST: $$$

Screen printing, also known as silk screening or serigraphy, is a form of printmaking that involves creating a stencil (called a screen) and then using it to apply layers of ink onto a printing surface, typically fabric or paper. Screen printing originated in China during the Song Dynasty (960–1279 CE), and was later adopted in Japan and other Asian countries as a popular method for decorating textiles. Modern screen printing developed in the early twentieth century with the introduction of photoreactive chemicals.

GET STARTED

1. **Gather the materials.** Basic materials include a screen, photo emulsion, a squeegee, inks, and your chosen printing surface (for example, a T-shirt or paper).

2. **Create your design and prepare your screens.** Start with a simple, high-contrast design. Each color in your design will require a separate screen (or stencil). Coat the screen with a photosensitive emulsion, place your design on the screen, and expose it to light.

3. **Print your design.** Place the screen on your printing surface, apply ink to the screen, and use the squeegee to press the ink through the screen. Print from light to dark colors, waiting until each layer of ink is dried before moving on to the next.

* Jennifer Roach, "Eastman Musician Has 'Hidden Passion' for Fabrics with Flow," University of Rochester, November 4, 2016, https://www.rochester.edu/newscenter/fabrics-with-flow -196582/.

Scuba Diving

"I call it scuba therapy because when you're floating among the fish you forget about any challenges you might be facing and come back feeling refreshed with amazing stories many people will never experience."

—BETH BURRELL,
Communications Professional

PHYSICAL FITNESS   **COST: $$$**

Scuba diving is an exhilarating underwater activity that allows you to explore the wonders of the oceanic world. SCUBA, an acronym for Self-Contained Underwater Breathing Apparatus, enables divers to breathe underwater using a tank of compressed air and a breathing regulator. This equipment allows divers to descend deep below the water's surface and experience its myriad of aquatic life, coral reefs, and underwater land-scapes. Jacques Cousteau and Émile Gagnan are widely credited with inventing modern scuba diving in 1943. They developed the first reliable and safe open-circuit scuba technology, known as the Aqua-Lung. Scuba diving opens up a new realm of exploration and appreciation for the ocean's biodiversity and ecosystems.

GET STARTED

1. **Get certified.** The first step is to obtain a scuba diving certification from a recognized organization like PADI (Professional Association of Diving Instructors) or NAUI (National Association of Underwater Instructors). This involves completing a course that includes classroom learning, pool training, and open-water dives.

2. **Rent or invest in equipment.** Beginners often rent scuba equipment, but as you dive more frequently, investing in your own gear becomes beneficial. Basic scuba gear includes a mask, snorkel, fins, regulator, buoyancy control device (BCD), dive computer, and a scuba tank.

Sepak Takraw

*"The most challenging part of sepak takraw is the acrobatics. It's the jumping and somersaulting in the air and hitting the ball as you're flying."**

—SAIFUL RIJAL,
Government Worker

GAMES/SOCIAL   COST: $

Sepak takraw, sometimes referred to as kick volleyball, is an exhilarating team sport from Southeast Asia that combines elements of soccer, volleyball, and gymnastics. Played with a small rattan ball, players must keep the ball in the air and send it over the net into the opponent's court. The rules are similar to volleyball, but players use their feet, knees, chest, and head to touch and maneuver the ball. The term *sepak* is from the Malay language, meaning "kick," while *takraw* is Thai for "ball." Therefore, the name of the sport essentially translates to "kick ball," aptly describing the primary action of the game.

GET STARTED

1. **Learn the basics.** Familiarize yourself with the rules and techniques of sepak takraw. Watching games and tutorials or joining a beginner's workshop can be helpful.

2. **Find space and equipment.** Essential equipment includes a rattan or synthetic ball and a net. You need a flat, open space to play on like a volleyball court or gymnasium.

3. **Practice with others.** Find a local sepak takraw club or team to join or simply gather friends to play. The game typically requires three players per team.

---

* *John O'Callaghan, "Sepak Takraw Takes Flight,"* AramcoWorld, *March/April 2020, https://www.aramcoworld.com/Articles/March-2020/Sepak-Takraw-Takes-Flight.*

Skateboarding

*"My entire professional career has been marked by trying to replicate the success of my peers. Trying to learn how to skate in my thirties has led me to question that."**

—STEVE ROUSSEAU,
Writer

PHYSICAL FITNESS   COST: $$

Skateboarding originated in the United States in the late 1940s to early 1950s, born out of the surfing culture in California. Surfers looking for an alternative during the low surf season started attaching roller skate wheels to wooden planks, creating the first rudimentary skateboards. The sport quickly evolved, gaining popularity and sophistication in terms of both equipment and techniques. Skateboarders, or skaters, ride their boards on various terrains and structures from smooth pavements to stairways and railings in urban landscapes. Skateboarding has often been associated with countercultural movements for embodying a form of rebellion against mainstream norms.

GET STARTED

1. **Visit an indoor skate park.** If available in your area, you can rent all the gear you need and practice within an indoor skate park. Many of them offer introductory skateboarding lessons as well.

2. **Equip yourself.** A visit to a local skate shop can provide personalized advice and the opportunity to feel the board before buying. Safety gear, including a helmet, knee pads, and elbow pads, is also essential.

3. **Practice regularly.** Master the fundamentals, such as balancing on the skateboard, pushing off with your foot, and basic turns. Like any sport, skateboarding requires regular practice to progress in skill.

* *https://www.vox.com/the-goods/21422884/best-money-skateboard-learning-adult*

Skiing

"I started skiing as a kid with after school programs. When you drop into a line in the back country there's just nothing like that feeling. Powder skiing is the best feeling in the world."

—IAN EHRLICH,
Actuary

NATURE/OUTDOOR   **COST: $$$**

Skiing, known for its dynamic speed, twists, and turns down snowy mountains, is an exhilarating hobby that offers sport, adventure, and recreation during the cold winter months. Skiing has roots that stretch back thousands of years with early evidence found in Russia, Scandinavia, and China. Skis are long, flat, narrow pieces of semi-rigid material worn on the feet to promote gliding on snow and were originally used for transportation. The evolution of skiing into a recreational and competitive sport began during the nineteenth century in Norway, thanks to pioneers like Sondre Norheim (1825–1897), who is often regarded as the father of modern skiing for his innovations in ski design and technique.

GET STARTED

1. **Acquire the appropriate gear.** Essential gear includes skis, ski boots, bindings, a helmet, and ski goggles. You can rent everything you need at ski lodges and resorts.

2. **Take lessons.** Professional instruction is invaluable when starting. Consider investing in lessons, which can help you learn the fundamental techniques and safety practices of skiing.

3. **Start on beginner slopes.** Begin your journey on bunny slopes, which are designed for beginners. These areas have gentle slopes that allow you to practice and build confidence at your own pace.

Skydiving

"There is something so exhilarating about hurtling through the air. There is no feeling like it."*

—DYLAN KAUFFMANN,
Student

NATURE/OUTDOOR   **COST: $$$**

Skydiving involves jumping from an aircraft and free-falling before deploying a parachute to slow the descent to the ground. It's a blend of adrenaline, freedom, and serenity, offering an unparalleled experience of flying through the air. Modern skydiving as a recreational sport began to develop in the early twentieth century, particularly after World War II, with advancements in parachute technology and the increased availability of aircrafts. Skydiving is suited for those who are physically fit, have a good level of mental resilience, and are not afraid to step out of their comfort zone.

GET STARTED

1. **Start with tandem jumps.** The safest and most common way to experience skydiving is a tandem jump, where you're attached to an experienced instructor using a harness. This requires minimal training and allows you to experience the thrill under expert supervision.

2. **Get certified.** If you wish to pursue skydiving more seriously, enroll in a skydiving course to get certified. Training programs like Accelerated Free Fall (AFF) teach you the skills needed to skydive independently. Be sure you're in good physical health with a medical checkup before beginning your training, as the sport can be physically demanding.

---

*   Noah Gold, *"Thrill-Seeking Seniors Embrace a New Hobby: Skydiving,"* The Catalyst, *May 23, 2022, https://recatalyst.org/3473/news/thrill-seeking-seniors-embrace-a-new-hobby-skydiving/.*

Slacklining

"To slackline, you cannot think about anything else or else you'll fall off. It was kind of like mediation. I started calling it the cheapest therapy." *

—CHERRYL GLOTFELTY,
Retired Professor

PHYSICAL FITNESS   COST: $$

Slacklining is the art of walking, balancing, and performing various tricks on a piece of flat, flexible webbing suspended between two anchor points. At first glance, slacklining can appear similar to tightrope walking. However, slacklining distinctly features a line that remains slightly loose, allowing the line to stretch and bounce like a narrow trampoline. This dynamic nature of the slackline adds unique levels of challenge and excitement to the activity. Slacklining emerged from the rock-climbing community during the 1970s in Yosemite Valley, California, as a way to improve balance and concentration during downtime at camp. What started as a fun and informal way for climbers to hone their skills quickly grew into a standalone activity with a dedicated following.

GET STARTED

1. **Acquire the equipment.** Start with an introductory slackline kit that includes the line, ratcheting mechanism, and tree protection. These kits are designed for beginners and offer a good balance of safety and usability.

2. **Find a spot.** Look for two sturdy anchor points, like trees, about 10 to 20 feet (3 to 6 meters) apart. Ensure they are robust enough to support your weight and that the area around them is free of hazards.

---

* Amy Alonzo, *"Sparks Woman Reaches New Slacklining Heights, Aims to Become World's Oldest Highliner,"* Reno Gazette Journal, *March 10, 2021, https://www.rgj.com/story/news /2021/03/10/nv-woman-aims-become-worlds-oldest-highliner-yosemite-feat/4633779001/.*

Sleuthing

"My brain is constantly curious. I always want to know how, who, why, where." *

—JANE,
Mother

EDUCATIONAL   COST: $

Sleuthing is often synonymous with amateur detective work but is usually pursued as a recreational or intellectual challenge. It requires skills of critical thinking, keen observation, and puzzle-solving, which is akin to what a professional detective embodies. The hobby also extends into the realm of community service, where hobbyists can contribute to local law enforcement efforts in solving crimes. With modern technological advancements, the scope and accessibility of sleuthing have significantly expanded to include analyzing social media footprints to utilizing public records.

GET STARTED

1. **Educate yourself.** Begin by understanding the basics of traditional and digital sleuthing. This can include online courses in digital forensics, research techniques, and legal guidelines.

2. **Participate in volunteer programs.** Look for opportunities to volunteer with local law enforcement or community groups. These programs should be approached with a strong sense of responsibility and a commitment to ethical sleuthing. Always prioritize safety and privacy, both for yourself and those you're investigating. Respect legal boundaries and avoid invasive or risky practices.

---

* Ellie Abraham. "True-Crime Fanatics on the Hunt: Inside the World of Amateur Detectives," The Guardian, *March 28, 2021, https://www.theguardian.com/uk-news/2021/mar/28/give-us -a-clue-inside-the-world-of-amateur-crime-solvers-and-sleuths.*

Snorkeling

"All the outside world is gone. You just hear the water. It's pleasant. You're in a whole other world. The fish's world." *

—TIM ALDRIDGE,
Former U.S. Marine

NATURE/OUTDOOR   COST: $

Unlike diving in deep water, snorkeling is done near the surface, allowing you to breathe through a tube called a snorkel while floating and viewing the marine environment below. Historically, the practice of snorkeling can be traced back thousands of years to sponge farmers and pearl divers in ancient civilizations using hollow reeds to breathe while submerged. Modern snorkeling took shape with the development of the diving mask and snorkel in the early twentieth century. Snorkeling requires minimal training and is accessible to people of all ages and skill levels.

GET STARTED

1. **Acquire the gear and learn the basics.** Essential gear includes a snorkel, a diving mask, and fins. Be sure that your diving mask fits snugly. You'll need to be familiar with floating to move efficiently in the water while exploring.

2. **Choose a location.** Look for snorkeling spots known for clear water and abundant marine life. Many coastal areas have designated snorkeling areas with guides and gear for rent.

3. **Understand safety and conservation.** Research different aspects of marine safety, including how to identify hazardous marine life and currents. Be mindful of marine conservation practices, such as not touching or disturbing wildlife.

---

* *Vincent Gabrielle, "Southern Appalachian Rivers Are Home to Incredible Fish. Meet Snorkelers Who Hunt for Them," The Guardian, July 25, 2021, https://www.knoxnews.com/story /exploretennessee/2021/07/25/east-tennessee-mountain-rivers-biodiversity-fish-attract -snorkelers/7937755002/.*

Soap Carving

"I consider my dad my hero and wanted to gift him something unique. I checked out every gift shop in town but was not satisfied. That's when I decided to experiment with soap."*

—ASWIN MANIKANDAN,
Engineer

ART   COST: $

Soap carving is an art form that emerged in various cultures with notable traditions in places like Thailand where elaborate soap flowers are a traditional craft. In the Western world, soap carving became popular as a simple and safe way to introduce children to the art of carving, particularly during the twentieth century when commercially produced soap became widely available. Unlike wood or stone carving, the soft and malleable nature of soap makes it an easy medium for carving and consequently a more approachable activity for casual hobbyists. Scented soaps offer an additional sensory experience that can feel extra therapeutic, while its texture allows for intricate details and smooth finishes that can be more challenging to achieve with harder materials. Soap carving is a low-cost hobby that appeals to those who enjoy detailed, hands-on craft activities.

GET STARTED

1. **Gather the materials.** All you need to start is a bar of soap, a small carving tool (like a craft knife or butter knife), and a simple design.

2. **Master the basics.** Practice basic carving techniques like cutting, shaving, and sculpting. Online tutorials or craft books can provide guidance and inspiration.

---

* Aathira Ayyappan, "How Aswin Manikandan Went from Engineer to 3D Soap-Carver Is All About #lifegoals," Edex Live, September 18, 2019, https://www.edexlive.com/people/2019/sep/18/check-out-this-final-year-engineering-students-stunning-3d-models-8212.html.

Soapmaking

"My mother-in-law taught me how to make homemade soap. Once I got a good handle on it, I started exploring with different organic additives, clays, and essential oils."

—MALINDA YOUNG,
Home Health

HOME · COST: $$

The earliest recorded evidence of soap dates to around 2800 BCE in Babylon. It was a practice that evolved over time in various ancient civilizations, including the Egyptians and Romans. Modern soapmaking involves basic ingredients like fats or oils, lye (sodium hydroxide), and water. Often enhanced with fragrances, colors, and other natural additives, soaps can be highly personalized to match the needs and preferences of its maker or user. Soapmaking is an attractive hobby for individuals who enjoy crafting, are interested in natural and homemade products, and appreciate the chemistry behind turning raw ingredients into usable soap (a process called saponification).

GET STARTED

1. **Research and learn.** Understand the basics of soapmaking, especially working safely with lye, which is a highly caustic and potentially dangerous chemical. There are plenty of resources available, including books and online tutorials.

2. **Gather the supplies.** Basic soapmaking supplies include safety gear like gloves and goggles, lye, fats or oils, a thermometer, molds, and any desired fragrances or additives.

3. **Start simple and experiment.** For your first batch, choose a simple recipe with a few ingredients. As you gain confidence, experiment with different ingredients, scents, and techniques, such as layering or swirling colors, to create artisanal soaps.

Soccer (Fútbol)

"Soccer has taught me the importance of preparation, confidence in your abilities, and how to lead and be part of a team."

—PAV GEE,
Product Manager

PHYSICAL FITNESS   COST: $

Soccer, known as football or fútbol in many parts of the world, is a team sport played between two teams of eleven players. The game's objective is to score by getting the soccer ball into the opposing team's goal using any part of the body except the arms and hands; only the goalkeeper, who guards the goal, is allowed to use their hands within a designated area. The origins of soccer trace back over two thousand years to ancient China, Greece, Rome, and parts of Central America. Its modern iteration began in nineteenth-century England, where it was formalized with a set of rules. Soccer's major appeal lies in its simplicity and the minimal equipment required, making it accessible to people from all walks of life.

GET STARTED

1. **Learn the game.** Familiarize yourself with the basic rules of soccer, such as the offside rule, fouls, and how the game is played.

2. **Equip yourself.** Essential equipment includes a soccer ball, cleats for outdoor play, and comfortable athletic wear. Shin guards are also recommended for protection.

3. **Practice and join others.** Start by mastering basic skills like passing, dribbling, and shooting, which can be practiced alone or with friends. Look for local soccer clubs, pickup games, or community teams to join. These provide opportunities to play regularly, improve your skills, and enjoy social aspects of the game.

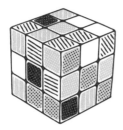

Speedcubing

"You can never learn enough about how to solve such a simple puzzle."

—PHILLIP ZHAO,
Student

COMPETITIVE   COST: $

Speedcubing is a hobby that combines cognitive exercise with competitive thrill, where individuals solve the Rubik's Cube, a 3D combination puzzle, in the shortest time possible. Also known as competitive Rubik's Cube solving, this activity involves rapidly twisting the cube's segments to achieve a uniform color on each of its six faces. Speedcubers often compete in timed events, striving to improve their solving speed with each attempt. Speedcubing originated in the early 1980s, shortly after the invention of the Rubik's Cube by Hungarian architect Ernő Rubik in 1974. The first World Rubik's Cube Championship was held in 1982 in Budapest, Hungary, marking the official beginning of competitive speedcubing. Speedcubing is well-suited for those who enjoy problem-solving, have a competitive spirit, and are fascinated by puzzles.

GET STARTED

1. **Get a Rubik's Cube.** Start with a standard 3-x-3 Rubik's Cube; however, there are cubes specifically designed for speedcubing that offer smoother and faster turns.

2. **Master the basics.** Speedcubing involves learning and memorizing a series of algorithms to solve the Rubik's Cube efficiently. Start by familiarizing yourself with basic techniques. There are numerous tutorials and guides available for beginners. Regular practice is key to improving your speed.

Spelunking

NATURE/OUTDOOR   COST: $$$

Spelunking, also known as caving, is the adventurous activity of exploring cave systems in their natural state. The term "spelunking" derives from the Greek word *spelaion,* which means "cave," and the Latin word *spelunca,* which also means "cave" or "cavern." Spelunking involves navigating through caves and underground passages, encompassing everything from walking in large caverns to crawling through narrow passages. Spelunkers often enjoy the thrill of discovery and exploration as they encounter a variety of geological formations like stalactites and stalagmites, underground rivers, and diverse ecosystems.

GET STARTED

1. **Start with safety.** Understanding safety protocols is crucial in spelunking. Beginners should familiarize themselves with cave navigation techniques, risk assessment, and emergency procedures. Begin by participating in guided cave tours to gain experience and understand what spelunking entails.

2. **Acquire the gear.** Essential gear for spelunking includes a helmet with a headlamp, sturdy footwear, gloves, and appropriate clothing. Advanced equipment might include ropes and climbing gear for more complex caves.

* Andrea Mustain, *"Modern-Day Cavewoman Has Spelunk,"* NBC News, *April 25, 2011,* https://www.nbcnews.com/id/wbna42752602.

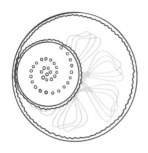

Spirographing

*"If you remember, back in the eighties they were quite big. I do big ones, like up to about A2 size."**

—CAT,
Supermarket Auditor

ART   COST: $

The Spirograph is a toy invented by British engineer Denys Fisher in 1960. Characterized by plastic rings, wheels, and other shapes that resemble gears with teeth that interlock, Fisher's invention was inspired by the principles of mathematical curves and mechanics. Uniquely combining geometry with art, the Spirograph allows you to move a pen around the inside and outside of these gears in various ways to produce hypnotic, swirling designs. The resulting patterns are known as hypotrochoids and epitrochoids and can be endlessly varied by changing gears, colors, and the way the gears are moved.

GET STARTED

1. **Buy a Spirograph kit.** A basic Spirograph kit includes several wheels, rings, and pens. These kits are widely available and suitable for beginners.

2. **Practice and explore.** Begin with simple patterns using the larger gears and rings to understand how the gears interact with each other and how different movements create different designs. As you become more experienced, use different color pens and gear combinations. You can also try overlaying different patterns or using multiple colors in a single design.

* Siobhan Macdonald, "ITV The Chase Fans in Tears at Lanarkshire Contestant's Unusual Pastime," Daily Record, February 17, 2022, https://www.dailyrecord.co.uk/entertainment /tv-radio/itv-chase-fans-gobsmacked-lanarkshire-26255731.

Spoken Word

"It gives us a sense of self-affirmation for our lives—joys, pain, shame, struggles— and things we have to say." *

—UJJWALA MAHARJAN,
Poet and Educator

`ART` `COST: $`

Spoken word is a performance art that centers around the verbal delivery of poems, stories, or monologues. It's an expressive form of storytelling where the artist uses their voice, intonation, and sometimes gestures to convey emotions and narratives. Unlike traditional poetry or theater, spoken word often emphasizes a free-flowing, rhythmic, and conversational style. Spoken word has roots in ancient oral storytelling traditions and poetic performances. As a modern expressive arts form, it became particularly prominent during the twentieth century, influenced by the Beat poets of the 1950s and 1960s and later by the rise of hip-hop culture. Whether exploring intricate narratives or sociopolitical commentary, spoken word provides a powerful platform for expressing raw emotions.

GET STARTED

1. **Watch spoken word performances.** Familiarize yourself with spoken word by watching videos online or attending local open mic nights and poetry slams. This can help you understand the nature of spoken word and influence your own style.

2. **Write material and practice performing.** Begin by writing your own pieces, focusing on subjects that are meaningful to you. Spoken word is as much about performance as it is about writing. Practice your delivery, paying attention to your voice modulation, pacing, and body language.

---

* Yuanyuan Kelly, "Nepali Youth Are Raising Their Voices, But Not in the Way You'd Expect," Global Citizen, *August 15, 2015,* https://www.globalcitizen.org/en/content/nepali-youth-are -raising-their-voices-but-not-in-t/.

Squash

"You can play at any time and you only need one other person to play. And it's the kinda thing that you can keep playing, as I am now demonstrating, until you're eighty-three." *

—STANLEY GREENFIELD,
Publishing Industry

PHYSICAL FITNESS   COST: $$

Squash is a high-paced racquet sport played by two or four players in a four-walled court with a small, hollow rubber ball. The game involves players taking turns to hit the ball onto the playable surfaces of the four walls within the court. The objective is to strike the ball in such a way that the opponent is unable to return it before it bounces twice. Squash birthed from an older game known as rackets, considered a pastime of prisoners who played in the enclosed courtyards of London's debtors' prisons. In the early nineteenth century at Harrow School in England, students discovered that a punctured rackets ball, which "squashed" on impact with the wall, produced a game with a greater variety of shots and required more athletic ability to play.

GET STARTED

1. **Learn the rules.** Familiarize yourself with the rules of squash, the dimensions of the court, and the scoring system. Consider taking beginner lessons or joining a squash clinic.

2. **Acquire the equipment and attire.** Purchase or rent the necessary equipment, which includes a squash racquet, balls, and appropriate footwear with non-marking soles.

3. **Practice and play.** Find a squash court to practice; many are available in public parks, gyms, or community centers.

---

* *Stephen Caruso, "Octogenarian Says Squash Is Serious Fun,"* The Riverdale Press, *March 27, 2008, https://www.riverdalepress.com/stories/octogenarian-says-squash-is-serious -fun,28070.*

Squeegee Painting

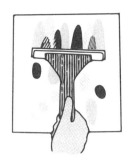

"Painting with a squeegee is a great form of 'process art'—it's all about the creation of the painting and experimenting." *

—DEBBIE CHAPMAN,
Website Owner

ART   COST: $

Squeegee painting is a unique and expressive form of art where a squeegee, typically a tool used for wiping liquid off a surface, is used to create paintings. While the technique itself isn't new, having been explored in various forms by artists in the twentieth century, its resurgence and adaptation for social media have brought it into contemporary artistic practice. Artists like Gerhard Richter were known for their use of the squeegee in creating abstract works, but today's social media artists have adapted and evolved the technique, often incorporating it into more accessible and engaging formats for a broader audience. Squeegee painting is attractive to those who enjoy experimenting with textures and colors and are open to the element of surprise in their creative process.

GET STARTED

1. **Gather the materials.** Along with basic painting supplies like paints, canvas, or paper, you'll need a squeegee. This can be anything from a traditional window-cleaning squeegee to a smaller, more flexible variant.

2. **Experiment with techniques.** You can squeeze or dab paint directly onto your canvas or place paint onto your squeegee. Explore different techniques with your squeegee by varying the pressure, angle, and direction.

* *https://onelittleproject.com/about-me/*

Stained Glass Art

"I asked my eighty-five-year-old uncle to teach me how to do stained glass art. His work is admired and treasured by family members, and I'm hoping to be able to continue that tradition."

—SHARON AKERS,
Retired Educator

LOW   COST: $

Stained glass art is created by assembling pieces of colored glass that are cut into specific shapes and sizes and held within a rigid frame. When illuminated, stained glass displays vibrant colors and intricate patterns, making it a unique and striking art form. Stained glass art particularly flourished in Europe during the Middle Ages, when it was featured in the windows of churches and cathedrals. Hobbyists often work on smaller decorative items, but many also carry on the tradition of creating large window art. Creating stained glass art requires patience, precision, and a sense of artistic composition. It's a hobby that can feel satisfying to those who are attracted to its unique aesthetic qualities, historical and cultural significance, and the physical process of cutting, assembling, and soldering glass.

GET STARTED

1. **Learn the basics.** Familiarize yourself with the fundamental techniques of creating stained glass art, including cutting glass, leading, and soldering. Seek online tutorials, books, or workshops.

2. **Gather the supplies.** Essential supplies include colored glass, a glass cutter, lead came (H-shaped rods) or copper foil (metal strips that join pieces together), a solder, and a soldering iron. Safety equipment like gloves and eye protection is also crucial.

3. **Start simple.** Begin with a small, manageable project to practice cutting and assembling glass. This could be a simple geometric design or a small suncatcher.

Stair Climbing

"They're all so different. It's such a fun way to navigate a neighborhood." *

—ALEXANDRA KENIN,
Part-time Marketing

PHYSICAL FITNESS   COST: $

Stair climbing is an invigorating activity that can be pursued as a high-intensity sport or as a fitness routine. In its competitive form, known as tower running or vertical running, the challenge lies in ascending stairs in tall buildings or stadiums as quickly as possible. For those focused on a unique form of fitness, stair climbing offers a robust workout that promotes strength and endurance. While stair climbing as a form of exercise has likely been around since the inception of stairs, its organized form as a competitive sport is relatively recent. The first recorded stair climbing event was in 1978 with the Empire State Building Run-Up in New York City. Stair climbing appeals to both athletes seeking the thrill of a race and to individuals looking for an effective, low-cost fitness regimen.

GET STARTED

1. **Learn techniques.** It's worthwhile to learn climbing techniques to maximize efficiency and minimize the risk of injury. These can include a step strategy (such as one step at a time versus two) or proper breathing and body positioning. Pay attention to hydration and stretching as well.

2. **Create a routine and join others.** Commit to a stair climbing routine to build your endurance. If you're inclined toward competition, participate in stair climbing events.

---

* *Heather Knight, "Climbing S.F.'s Beloved Staircases with a Guide Who's Vowed to Conquer Them All,"* San Francisco Chronicle, *September 22, 2020, https://www.sfchronicle.com /bayarea/heatherknight/article/Isn-t-it-incredible-Climbing-S-F-s-15585110.php.*

Stamp Collecting

"I have a scientific background, so the analytical side really appeals. My personal philatelic interest is crash mail, envelopes salvaged from plane crashes. Definitely morbid but equally fascinating." *

—CONSTANZE DENNIS,
Auctioneer

COLLECTING   COST: $

Stamp collecting, known as philately, is the hobby of collecting and studying postage stamps, postmarks, and related materials. The hobby began shortly after the issuance of the first adhesive postage stamp, the Penny Black, in 1840 in the United Kingdom. Stamp collecting gained popularity in the late nineteenth century as postal systems worldwide expanded and stamps became more intricate and varied. While the digital age has led to a significant decline in the everyday use of postage stamps, the hobby has adapted and endures, continuing to captivate enthusiasts around the world with its blend of historical richness, artistic beauty, and educational value.

GET STARTED

1. **Gather the supplies and choose a focus.** Start with essential supplies like a stamp album, stamp tongs (to handle stamps without damaging them), and a magnifying glass. It can be enjoyable to focus on a particular theme, such as stamps from a certain country or era.

2. **Start collecting.** You can purchase stamps from postal services or stamp dealers, trade with other collectors, or acquire them from friends, family, or pen pals via mail they send you.

---

* Nicole Mowbray, "Post Modern: Why Millennials Have Fallen in Love with Stamp Collecting," The Guardian, *April 11, 2020, https://www.theguardian.com/artanddesign/2020/apr/11/post-modern-why-millennials-have-fallen-in-love-with-stamp-collecting.*

Stamping

"Creating cards, scrapbook pages, and gift items is about more than just stamps and ink— it's about sharing a part of yourself with the people you love." *

—RHONDA K. AMOROSO,
CEO of Publishing Company

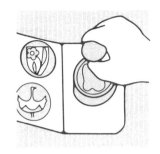

ART   COST: $

Stamping is a satisfying hobby for those who enjoy crafting and seek an easy yet fulfilling way to embellish and personalize artistic projects. Pressing ink-coated stamps onto various surfaces to create images or patterns, the allure of stamping lies in its simplicity and the boundless creativity it offers. Stamping blossomed into a crafting hobby in the twentieth century with the advent of vulcanized (hardened) rubber. More recently, clear stamps have grown in popularity since the early 2000s. Also known as acrylic stamps or photopolymer stamps, the transparent nature of clear stamps allows for greater precision, making it preferred for card making and scrapbooking. Stamping is a versatile craft accessible to all ages and skill levels that makes it easy to infuse art into everyday life.

GET STARTED

1. **Gather the supplies.** Begin with a selection of stamps that resonate with your style, an ink pad in your preferred color, and paper or cardstock.

2. **Find inspiration.** Start with simple projects like creating greeting cards, customizing stationery, or decorating a journal. Engage with other stamping enthusiasts through online forums, social media groups, or local crafting workshops to share inspiration and tips.

* *https://stampingthrulife.stampinup.net/about_me*

Stand-Up Paddleboarding

"I feel strong and deeply in touch with nature when paddleboarding and I love how meditative it is!"

—ELIZABETH MARIE CHEON SWEET,
Nonprofit Community Engagement Manager

NATURE/OUTDOOR   COST: $$$

Stand-up paddleboarding (SUP) is a water sport where you stand upright on a large, stable board and use a long paddle to navigate through water. SUP combines elements of surfing and paddling and offers a uniquely serene way to traverse rivers, lakes, or oceans. SUP is often attributed to the surf culture of Hawaii in the twentieth century. In the 1940s, Hawaiian surf instructors began standing on their boards to better see and manage their students, using paddles to maneuver. This practice evolved into its modern iteration that many enjoy as a hobby today. SUP offers a harmonious blend of physical activity and the tranquility of being on the water.

GET STARTED

1. **Learn the basics.** Essential skills include standing up on the board, balancing, and paddling techniques. Lessons from a certified instructor or tutorials can be very helpful.

2. **Choose the right equipment.** Start with a beginner-friendly paddleboard, which should be wide and stable. You'll also need a suitable paddle, a personal flotation device, and a leash to connect you to the board.

3. **Start on calm water.** Practice balancing and paddling on your board in calm, flat water. Understand basic water safety rules and always check the weather and water conditions before paddling.

Stickers

*"I seek out stickers that I remember that I had—those are the ones I always want."**

—RACHEL LLOYD,
Digital Creator

COLLECTING   COST: $

The appeal of stickers lies in their versatility and the joy of expression they offer. The act of peeling and placing a sticker is satisfying, offering a tangible way to showcase individuality. Stickers were initially adhesive labels used for marketing and promotional purposes until gaining significant popularity in the mid-to-late twentieth century with the advent of more varied and creative designs. Whether you're a collector, an artist, or someone who enjoys personalizing your space and belongings, the world of stickers offers endless possibilities for creativity and self-expression.

GET STARTED

1. **Begin collecting.** Look for designs that catch your eye or resonate with your personal interests. Craft stores, online marketplaces, and specialty shops offer a wide range from decorative and thematic to vintage and handmade.

2. **Play and create.** You can use stickers to decorate your laptop, phone case, notebooks, or water bottles. Also, consider making your own stickers. This can be as simple as drawing designs directly onto adhesive paper or exploring digital design software for a more professional finish.

---

* *Rachel Kramer Bussel, "Inside the New World of Sticker Enthusiasts,"* Glamour, *December 9, 2020, https://www.glamour.com/story/inside-the-new-world-of-sticker-enthusiasts.*

Stone Skipping

*"I love being outside. I can really appreciate the beauty of a good skim in a beautiful setting; it's a lovely, fleeting moment."**

—LUCY WOOD,
Photographer

NATURE/OUTDOOR   COST: $

Stone skipping is a simple yet captivating outdoor activity that involves throwing a flat stone across the surface of a body of water in such a way that it bounces or "skips" along the surface multiple times before sinking. The appeal of stone skipping lies in the challenge of achieving the most skips from a single throw. The current world record for stone skipping is held by Kurt Steiner who achieved eighty-eight skips at the Red Bridge campgrounds in the Allegheny National Forest on September 6, 2013. Whether striving to break personal records or just enjoying the serenity of a peaceful setting, stone skipping is an accessible pastime that allows you to engage with nature, practice mindfulness, and enjoy a moment of simplicity.

GET STARTED

1. **Find stones.** Look for palm-sized stones with smooth, flat surfaces. Riverbeds, lakeshores, or beaches are ideal places to find suitable stones for skipping.

2. **Find a location.** Choosing the right location is as key as choosing the right stones. Look for still or gently moving water bodies such as lakes, ponds, or quiet riverbanks. Be aware of your surroundings and avoid skipping stones in the direction of others who might be in the water.

---

* *Ella Benson Easton, "Stone Skimming Is a World Champion Sport—And a Model for Space-ships," Atlas Obscura, October 19, 2023, https://www.atlasobscura.com/articles/stone-skimming-championship-spaceship-studies.*

Stop Motion Animation

"Making stop motion animation is like watching my imagination come to life. It's always a surprise, and it always makes me laugh!"

—KALLY,
Graphic Designer

TECH   COST: $$

Stop motion animation is an enchanting form of filmmaking where physical objects are moved in small increments among individually photographed frames. When these frames are played in sequence, they create the illusion of movement. This technique can bring to life everything from inanimate objects and clay figures to puppets and paper cutouts, creating a whimsical and often surreal visual narrative. Pioneers like J. Stuart Blackton and Émile Cohl are among the earliest animators to experiment with stop motion techniques. Stop motion animation is a time-intensive hobby that demands patience and precision but yields the highly rewarding result of manifesting imaginative concepts into tangible, visual stories.

GET STARTED

1. **Gather the materials.** At the minimum, you'll need a camera or a smartphone with a good camera, a tripod, and materials for creating your subjects, such as clay, paper, or puppets.

2. **Start simple.** To understand the process, a straightforward project works best for beginners. It could be as simple as making an inanimate object move across a table or animating a plain clay figure.

3. **Learn and experiment.** Experiment with different materials, settings, and storytelling styles. Utilize online tutorials, books, or workshops to refine your techniques.

Story Time at the Library

"I love when the children interact during my story readings. Hearing their giggles and laughs brings me a lot of joy." *

—STELLA SAMEREIE,
Student

VOLUNTEERING   COST: $

Volunteering for story time at libraries is a highly rewarding hobby for those who enjoy public speaking, have a passion for children's literature, and possess a knack for engaging with young audiences. Story time sessions at libraries usually go far beyond the simple act of reading books. It's an interactive experience that can include songs, rhymes, finger plays, and crafts—all designed to foster a love for reading and develop early literacy skills in children. Anne Carroll Moore (1871–1961), a prominent figure in the development of children's library services in the United States, played a key role in popularizing the concept, which has since become a fundamental service in library communities around the world.

GET STARTED

1. **Learn storytelling techniques.** Begin by familiarizing yourself with effective storytelling techniques like voice modulation, facial expressions, and audience engagement strategies. Online tutorials and workshops can help, and the library may also offer some training.

2. **Sign up to volunteer.** Reach out to your local library to inquire about volunteer opportunities for story time. Most will require safety clearances like a background check.

---

* Ashley Atkinson, "Our Library, Our Stories: Stella Samereie," Fairfax County, n.d., https://www.fairfaxcounty.gov/library/branch-out/our-library-our-stories-stella-samereie.

Sudoku

"Other than I just enjoy the process of doing the puzzle and the satisfaction that comes with completing one, I really love that it's easy to fit into my day."*

—CHARMAINE DIAMOND,
Copywriter

INTROSPECTIVE   COST: $

		1				4	2	
2								
				2				9
						4		
8								
					5			
	4					2		
		5						4

Sudoku is a logic-based, combinatorial number-placement puzzle that has become one of the world's most popular brain teasers. The classic Sudoku puzzle consists of a 9-x-9 grid, divided into nine 3-x-3 subgrids or "regions." The objective is to fill the grid with digits so that each column, each row, and each of the nine 3-x-3 subgrids contain every digit from 1 to 9. The puzzle starts with a partially completed grid, which provides a unique solution. Sudoku was popularized in Japan during the 1980s where it gained its name—meaning "single number." It was introduced to the Western world in the early twenty-first century and quickly became a staple in newspapers and puzzle books. Sudoku offers a perfect blend of mental exercise and leisure, making it ideal for those looking for an intellectually rewarding pastime.

GET STARTED

1. **Understand the rules.** Familiarize yourself with the basic rules of Sudoku. The key is understanding how the numbers 1 through 9 must be uniquely placed in each row, column, and region.

2. **Start with easy puzzles.** Begin with simpler puzzles, which often have more numbers pre-filled in the grid. Practice regularly, and you'll master strategies and enhance your abilities to complete the puzzles.

* *https://hobbiesarefun.substack.com/p/do-you-sudoku*

Surfing

"I love surfing because it allows me to connect with nature in a way that's almost indescribable. It brings a sense of peace and calming to the mind but also excitement and adventure for the spirit."

—JACOB CHO,
Entrepreneur

PHYSICAL FITNESS   COST: $$$

Surfing is the practice of riding on the waves of the sea using a surfboard. The roots of surfing can be traced back over a thousand years to the Polynesian islands, where it was not just a pastime but a pivotal part of their culture. However, it was the Hawaiian Islands that became synonymous with surfing, with key figures contributing to its modern evolution, like Duke Kahanamoku, a Hawaiian Olympic swimmer who popularized surfing in the United States and Australia during the early 1900s, and Tom Blake, who in the 1930s introduced significant improvements to surfboards that made them lighter and faster. If you cherish adventure, the outdoors, and a bit of a challenge, surfing can provide a journey of exhilarating discovery and profound connection with the elemental power of the sea.

GET STARTED

1. **Start with lessons.** Professional instruction is invaluable as a novice. A certified surf instructor can provide crucial insights on techniques, wave reading, and safety protocols. Proficiency in swimming is also essential for safety and confidence in the water.

2. **Choose the right board.** Beginner's surfboards are typically longer and thicker for stability. Wetsuits are also recommended for comfort and protection.

Swimming

"The doctor said that I have problems with my body, such as joints and spine, so the only exercise suitable for me is swimming."

—CHUNYING LIN,
Professor

PHYSICAL FITNESS **COST: $**

Swimming can be enjoyed in various forms from a leisurely float to competitive lapping. It offers a full-body workout that improves cardiovascular health, strength, and flexibility without stressing the joints. Beyond the physical benefits, swimming is also known for its calming effects, often seen as a form of moving meditation. Cave paintings from the Stone Age discovered near southwestern Egypt depict figures that appear to be swimming in different styles, suggesting that this activity has been a part of human life for thousands of years. Whether it's for fitness, relaxation, or the sheer joy of being in the water, swimming is a hobby that can suit a wide range of people, regardless of age or fitness level.

GET STARTED

1. **Learn the basics.** Enroll in swimming lessons at a local pool, gym, or community center. These lessons provide essential skills like floating, swimming strokes, and water safety.

2. **Choose the proper gear.** Invest in a comfortable swimsuit, goggles, and a swimming cap.

Swing Dancing

"I started dancing Lindy Hop when I first arrived in a new city. To this day, many of my closest friends are dancers as a result of that choice."

—ARTHUR PANG,
Marketing and Communications

DANCE   COST: $

Swing dancing is a social dance that originated in the United States during the 1920s and 1930s. It's a vibrant, energetic style that typically pairs a lead and a follow, moving rhythmically to the swinging tunes of jazz music. The roots of swing dancing are in the African-American communities of the Harlem Renaissance. During this time, the most iconic style of swing dance emerged—the Lindy Hop—named after Charles "Lindy" Lindbergh's transatlantic flight in 1927. The Lindy Hop is characterized by its aerial moves, where dancers perform lifts and jumps, and is often considered the original form of swing dance. Other styles include the West Coast Swing, which features a smooth, linear style of dancing; and the Charleston, known for its high-energy kicks and distinctive 1920s flair. Swing dancing provides a wonderful way to socialize, exercise, and indulge in the lively rhythms of jazz music.

GET STARTED

1. **Learn the basics.** Taking beginner classes and immersing yourself in the music are great ways to learn the steps and familiarize yourself with the rhythms of swing dancing. Start with comfortable and breathable attire that allows you to move freely, with flat or low-heeled shoes that make it easier to slide and turn.

2. **Embrace the community.** Swing dancing boasts a vibrant and welcoming community. Attend social dances and related events to engage with fellow enthusiasts.

Table Tennis (Ping-Pong)

"It has become an example of the power of passion to fuel your life, both recreationally and professionally." *

—KINSEY CROWLEY,
Reporter

GAMES/SOCIAL　　COST: $

Table tennis, also known as Ping-Pong, is a fast-paced, competitive game where players use small paddles to hit a lightweight, hollow ball back and forth across the table. The game was originally called "Ping-Pong," derived from the sound the ball makes when hit back and forth, but the name "table tennis" was adopted in 1921. With origins in Victorian England as an after-dinner parlor game among social elites, the game gained widespread popularity in the late nineteenth and early twentieth centuries, evolving from a casual indoor pastime to a formalized sport with standardized equipment and rules. Table tennis can be enjoyed casually or competitively and is accessible to people of all ages and fitness levels. The game is celebrated for its ability to sharpen reflexes, improve hand-eye coordination, and offer both a social and competitive environment.

GET STARTED

1. **Find a playing space.** Table-tennis tables can be found in community centers, sports clubs, or recreational areas. Portable or foldable tables can also be purchased for home use.

2. **Acquire the equipment.** Start with a basic set of table-tennis paddles and a few balls. These are readily available and affordable at most sporting goods stores.

---

*　https://www.forbes.com/sites/kinseycrowley/2018/08/09/how-ping-pong-helped-me-get-ahead-at-work/?sh=3fa62a6fa08e

Tae Kwon Do

"I feel myself progress, and it shows me the power of thought and action on self-conceived limitations."

—JOSLYN LEE,
Small Business Owner

PHYSICAL FITNESS   COST: $$

Literally translating to "the way of the hand and foot," the Korean martial art style of Tae Kwon Do dates back over two thousand years but started gaining worldwide recognition after debuting as a demo sport in the 1988 Olympics. Tae Kwon Do has always been distinguished by its arsenal of flying, jumping, and spinning kicks, but modern performances that include music and dance have made it even more comparable to stunning acrobatics. If you enjoy competing, Tae Kwon Do boasts a strong tournament circuit around the world. Tae Kwon Do also includes a system of sequenced forms called "patterns" or *poomsae* that hold cultural and historical significance and are practiced like a physical meditation. Tae Kwon Do is a comprehensive art that offers physical fitness, self-defense, and spiritual development, making it great for both children and adults.

GET STARTED

1. **Find a school.** Tae Kwon Do studios and clubs will vary in systems and affiliations. Most schools will allow you to observe a class or participate in a trial lesson.

2. **Prepare to invest in gear.** You'll start with a traditional Tae Kwon Do uniform called a *dobok*, which consists of a long-sleeve jacket, pants, and white belt. As you progress in rank, be prepared to invest in sparring equipment.

3. **Plan to attend regularly.** Tae Kwon Do is usually based on a curriculum. You'll need to demonstrate mastery to progress in belt rank, so training consistently will help you retain what you learn.

Tai Chi

"Tai chi helps me strengthen my leg muscles, be more aware, and connect me to my body."

—JENNY,
Accountant

PHYSICAL FITNESS   COST: $

Tai Chi, short for *Taijiquan*, is a martial art that embodies principles of balance, harmony, and the integration of opposing forces, both in a physical and metaphysical sense. Tai Chi originated in China around the sixteenth century and is often associated with the legendary Taoist monk Zhang Sanfeng. It is believed that the monk witnessed a fight between a snake and a crane and became inspired to develop a martial arts form that emphasized softness, yielding, and using an opponent's force against them. Distinct from many other martial arts styles, Tai Chi focuses on breath and mindfulness through a series of slow, deliberate movements designed to cultivate energy, or *qi* (chi). It's often described as meditation in motion and is a suitable for all fitness levels, making it a peaceful yet powerful experience that enhances one's physical and mental well-being.

GET STARTED

1. **Choose a style.** Tai Chi has several styles, with the major styles being Yang, Wu, Chen, and Sun. Yang style is known for its gentle and flowing movements, while Chen style is a more dynamic mix of fast and slow movements. As a beginner, you might prefer the gentler styles, but explore and find one that resonates with your physical abilities and interests.

2. **Learn the basics.** Look for classes taught by experienced Tai Chi instructors who not only teach the movements but explain the philosophy and principles behind them. Proper guidance is crucial for learning the correct techniques and forms.

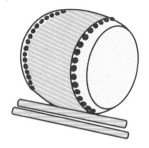

Taiko

*"I can come in here and hit the drums
as hard as I want. And I can yell as loud as
I want, and it's totally fine."* *

—RYAN KIMURA,
Business Owner

GAMES/SOCIAL   COST: $$

Taiko is a traditional Japanese drumming form that embodies the spirit of ensemble play and often features choreographed movements that amplify the power of the percussive elements. With influences from China and Korea, it was originally used in religious ceremonies, festivals, and warfare before evolving into a modern performance art. The term *taiko* literally translates to "big drum," aptly describing the large size of the drums used in Taiko drumming, hit by long wooden sticks called *bachi*. Taiko drumming is distinguished by its physical and rhythmic dynamism. It's a hobby that combines musical skill with teamwork and theatrical flair. Taiko offers the chance to immerse yourself in a cultural tradition that is vibrant, powerful, and deeply communal.

GET STARTED

1. **Learn the performance.** Attend a Taiko performance or watch videos to understand its style and energy. This will give you a feel for the art form and its physical and musical demands.

2. **Join a class and practice regularly.** Look for local Taiko groups or workshops. Many communities have Taiko classes for beginners. Learning in a group setting is essential, as Taiko is about ensemble play. Keep in mind that Taiko is physically demanding. Maintaining good fitness in addition to regular Taiko practice can be beneficial.

---

* *"Drumming to De-Stress at SF Taiko Dojo,"* KALW Public Media, *November 5, 2013,*
https://www.kalw.org/show/crosscurrents/2013-11-05/drumming-to-de-stress-at-sf-taiko-dojo.

Tap Dancing

*"For at least one hour a week in tap class, I had permission to be terrible. Instead of obsessing over how I looked or whether I was meeting some unattainable standard, I was focusing on how it actually felt to dance."** *

—JULIE KING,
Humor Writer

DANCE   **COST: $$**

Tap dancing is a dynamic dance form where the dancer's feet become percussive instruments. The dance involves wearing shoes fitted with metal taps on the heels and toes, creating distinctive sounds as the dancer strikes the floor. Each movement, from simple heel drops to complex combinations of steps, produces a unique sound, blending dance and music into one art form. Tap dancing emerged during the nineteenth century from the fusion of several ethnic dance forms in America, particularly African tribal dances and Irish and English clog dances. It can be performed to a wide range of music genres from jazz to pop and even rock, but the sounds of the tap shoes themselves play a focal role. The allure of tap dancing lies in its combination of rhythm and movement that you get to create directly from your soul with your soles!

GET STARTED

1. **Master the basics.** Focus on learning basic tap steps, such as shuffles, ball changes, and simple toe taps. Mastery of these foundational movements is necessary to progress onto more advanced techniques. Look for beginner classes at local dance studios or community centers.

2. **Invest in tap shoes.** Proper tap shoes are essential. They don't have to be expensive; beginner tap shoes are sufficient to start and can be found at dance supply stores or online.

* *https://sports.yahoo.com/news/struggled-accept-postpartum-body-then-170001344.html*

Taphophilia

"I began to regularly explore and appreciate our local cemeteries as a peaceful, green space, and occasionally a nighttime destination."

—SELENA ORKWIS,
Chef and Entrepreneur

INTROSPECTIVE   COST: $

Taphophilia is the deeply expressed interest in cemeteries, tombstones, and the art of memorials. Taphophiles find beauty in cemeteries, exploring them with a deep appreciation for their cultural, artistic, and historical significance. As a hobby, it involves visiting graveyards, appreciating the craftsmanship of tombstones, understanding epitaphs, and learning about different burial practices and their historical contexts. Taphophilia offers a unique way to connect with the past, understand the present, and contemplate the universal human experience. It's a hobby for individuals who find solace and intrigue in the quiet, often overlooked corners of stories that cemeteries hold.

GET STARTED

1. **Educate yourself.** Learn about cemetery etiquette and the cultural significance of graveyards. Understanding how to respectfully visit these places is imperative. Study funerary art, epitaphs, and cemetery symbolism, which can enrich your visits with a deeper understanding.

2. **Visit local cemeteries.** Begin by researching local cemeteries. Explore their history, observe the different styles of tombstones and monuments, and read the inscriptions. Consider documenting your experiences by keeping a journal or taking photographs (where permitted) of interesting gravestones and cemetery landscapes.

Tarot

"I love tarot because the meaning of the cards is always changing, and tarot not only helps me better understand myself but also helps me feel more at peace with the world."

—JEN K.,
Writer

INTROSPECTIVE   COST: $

Tarot, often associated with divination and fortune-telling, is the practice of using a deck of symbolically rich cards to gain introspection and guidance. The deck contains seventy-eight cards and is divided into two main categories: the Major Arcana, which consists of twenty-two cards that represent life's significant themes and lessons, and the Minor Arcana, comprised of fifty-six cards that reflect day-to-day events. The origins of tarot are not definitive but trace back to playing cards created for the Milanese court in the mid-fifteenth century. Over time, these playing cards began to acquire esoteric significance that incorporated symbolism from a variety of sources, including medieval and Renaissance Europe, Christian mysticism, and Kabbalah.

GET STARTED

1. **Choose a deck and learn the cards.** The deck should resonate with you visually and symbolically. Familiarize yourself with the meanings of the cards. This involves not just memorizing their traditional interpretations but also tuning into your own intuition and understanding of the imagery.

2. **Practice and connect with others.** Begin by pulling a card each day to reflect on its meaning and how it might relate to your daily experiences. Sharing readings and insights with others can help deepen your understanding and appreciation of the tarot.

Taxidermy

*"There's a lot to learn from taxidermy:
It's art, it's nature, and there's
also a conservation aspect to it."* *

—JESSICA DRAGO,
Artist

ART   COST: $$$

Taxidermy is an intricate art form focused on the preservation and display of animals. It involves carefully preparing, stuffing, and mounting animal skins to create lifelike representations. Taxidermy began to emerge as a modern scientific art form in the eighteenth century, as early European taxidermists like Jean-Baptiste Bécœur developed methods to preserve specimens for natural history museums, private collections, and wildlife study. Modern taxidermists often work with specimens that have died naturally or as part of population control efforts. As a hobby, taxidermy satisfies scientific interests, the desire for artistic expression, and a curiosity for wildlife.

GET STARTED

1. **Educate yourself and take a class.** Start by learning about the process, including ethical sourcing and legal considerations. Books, online resources, and taxidermy associations can provide valuable information. Look for beginner classes or workshops, as hands-on learning is crucial in taxidermy.

2. **Gather the tools and animal remains.** Purchase the essential tools, like scalpels, scissors, preservatives, and mounting materials. Many taxidermists obtain animals that have died naturally or as a result of population control measures. There are also licensed suppliers who sell specimens specifically for taxidermy.

* Jacqueline Mroz, "Taxidermy Isn't Dead! And for These NJ Women, It's Cooler than Ever Before," New Jersey Monthly, *November 30, 2023, https://njmonthly.com/articles/arts -entertainment/taxidermy-isnt-dead-and-for-these-nj-women-its-cooler-than-ever-before/.*

Tea Ceremony

*"Gongfu tea ceremony is special to me ecause it ties back to why I started drinking tea to begin with: to ground myself."**

—**CYNDY SPICE,**
SEO Copywriter

INTROSPECTIVE   COST: $$

The tea ceremony, based in Japanese culture, is a ritualized form of making and drinking tea. Known as *chado* in Japanese and translating to "The Way of Tea," the tea ceremony is a ritual that combines elements of philosophy, spirituality, and aesthetics. Its earliest origins trace to ancient China in the third century CE. The Chinese *gongfu cha* ceremony, characterized by its meticulous brewing technique and intimate setting, laid the foundational aesthetics for tea rituals. Japanese chado transformed these early practices into a spiritual and philosophical pursuit influenced by Zen Buddhism.

GET STARTED

1. **Research and learn.** Understanding the cultural background and Zen philosophies underpinning the tea ceremony is essential. Reading books or watching documentaries about its history can provide valuable insights. Look for classes or workshops, often available at cultural centers or through tea ceremony schools. Learning from an experienced instructor is important, as the ceremony involves specific techniques and etiquettes.

2. **Gather the supplies.** For chado, essentials include matcha powder, a bamboo whisk, tea bowl, and tea scoop.

* Deanna Schwartz, "From Rapping to Raising Goats, You've Got Some Wonderful Hobbies," NPR, *August 7, 2022, https://www.npr.org/2022/08/07/1112564993/hobby-ideas #johnny-tang.*

Tennis

"Being a coach for blind tennis allows me to think creatively about how to integrate coaching skills with my knowledge of how the brain processes sound."

—JENNIFER ROTH,
Professor

PHYSICAL FITNESS   COST: $

Tennis is a globally popular racket sport that blends physical agility, strategic thinking, and mental endurance. Involving two players (singles) or two teams of two players (doubles), the objective is to hit a lightweight ball over a net into the opponent's court in such a way that the opponent is not able to return it. Originating in nineteenth-century England, tennis is a fast-paced game that distinguishes itself from other racket sports through its unique scoring system, court dimensions, and playing techniques. It is typically played on large outdoor courts and involves distinct strokes, such as serves, volleys, and groundstrokes. Adaptations like blind tennis, where the ball emits a sound, and wheelchair tennis, with modified rules to accommodate athletes in wheelchairs, also showcase the sport's accessibility to a broader range of players.

GET STARTED

1. **Acquire the equipment.** The basic equipment you'll need includes a tennis racket suited to your size and skill level, tennis balls, and comfortable athletic shoes.

2. **Learn the basics.** Consider taking lessons from a certified coach or join a beginner's clinic to master the fundamental strokes, rules, and techniques of the game. If you want to practice alone, you can use a backboard at a tennis facility or construct one at your home if you have space.

Terrarium Building

"You get the 'I want to live here' feeling inside your chest. I try to create something like that inside each tiny glass container." *

—PATRICIA BUZO,
Author

`NATURE/OUTDOOR`   `COST: $`

Terrarium building is the art of creating miniature ecosystems within transparent containers like glass jars, bowls, or tanks. The concept of terrariums was developed by Nathaniel Bagshaw Ward, a physician from London with a penchant for botany. His experiments with glass cases during the early nineteenth century led to the discovery that sealed containers could support plant life independently by creating a unique microclimate. Subsequently, one of the first terrarium designs was named after him—the Wardian case—and used to transport plants overseas. Building and maintaining a terrarium rewards hobbyists with the ability to enjoy lush, green vistas in a compact form.

GET STARTED

1. **Gather the materials.** Select a glass container first; it can be fully enclosed with a (removable) lid or kept open. You'll need small plants like ferns or mosses, along with gravel, charcoal, potting soil, and decorative elements like rocks or figurines.

2. **Arrange and maintain your terrarium.** Start with a layer of gravel for drainage, followed by a thin layer of charcoal, which prevents odors and bacteria buildup. Add soil and then your plants. Arrange the decorative elements according to your desired design. Place your terrarium in indirect light. Water sparingly, as terrariums retain moisture efficiently.

---

* Margaret Roach, *"Inside a Terrarium, It's Always Gardening Season,"* The New York Times, November 26, 2021, https://www.nytimes.com/2021/11/26/realestate/how-to-build-a-terrarium.html.

Terrazzo

"It's become more than a bit of an |obsession. I'm at the point where I notice it EVERYWHERE. And I'm pinning it all the time. And I want to terrazzo all the things."*

—MARLENE SAUER,
DIY Blogger

ART   COST: $

Terrazzo is an artistic hobby that involves taking chips of marble, glass, and other similar materials, setting them in concrete or epoxy resin, and then polishing to a high shine. The result is a beautifully glossy, mosaic-like pattern distinguished by its durability and uniform texture. Terrazzo is often seen in flooring and countertops, but hobbyists also enjoy using this technique to create small household items like decorative coasters and trays. Terrazzo developed in the eighteenth century when Venetian workers looked for a cost-effective way to use marble remnants. Its combination of creativity, sustainability, and practicality continues to enchant those who enjoy hands-on crafting and design.

GET STARTED

1. **Gather the materials.** You'll need a base material like cement or resin, along with decorative chips of marble, glass, or other stones. Depending on the scale of your project, other essential tools might include molds, a trowel, a wooden dowel or stick for mixing, a grinder or sander, and a polisher.

2. **Start with small projects.** Making a coaster or jewelry are a good place to start and often come in beginner-friendly starter kits. Tap into online tutorials, books, or workshops to master the process of mixing, setting, and polishing the terrazzo.

*   https://idlehandsawake.com/diy-terrazzo-tile-wall-hanging/

Theater

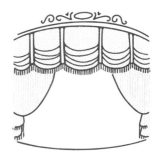

"It all comes down to sharing stories and being able to see people's reactions to the story as it happens."

—CARYL LORIA ILLANA,
Policy Analyst

GAMES/SOCIAL   COST: $$

Theater, an art form that combines elements of drama, speech, music, and dance, is a powerful medium for storytelling and human expression. It involves the portrayal of characters and narratives in a live performance, transporting both the performers and the audience to different worlds, times, and situations. The origins of theater trace to ancient civilizations, notably in Greece around the sixth century BCE, when staged performances were used to honor deities and bring alive notable tragedies and comedies. This hobby offers multiple avenues to get involved whether you want to be on stage or behind the scenes. Theater also fosters a deep sense of collaboration, as it typically involves working with a diverse group of people, including directors, fellow actors, and stage crew.

GET STARTED

1. **Familiarize yourself with theater.** Learn about different aspects of theater. Consider enrolling in theater classes or workshops to develop specific skills, whether in acting, stagecraft, or dramatic writing. Understanding the various elements gives a comprehensive view of what theater entails and which area you might want to focus on as a hobby.

2. **Get involved locally.** Participate in local theater productions, whether as an actor, crew member, or as part of the audience. Community theaters often welcome newcomers and are great places to get hands-on experience.

Thrifting

"Vintage clothing allows me to share a story, care for beautiful pieces, and connect with other vintage fashion-enthusiasts."

—LINDSAY ANNE HERRING,
Anthropologist and Storytelling Facilitator

FASHION/BEAUTY   COST: $

Thrifting is the practice of shopping for secondhand items at thrift stores, flea markets, garage sales, and charity shops. It involves scouring through various used goods, from clothing and accessories to furniture and home decor, in search of unique, affordable, and often vintage items. Thrift stores initially emerged in the twentieth century as a way of providing affordable clothing and goods to those in need while raising funds for charitable causes. Over time, thrifting evolved into a popular activity for a broader audience from budget-conscious shoppers to environmental advocates and vintage collectors. Thrifting is suited for individuals who appreciate sustainable living, as it is an eco-friendly alternative to buying new, helping to reduce waste and support recycling.

GET STARTED

1. **Plan visits locally.** Identify thrift stores, flea markets, and garage sales in your area. Thrifting can be overwhelming, so it's helpful to have a plan. Decide what you're looking for, whether it's vintage clothing, rare books, unique furniture, or quirky home decor. Each visit can offer a new adventure.

2. **Learn the art of bargaining.** Bargaining can be part of the experience, especially at flea markets and garage sales. Start by offering a price that is lower than the asking price, but still reasonable. If you're interested in multiple items, ask if a combined discount is possible.

Tie-Dyeing

"I started about eight years ago as a hobby to do as a stay-at-home mother. I love being able to create every day, and I love seeing people's faces when they see my art."

—MARLAINA FETTE,
Artist

ART   COST: $

Tie-dyeing is achieved by tying or folding fabric in various ways before applying dyes, resulting in distinctive designs where the tied areas resist the dye. The outcome is often a surprise, as the patterns are only revealed once the fabric is untied and dried. Early forms of tie-dyeing have been seen in ancient cultures from Asia to Africa, but its modern form became famously associated with the counterculture movement of the 1960s and 1970s in the United States, symbolizing freedom of expression and creativity. Tie-dyeing is an accessible craft suited for all ages and skill levels.

GET STARTED

1. **Prepare the materials and workspace.** You'll need a tie-dye kit, which typically includes fabric dyes, rubber bands, and gloves. You'll also need white cotton items to dye, like T-shirts, socks, or pillowcases. Tie-dye can be messy, so cover your workspace with plastic sheets or newspapers. Wear old clothes or an apron and use gloves to protect your hands.

2. **Experiment with patterns.** Explore different ways to fold, twist, and tie your fabric using rubber bands or strings. Squeeze the dyes onto the fabric according to your desired pattern. Common techniques include spirals, stripes, and circles.

3. **Set and rinse.** Let the fabric sit for several hours or overnight to set the colors. Rinse the fabric in cold water until the water runs clear, untie, and hang it to dry.

Tintype Photography

*"There's a hyper-real, yet other-worldly nature to each image."**

—ADRIAN WHIPP,
Fine Art Photographer

ART   COST: $$$

Tintype photography refers to a process of capturing images on thin sheets of metal. Initially known as melainotype or ferrotype from the use of iron plates, the process was invented in the 1850s and involves coating a thin sheet of metal with a light-sensitive chemical and then exposing it in a camera while still wet. Rather than recording colors, the process captures varying intensities of light, producing monochromatic images that feature a distinctive vintage look that many hobbyists find charming.

GET STARTED

1. **Consider safety measures.** Understand the chemistry and techniques involved by studying books, online resources, or workshops.

2. **Gather the supplies.** You'll need a camera capable of holding metal plates, usually known as large format cameras. The process also requires chemicals like collodion, silver nitrate, and developer in addition to gloves and several metal plates. Pre-coated aluminum plates are recommended for beginners.

3. **Create a darkroom.** Tintype photography requires a space with minimal light to develop. If you're unable to access or create a darkroom, a portable dark tent can also be used. Tintype photos typically take fifteen to thirty minutes to develop.

* *Joy Celine Asto, "Lumiere Tintype: Inspired by Traveling Photographers of Centuries Past,"* The Phoblographer, *February 3, 2019, https://www.thephoblographer.com/2019/02/03/lumiere-tintype-adrian-whipp/.*

Toastmasters

"The exciting part about Toastmasters is finding ways to connect with others better." *

—KATE MACEACHERN,
Content Consultant

GAMES/SOCIAL   COST: $$

Toastmasters International, often referred to as just Toastmasters, is a global organization dedicated to improving communication, public speaking, and leadership skills. Members deliver speeches, receive feedback, take on leadership roles, and participate in impromptu speaking exercises, all within the framework of regular group meetings. Toastmasters started as a small club created by Ralph C. Smedley in Bloomington, Illinois in 1924. Its particular focus on helping individuals overcome a fear of public speaking resonated with a broad audience, growing it into a worldwide network.

GET STARTED

1. **Find a chapter or club.** You can visit the Toastmasters International website to find a club near you. Most clubs welcome guests, allowing you to attend and observe a meeting before deciding to join for a minimal fee.

2. **Attend and embrace opportunities.** Regularly participating in club meetings is key. As a member, you'll work through different educational projects at your own pace. Take advantage of various opportunities and challenges presented in club meetings to gain as much practice as you can and reach your goals.

* *"Hobbies & Side Projects of Employees #workingatTR,"* Thomson Reuters, *n.d., https://www.thomsonreuters.com/en/careers/careers-blog/hobbies-and-side-projects-of-employees.html.*

Trainspotting

*"The train kind of becomes the secondary event, and it's the time with your friends, getting out and about, that becomes the main event."**

—KANE STEVENSON,
Graduate Student

NATURE/OUTDOOR   COST: $

Trainspotting is a hobby for anyone with a passion for railways and a keen appreciation for the mechanical and historical aspects of trains. It involves observing and recording details about trains, including their types, numbers, routes, and schedules. Trainspotters, or railfans, visit railway stations, bridges, and other vantage points to observe trains and document their findings in notebooks or with a camera. This hobby emerged in the United Kingdom during the mid-twentieth century, coinciding with the rise of rail transport. Over the years, trainspotting has evolved into a well-organized activity with dedicated clubs and societies who share a delight in the engineering marvels of locomotives.

GET STARTED

1. **Educate yourself.** Familiarize yourself with different types of trains, railway companies, and railway history through books and websites.

2. **Visit train stations and tracks.** Spend time at local train stations, bridges, or public railway crossings where you can safely observe trains. Each location offers a different experience.

3. **Document and connect.** Get a notebook or a digital device to record details of the trains you spot. You can also connect with other trainspotters online or in person to share tips, information, and organize group spotting trips.

---

* Caroline Horn, "Trainspotting Hobby Forges Friendships and Worldwide Connections for Adelaide Student," ABC South East SA, *January 19, 2024, https://www.abc.net.au/news /2024-01-20/kane-stevenson-takes-sa-rail-global-trainspotting-connections/103292426.*

Trampolining

*"My kids refused to go on the trampoline;
I guess they thought they're too old for it,
but I still love it."**

—SALMA HAYEK,
Actress

PHYSICAL FITNESS   COST: $$

The modern trampoline was invented as a training tool for acrobats and gymnasts in the 1930s by George Nissen, an American gymnast. He was inspired by the safety nets used by circus trapeze artists and aimed to create a bouncing apparatus that could help with training and provide entertainment. Trampolining has since evolved from a gymnastic tool to a popular recreational activity and competitive sport, even making its way into the Olympics in 2000. Trampolining appeals to a wide audience, from children enjoying the thrill of bouncing to adults seeking a fun and unconventional way to stay fit. You can perform a range of aerial acrobatics from basic jumps to complex flips and twists. It's a joyful form of exercise that allows you to defy gravity.

GET STARTED

1. **Find or acquire a trampoline.** Search for a local trampoline park. They offer a safe, recreational environment for all ages to enjoy. You can also purchase your own trampoline, which range in size from small fitness tools to large, covered trampolines that can be housed in a backyard.

2. **Take a class.** Though jumping on a trampoline can feel straightforward, there are classes that can provide greater instruction on techniques, safety, and more advanced moves.

---

* Hannah Coates, *"Salma Hayek's High-Flying Hobby Might Surprise You,"* British Vogue, January 10, 2023. *https://www.vogue.co.uk/beauty/article/salma-hayek-trampoline.*

Traveling

"Hemingway said that the best cure for ignorance is travel. I've found it especially true when it comes to the bias we have of people and their countries. You don't have to like a country's leaders and government to love their people."

—MICHAEL VU,
Self-employed

NATURE/OUTDOOR   COST: $$$

Traveling is an exploration not just of places but of oneself, as travelers often find that they learn as much about themselves as they do about the world. Unlike a vacation where the focus is on relaxing, traveling as a hobby is about actively seeking new experiences and insights. Journeying to different places, whether near or far, allows you to experience new cultures, landscapes, cuisines, and ways of life. It satisfies those with a deep thirst for knowledge and adventure and can deepen your connection with the world in ways few other activities can. Traveling is a hobby that offers endless possibilities for fun and excitement as much as meaningful personal growth.

GET STARTED

1. **Plan and research.** Though some might prefer to be spontaneous, planning and research are key to understanding the history, culture, customs, and attractions of a place you're interested in exploring. Having an itinerary while remaining open to changes in your plans can lead you to new experiences that are pleasantly rewarding.

2. **Set a budget.** Traveling can be expensive, but it doesn't have to be. Set a budget and look for ways to travel economically, such as off-season travel, staying in hostels, or using public transportation.

Trivia

"Hosting my many trivia events has been a wonderful opportunity to watch long-lasting friendships begin and relationships grow through a trivia team."

—CHRIS V.,
Library Retail Marketing

GAMES/SOCIAL   COST: $

A Vexillology

B Mycology

C Galanthomania

D Phillumeny

Trivia is a hobby that many find both entertaining and intellectually stimulating. It involves the mastery of random, interesting facts across a wide range of subjects from history and science to pop culture and sports. Beyond just the accumulation of knowledge, trivia offers the pleasure of learning diverse tidbits about our world. Trivia grew into a beloved pastime around the globe in the twentieth century with the advent of quiz games like *Jeopardy!, Who Wants to Be a Millionaire,* and Trivial Pursuit. It's the perfect hobby for those who are naturally curious and enjoy a good challenge. Frequently involving group participation, it also offers a way to connect with others who share similar interests. For the inquisitive mind, trivia is a hobby that never grows old, as there's always something new to learn.

GET STARTED

1. **Expand your knowledge.** Begin by reading widely and watching educational programs. There's no set curriculum for trivia, so a broad base of general knowledge is beneficial.

2. **Participate in games.** Many bars and restaurants host trivia nights where teams compete against each other. This is a great way to dive into the trivia community and test your knowledge. You can also play trivia apps and games for practice.

337

Tufting

"I think tufting is very stress-relieving." *

—NORA PENG,
Student

HOME   COST: $$

Tufting is a craft hobby that involves making tufted textiles like rugs, wall hangings, and upholstery. The process entails pushing yarn through a fabric base, typically using a special tool called a tufting gun, to create dense loops or piles. These loops can then be cut or left intact to form various textures and designs. Tufting gained industrial prominence in the twentieth century with the mechanization of the tufting process, particularly in the carpet industry. It has experienced a recent renaissance as a hobby thanks to creators on social media platforms who showcase their tufting projects from start to finish. Tufting offers a unique way to explore creativity and produce works of art that are both visually stunning and functional.

GET STARTED

1. **Gather the supplies.** Essential tools include a tufting gun (either manual or electric), tufting cloth, yarn in various colors, and a frame to stretch the cloth.

2. **Master the basics.** Learn the basics of using a tufting gun and techniques for creating different textures and patterns. Online tutorials, workshops, and community classes can be great resources for beginners.

3. **Start with small projects.** Begin with small, manageable projects like coasters or small rugs to practice and gain confidence. Geometric shapes or abstract patterns are great for beginners.

---

* Agence France-Presse, "Tuft Times: The New Craft Hobby That Sparked a Craze Among Young Chinese," South China Morning Post, *April 22, 2022, https://www.scmp.com/news /china/article/3175157/tuft-times-new-craft-hobby-sparked-craze-among-young-chinese.*

Tutoring

"The most rewarding aspect of tutoring is feeling like I'm actually making a difference in the lives of the students."

—LOGAN TAYLOR BLACK,
Student

`VOLUNTEERING`   `COST: $`

Tutoring involves teaching or guiding individuals or small groups in specific subjects or skills. Whether helping a student grasp a difficult concept, learn a new language, or master a musical instrument, tutoring allows you to share your passion and expertise in a meaningful way. Tutors often find joy in the "aha" moments of their students, witnessing the direct impact of their teaching on someone's understanding and growth. It's a hobby that not only enriches the minds of those you teach but also provides continuous learning and personal growth for the tutor.

GET STARTED

1. **Identify your expertise and audience.** Consider subjects or skills you are knowledgeable and passionate about. This could be an academic subject, a language, a musical instrument, coding, and so on. Decide on the age group or skill level you are most interested in teaching. Tutoring styles and content can vary greatly among young children, high school students, college students, and adults.

2. **Find opportunities.** Start by offering tutoring services in your community through local schools, libraries, or community centers. Online platforms also offer opportunities to tutor students virtually.

* *Zareen Syed, "At West Ridge Tutoring Center, Multilingual Refugees Given Safe Space to Learn with Help from College Students," Chicago Tribune, November 26, 2023, https://www.chicagotribune.com/2023/11/26/at-west-ridge-tutoring-center-multilingual-refugees-given-safe-space-to-learn-with-help-from-college-students/.*

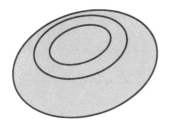

Ultimate Frisbee

"I was never really into sports until we played Ultimate Frisbee in gym. There was a wild joy in rushing down the field with your team and figuring out how to score a point."

—SAM MOREY,
Freelance Writer

GAMES/SOCIAL   COST: $

Ultimate Frisbee, often simply called Ultimate, is a fast-paced, noncontact team sport played with a flying disc, commonly known as a Frisbee. The game combines elements of soccer, football, and basketball, but instead of a ball, players use a Frisbee. The objective is to score points by catching the Frisbee in the opposing team's end zone, much like scoring a touchdown in American football. What sets Ultimate apart is its emphasis on sportsmanship and the "Spirit of the Game," a guiding principle that promotes fair play, respect, and the joy of play among all participants. Originating in 1968 in Maplewood, New Jersey, Ultimate was created by a group of students at Columbia High School, led by Joel Silver. The game quickly spread for its fun and inclusive nature, now played worldwide in pickup games, leagues, and even at professional and international levels.

GET STARTED

1. **Learn the rules.** Familiarize yourself with the basic rules of Ultimate, including throwing and catching techniques. Online tutorials, instructional videos, and local clinics can be great resources.

2. **Get an Ultimate Frisbee.** Purchase a standard Ultimate Frisbee. Unlike regular Frisbee discs, these are slightly heavier and designed for the sport, providing better stability and accuracy.

3. **Join others.** Many communities have Ultimate clubs or regular pickup games. These are great for beginners to learn in a friendly, noncompetitive environment.

Unicycling

"I feel like I'm bringing joy to people's days when they see me riding by. It brightens my day as well." *

—PETER FORNELL,
Student

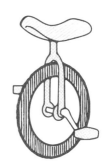

PHYSICAL FITNESS   **COST: $$$**

A unicycle is a single-wheeled vehicle that consists of a frame, pedals, and a seat, but lacks handlebars like in traditional bicycles. Riders must maintain balance through constant motion and skillful control of their body, providing a unique challenge that many find satisfying to master. The unicycle likely evolved from the penny-farthing, a bicycle from the nineteenth century that featured a large front wheel and tiny rear wheel. Daring cyclists would ride the penny-farthing with the rear wheel lifted off the ground, eventually leading to the creation of the unicycle and its many styles of riding. Unicycling can be enjoyed in many contexts from performance art to sports or as a solitary passion.

GET STARTED

1. **Choose a unicycle.** Start with a basic unicycle suitable for beginners. The wheel size and type of unicycle will depend on your interest, whether it's road, off-road, or performing tricks.

2. **Wear safety gear.** Wear a helmet, knee pads, and elbow pads to protect yourself in case of falls.

3. **Master the basics.** Begin by practicing mounting the unicycle and maintaining balance. This can be done by holding onto a wall or a rail. Start riding on smooth, flat surfaces. Consult online tutorials or local classes to improve your skills.

*   Ariella Kissin, "One Wheel, No Worries: Introducing Kenyon's Local Unicyclist," *The Kenyon Collegian, March 25, 2021, https://kenyoncollegian.com/features/2021/03/kenyons-local-unicyclist/.*

Upcycling

HOME   COST: $

Upcycling is a creative and environmentally conscious hobby that involves repurposing and transforming discarded materials or old items into new, useful, or artistic objects. Unlike recycling, which breaks down materials to create something new, upcycling creatively reuses items in their existing form, giving them a second life and a new purpose. This process not only reduces waste but also allows for the creation of unique, personalized items, from home decor to clothing and beyond. The term "upcycling" gained popularity in the 1990s and is credited to Reiner Pilz of Pilz GmbH & Co., a German automation technology company. It has since evolved into a significant movement, inspiring people to embrace a creative approach to sustainability.

GET STARTED

1. **Gather the materials.** Look around your home for items that you no longer use or visit thrift stores and flea markets. Old furniture, clothing, and household items are great starting points.

2. **Choose an easy project.** Try a beginner project, like turning a glass jar into a planter or an old T-shirt into a tote bag. These types of projects require minimal tools and provide a great way to use what you've made.

3. **Learn DIY skills.** Depending on your projects, you might need to learn the basics of sewing, painting, or carpentry.

Vegetable Carving

*"Carving taught me to be more mindful and patient, and to live in the moment."** *

—TEERAPHON PONGKITTIPHAN,
Engineer

FOOD   COST: $

Vegetable carving is an artistic culinary hobby that transforms everyday vegetables into stunning sculptures and intricate designs. The origins of vegetable carving are believed to date back to ancient Asia, particularly in Thailand and Japan. In Thailand, it started during the Sukhothai Dynasty in the fourteenth century to decorate royal tables. The modern practice continues to focus on decorative pieces to enhance the presentation of dishes or for table centerpieces, but there's also been a growing trend of carving vegetables into playable musical instruments, showcasing the fun and versatility of this craft. Whereas the preservation of butter and ice can be prolonged, the perishable nature of vegetables is less controllable, enhancing the ephemeral nature of its beauty.

GET STARTED

1. **Gather the supplies.** You'll need a sharp paring knife and a few sculpting tools. Opt for affordable and abundant vegetables like carrots, potatoes, cucumbers, or zucchinis. Practice food safety by wearing gloves and maintaining a clean working station.

2. **Learn the techniques.** Familiarize yourself with basic carving techniques through online tutorials, books, or classes. Utilize scraps and design your carvings with the intention of them being consumed.

---

* *"Hobbies of Our People Around the World."* Goldman Sachs, *December 20, 2019. https://www.goldmansachs.com/careers/blog/posts/hobbies-of-our-people.html.*

Vexillology

"Maps and globes fascinated me, and I started to memorize all the capitals of countries and tried to identify flags. The interesting thing about it is seeing how things change over time."

—VICTOR VENABLE,
Autoclave Operator

EDUCATIONAL   COST: $

Vexillology—from the Latin word *vexillum,* meaning "flag" or "banner"—is the intellectual hobby revolving around the study and appreciation of flags. The term was coined in 1957 by Dr. Whitney Smith, a prominent flag scholar who also cofounded the North American Vexillological Association in 1967. Vexillologists delve into the stories and meanings behind various national, regional, organizational, and historical flags, exploring how they reflect cultural identities, historical events, and societal values. It offers endless avenues for exploration and discovery and attracts individuals with a keen interest in history, design, and symbolism.

GET STARTED

1. **Educate yourself.** Start by learning the basics of flag design, history, and symbolism. Books, online resources, and academic articles can provide a wealth of information.

2. **Join others.** Organizations like the North American Vexillological Association or other regional groups offer resources, publications, and a community of fellow flag enthusiasts. You can even participate in vexillological conferences to deepen your understanding.

3. **Start a collection.** Collecting flags can be another tangible way to connect with this hobby. Begin with flags that hold personal significance or interest you historically or culturally.

Video Gaming

"I've come to love video games for their immersive storytelling, brain-busting puzzles, and the challenge of mastering different game mechanics. It's also allowed me to keep in touch with friends across the world."

—HAROLD BAGUINON,
Software Engineer

TECH   COST: $$$

Video gaming is an immersive hobby that involves playing games on various electronic devices, including consoles, computers, and mobile phones. These games range from simple and classic formats like puzzles and platformers to complex, narrative-driven adventures or strategy games. The origins of video gaming can be traced back to the 1950s and 1960s, with the creation of early computer games. However, modern video gaming began to take shape in the 1970s with the introduction of arcade games like *Pong*, developed by Atari, and the subsequent advent of home gaming consoles. Video games can be enjoyed alone or with others. They can transport players to different worlds, with experiences ranging from high-octane action to thoughtful strategy and deep storytelling.

GET STARTED

1. **Choose a platform and your games.** Decide whether you prefer to play on a console (like PlayStation, Xbox, or Nintendo), a computer, or a mobile device. Each platform offers different types of games and experiences. There is a vast array to choose from, whether it's adventure games, sports simulations, puzzles, or role-playing games.

2. **Set time limits.** Gaming can be incredibly engaging, so setting time limits and balancing it with other life activities can help make it a rewarding part of a well-rounded life.

Vintage Car Restoration

"Vintage car restoration is a dance between engineering and artistry, where every rusted part has a story, and every polished surface reflects a piece of the past."

—BENJAMIN KOVAC,
Car Mechanic and Blog Owner

NATURE/OUTDOOR   COST: $$$

The hobby of vintage car restoration began to gain popularity in the post–World War II era, particularly in the United States, as a way to preserve the automotive heritage. It grew organically among car enthusiasts who saw value and beauty in older vehicle models and took pleasure in restoring them. Over the years, this pastime developed into a deeply respected craft, combining mechanical skill, historical research, and artistic talent. Restoring vintage cars can range from minor repairs and cosmetic touch-ups to complete overhauls, where every component of the vehicle is restored or replaced.

GET STARTED

1. **Educate yourself.** Learn about different vintage car models, their histories, and the specifics of car restoration. Joining other enthusiasts through local or online clubs and communities can be particularly invaluable with advice, source parts, and support throughout your restoration journey.

2. **Choose a project.** Start with a car that matches your skill level and budget. It's important to select a vehicle that you're passionate about and that has available parts.

3. **Equip a workspace.** Vintage car restoration requires a range of mechanical tools and enough space to work comfortably, such as a garage.

Vinyl Records

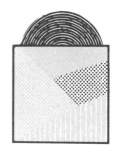

"My grandfather was a Saturday-morning Polka DJ on a college station for twenty-five years and would bring home as many free records as they would allow. I grew up looking at the covers and started collecting them."

—DEAN BISCAN JR.,
Creative Director

COLLECTING   COST: $

Vinyl records are flat, circular discs traditionally made from polyvinyl chloride and known for their distinctive grooves that capture sound in analog form. When played on a turntable, a needle traces these grooves, translating the movements into sound and producing music with a warmth and depth that many enthusiasts argue is unmatched by digital formats. Emile Berliner, a German American inventor, is credited with creating the flat disc record in the 1890s. Vinyl gained immense popularity in the mid-twentieth century, becoming the primary medium for commercial music until the rise of digital formats in the 1980s and 1990s. They have resurged and persist in popularity, cherished by music enthusiasts who value the format's audio qualities and the tangible connection it provides to music.

GET STARTED

1. **Acquire a turntable.** Look for one with a reliable mechanism and a good needle that will treat your records gently.

2. **Start your collection.** Begin with a few albums that you love or classics in your favorite genre. Flea markets, record stores, and online platforms are great places to find vinyl records.

3. **Learn about record care.** Understand how to properly handle and store your records to keep them in good condition. This includes cleaning them regularly and storing them vertically in a dry, cool place.

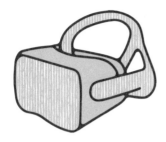

Virtual Reality (VR)

*"I started VR because I'm a social gamer.
Now I'm DJing virtual venues with the world's
biggest misfits, and honestly, I can say
something like, 'These people on VR.' But
I'm the people, and I'm amazing."*

—JOY,
Food Pantry Program Assistant

TECH   **COST: $$$**

Virtual Reality (VR) is an immersive technology that transports users into a digital world, offering an interactive experience that simulates physical presence in imagined or replicated real-life environments. Through a VR headset, users can look around a virtual space, move objects, and often interact with the environment using handheld controllers. The experience is not just visual; spatial, audio, and sometimes haptic (touch) feedback contribute to the illusion of reality. The development of VR technology began in the 1960s and 1970s with pioneers like Ivan Sutherland, known for creating the first VR headset. Morton Heilig's Sensorama, an early VR machine, and Jaron Lanier, who popularized the term "virtual reality" in the 1980s, also made significant contributions. VR has since evolved dramatically, with advancements in technology making it more accessible and realistic.

GET STARTED

1. **Purchase or rent a system.** Options range from stand-alone systems to tethered setups, each with different capabilities and price points. VR recreational rooms are growing and serve as a lower-cost option for you to rent the experience.

2. **Designate space.** Ensure you have a safe, open area to use the VR system. Space requirements can vary, but having enough room to move freely without obstructions enhances the experience.

Volunteering as a Docent

"I'm trying to point out things you wouldn't get just by reading the facts on the wall." *

—FRANK BUETHE,
U.S. Marine Veteran

VOLUNTEERING   COST: $

Volunteering as a docent involves serving as a guide in places like museums, art galleries, historical sites, and zoos. A docent's role is to enhance the visitor experience by providing insightful information, leading tours, and sometimes assisting with educational programs. The word "docent" derives from the Latin word *docere,* meaning "to teach," and has roots in the educational systems of Europe. Docent programs and opportunities grew as cultural and educational institutions recognized the need for informed guides to interpret and convey the significance of their collections to the public. Volunteering as a docent is fulfilling for those who enjoy sharing their passion for art, history, culture, or science with others.

GET STARTED

1. **Identify an institution.** Find a site that aligns with your interests and hosts volunteer docent programs. Docent programs usually require you to undergo training to learn about the institution's collection, tour techniques, and visitor engagement strategies. Being a docent also requires a regular commitment.

2. **Stay informed and engaged.** Continuously educate yourself about new exhibits, artifacts, or developments within your field of interest. Staying informed enhances your ability to engage and educate visitors effectively.

* Richard Hakes, "Senior Citizens Serve at the Stanley Museum of Art and the Hoover Museum, Learning Valuable History Lessons," Iowa City Press-Citizen, *July 15, 2023, https://www.press-citizen.com/story/news/2023/07/15/local-seniors-thrive-inmuseums-as -volunteer-docents/70413334007/.*

Watching Movies

"Some of my favorite memories are going to the video store to rent movies with my mom. Now I own almost four hundred movies, almost like having my own video store."

—ZACH MARKEL,
Valet

GAMES/SOCIAL   COST: $

The first public movie screenings in the 1890s marked the beginning of cinema as a popular form of entertainment. Since then, film has evolved into a diverse and sophisticated art form, with genres ranging from drama and comedy to action, science fiction, and beyond. Watching movies is an immersive experience that can evoke a wide range of emotions and thoughts. It's a hobby that appeals to a broad spectrum of people, from those seeking a brief escape from daily life to aficionados who appreciate the nuances of filmmaking. Watching movies is an endlessly varied hobby that can open windows into different cultures, eras, and perspectives, enriching one's understanding of the world.

GET STARTED

1. **Explore different genres.** Whether it's classic cinema, foreign films, independent movies, or mainstream blockbusters, each genre offers a different viewing experience.

2. **Join movie communities or clubs.** Engaging with other enthusiasts can enhance the movie-watching experience. Online forums, social media groups, and local movie clubs can provide recommendations, insights, and opportunities for discussions.

3. **Attend film festivals and screenings.** Attending film festivals and special screenings can offer unique cinematic experiences and the opportunity to see films not typically shown in mainstream theaters.

Watercolor Painting

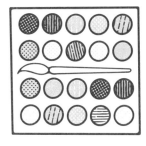

"There is something fascinating in the way water flows; it's captivating. You add different colors, and somehow the water takes the lead, flowing and mixing to create beautiful patterns and shapes."

—GUADALUPE MANRIQUE,
Science Communications Specialist

ART   COST: $

Watercolor painting involves the use of water-based pigments, often resulting in pieces that are distinguished by a soft, ethereal effect. Water is used as a diluting agent in this painting method, meaning that the more water you use, the lighter your pigments will appear. Watercolor painting can feel both forgiving and difficult to control. Some mistakes can be diluted out with water if you don't have dried layers of colors underneath, but the fluid nature of water can also be challenging to predict. This is why watercolor is a great therapeutic tool for encouraging flow—to let go of control and lean into the spontaneity.

GET STARTED

1. **Gather the supplies.** Start with a variety of brush sizes and a basic watercolor palette (also called a watercolor pan) or watercolor paint tubes, which allow for easier experimentation with color mixing. You'll need heavyweight paper specifically made for watercolor painting; this paper is designed to prevent tearing or bowing from the excessive use of water.

2. **Experiment with different techniques.** Two fundamental approaches to watercolor are a wet-on-wet or wet-on-dry techniques. Wet-on-wet involves applying wet paint onto wet paper and is a more fluid method that results in a misty or atmospheric texture. The wet-on-dry techniques allow for more controlled lines and shapes as you apply wet paint to dry paper.

Weightlifting

"I began working with a trainer for some real guidance and a set routine. There are so many little successes in weightlifting; it's hard not to fall in love with it!"

—LISA GOTTUSO,
Compliance Officer

PHYSICAL FITNESS   COST: $

Weightlifting is a disciplined hobby that enhances muscular strength, endurance, and overall physical fitness. It includes a variety of exercises where individuals lift barbells, dumbbells, or use weight machines to train different muscle groups. Weightlifting offers measurable progress, being well-suited for individuals who are motivated by tangible goals. It stands out from other fitness activities in its focus on strength and endurance rather than cardiovascular fitness.

GET STARTED

1. **Learn proper form.** Start by understanding the basic principles of weightlifting, including proper form and technique. Though you can learn through online resources or books, working with a certified trainer who can correct you along the way can be immensely helpful as a beginner.

2. **Access the equipment.** Join a gym that offers a variety of weight-training equipment or acquire your own basic equipment like a set of dumbbells.

3. **Follow a program.** Maintaining consistency is key in weight training. Follow a beginner weightlifting program that focuses on foundational exercises, ensuring a balanced approach to strength training.

Western Calligraphy

"I'm mesmerized by the flow of ink from the pen on paper while meditating on the beauty of language."

—KAREN NORDSTROM ROBERTS,
Community Art Teacher

ART   COST: $

Calligraphy in the Western world revolves around the mastery of lettering with ink and special writing instruments like nib pens and brushes. The roots of Western calligraphy are in ancient Greek and Roman civilizations that developed writing styles like the Roman Capitals (uniform and geometric), Rustic Capitals (rounded with varied strokes), and Uncial scripts (evenly sized and rounded). Distinguished by elements like flourishes, borders, and embellishments, Western calligraphy focuses on creating beautiful, decorative, and expressive letters and symbols. Calligraphy is often used for creating invitations, certificates, greeting cards, and personalized artwork. It is a popular hobby for those who appreciate fine detail and the meditative and creative aspects of the practice.

GET STARTED

1. **Gather the materials.** You'll need a calligraphy pen or brush, ink, paper, and a ruler or T square. Common inks for calligraphy are bottled fountain ink and India ink. Choosing the right paper to prevent bleeding or feathering of your ink is also important. Drawing paper, watercolor paper, and special calligraphy pads are great options to use.

2. **Choose a style.** Common lettering styles of Western calligraphy include Italic, Copperplate, and Gothic, and each has its own unique characteristics. Experiment with different scripts to find your favorite.

Whittling

"I found out it was something I could really do—I can't draw worth a hoot, I can't paint, but woodworking was something I really enjoyed and could spend hours doing."*

—DR. BOB BLOCK,
Pediatrician

ART   COST: $

Whittling is a form of wood carving characterized by its simplicity and the minimal tools required. Unlike other forms of woodcarving that may require a range of tools and a workshop, whittling is often done with just a single piece of wood and a pocketknife, making it a more accessible and portable craft. It has been a common pastime in many cultures throughout history, often associated with folk art and functional object creation. Whittling has a relaxing and meditative quality and is particularly great for anyone who appreciates the tactile experience of working with their hands.

GET STARTED

1. **Choose a knife.** Begin with a good-quality whittling knife. A simple pocketknife can work, but a knife specifically designed for whittling will provide better control and results.

2. **Select the wood.** Softwoods like basswood, pine, or cedar are ideal for beginners. They are easier to carve and require less effort to shape.

3. **Master the basics.** Learn basic whittling techniques and cuts. Always position the knife to carve away from your body, use a thumb guard, and work in a well-lit area.

---

* Grace Wood, *"Whittle by Whittle, the Woodworking Hobby Continues to Grow in Oklahoma,"* Tulsa World, *August 5, 2022, https://tulsaworld.com/life-entertainment/home-and-garden/diy /whittle-by-whittle-the-woodworking-hobby-continues-to-grow-in-oklahoma/article_3af3f3d0 -0f64-11ed-a94c-6ba36908ca3f.html.*

Wikipedia Editing

"When I improve an article, I feel like I've accomplished something. I see my editing as more of a mission."*

—RYAN NG,
Accountant

VOLUNTEERING   COST: $

Wikipedia, cofounded by Jimmy Wales and Larry Sanger in 2001, is a collaborative space where volunteers from around the globe write, update, and maintain a vast array of articles covering an almost infinite range of topics. The idea was to create a freely accessible online encyclopedia that anyone could contribute to and edit, democratizing the creation and dissemination of knowledge. The project has since grown into the world's largest online encyclopedia. Wikipedia editing is a great hobby for people who enjoy research, fact-checking, and writing.

GET STARTED

1. **Create an account and learn the rules.** Start by creating a free user account on Wikipedia. Understand Wikipedia's guidelines and editing protocols, which include their neutral point-of-view policy, verifiability standards, and rules on citing sources.

2. **Start with small edits.** To get accustomed to Wikipedia's editing process, start by making small edits to existing articles, such as correcting typos, fixing grammar, or updating outdated information.

3. **Engage with the community.** Engaging with community portals, discussion pages, and collaborating with other editors can enhance your experience.

---

* *Stephen Harrison, "If You See Something, Write Something." The New York Times, March 28, 2018, https://www.nytimes.com/2018/03/28/nyregion/if-you-see-something-write-something.html.*

Wood Sculpting

"I like the patience required to bring the piece to life and the wide variation of tools available to do so."

—TYLER CURREN,
Special Effects Technician

ART   COST: $$

Wood sculpting is an art form that involves shaping and carving wood with tools like chisels, gouges, hammers, and saws. It is distinct from other wood-carving activities in its scale and artistic focus. The process ranges from removing large sections of wood to create a rough shape to detailed work like adding intricate textures and features. While wood carving might include functional objects like utensils or decorative elements like ornate trim, wood sculpting often aims at creating stand-alone artistic pieces. It allows for more expressive freedom, often resulting in sculptures that can be both abstract and representational. For those drawn to the idea of creating art from a raw, natural medium, wood sculpting offers a fulfilling blend of artistry, craftsmanship, and connection to nature.

GET STARTED

1. **Learn the basics.** Consider taking a class, joining a wood sculpting workshop, or following online tutorials to learn from experienced sculptors. This can provide valuable guidance and improve your skills.

2. **Gather the materials.** Start with essential tools like a carving knife, chisels, gouges, and a mallet. The best woods for sculpting include basswood, pine, and butternut.

Worm Charming

"It's a bit of fun, really. I am interested in green issues, and this is a way of helping people connect with the earth." *

—REVEREND MIKE NORTH,
Priest

NATURE/OUTDOOR   COST: $

Worm charming is a fascinating hobby that involves coaxing earthworms out of the ground. Participants use various techniques to vibrate or shake the soil, mimicking the natural signals that encourage worms to surface, such as rain or the movements of predators. The charm lies not just in the number of worms collected but also in the technique and the sheer fun of the activity. While the precise origins of worm charming are unclear, this unique practice has been a part of agricultural societies for centuries, primarily as a means of gathering bait for fishing. It has since evolved into a competitive and recreational hobby, with events and competitions held in various parts of the world, particularly in the United Kingdom and the United States.

GET STARTED

1. **Learn about worms.** Understanding the behavior of earthworms and their natural habitat can significantly improve your chances of charming them effectively.

2. **Choose your techniques.** Common methods include tapping the ground rhythmically with a stick, vibrating a pitchfork tine inserted into the soil, or even playing music.

3. **Participate in events.** Joining a worm-charming event or competition can be a great way to learn, meet fellow enthusiasts, and enjoy the communal aspect of the hobby.

* *Paul Wilkinson, "Old Hobby Comes to the Surface," Church Times, September 5, 2014, https://www.churchtimes.co.uk/articles/2014/5-september/news/uk/old-hobby-comes-to-the-surface.*

Wreath Making

"All day long I use numbers and work on the financial side of things. Everyone needs to have something positive and something creative that uses a different part of your brain." *

—PENNY PARKS,
Financial Industry Executive

ART   COST: $

A wreath is typically circular in shape and is made from various natural or synthetic materials such as flowers, branches, ribbons, or wires. Often symbolizing unity, strength, and the cycle of life, wreaths have been a part of folklore and traditions throughout various cultures. Ancient Greeks and Romans used wreaths as crowns to symbolize victory, status, and achievement, while many European countries that celebrate May Day use them to symbolize the arrival of spring, fertility, and new beginnings. Over time, the making of wreaths evolved beyond symbolic headpieces to decorative items used to adorn doors, walls, and tables, especially during festive seasons or significant events.

GET STARTED

1. **Gather the supplies.** Materials can include natural elements like branches, flowers, and leaves, or artificial items like ribbons, fabric strips, and ornaments. The choice of materials often reflects the season or the theme of the wreath.

2. **Choose a base.** The base can be a metal, foam, or grapevine ring, depending on the style and design of your wreath. Each type of base offers different advantages in terms of structure and ease of attaching materials.

---

* *Grier Ferguson, "In Quest for Creative Outlet, Financial Industry Executive Turns to Wreaths,"* Business Observer, *January 11, 2019, https://www.businessobserverfl.com /news/2019/jan/11/penny-parks-links-financial-tampa-wreaths-makes/.*

Wushu

"I started Wushu as a means to attend a training camp in Shaolin to live out a childhood dream. I eventually fell in love with the movements and expression, as well as the endless ways to push my physical abilities."

—ALLEN PENG,
Civil Engineer

PHYSICAL FITNESS   COST: $

Wushu, which translates to "martial arts" in Mandarin, is often recognized in the West as Kung Fu. It is the collective term for martial art practices that originated in China and encompasses a vast array of styles and techniques, each with its own unique philosophy and aesthetic. Wushu is not merely a form of self-defense but an artful expression, a sport, and a means of preserving robust historical and cultural traditions. The roots of Wushu stretch back over millennia, with some accounts dating it as far back as the Zhou Dynasty (1046–256 BCE). However, it was during the Tang Dynasty (618–907 CE) that Wushu became systematized and practiced within the military. Wushu evolved through contributions from various warriors, monks, and philosophers over centuries, each leaving their mark on this multifaceted discipline.

GET STARTED

1. **Choose a style.** Research the different styles of Wushu to discover the one that resonates most with you—whether it's the fast-paced *Changquan* (Long Fist) or the precise movements of *Taijiquan* (Tai Chi).

2. **Locate a school or instructor.** Seek out a qualified instructor or school that specializes in the style you wish to learn. The guidance of an experienced teacher is invaluable in learning proper form and technique.

Yarn Wrapping

"Think of it as graffiti but using yarn." *

—MONA CHEAH,
Part-time Worker

(ART)   (COST: $)

Yarn wrapping is a highly therapeutic hobby that involves wrapping yarn around various objects from small stones and sticks to large furniture or even trees (often referred to as yarn graffiti or yarn bombing). The specific origins of yarn wrapping are difficult to trace, but similar techniques have been seen in various forms of traditional crafts around the world. The essence of yarn wrapping lies in the rhythmic process of winding colorful threads around an object, transforming it with layers of texture and hue. The tactile nature of yarn and the meditative act of wrapping make it a relaxing activity, perfect for those looking to unwind creatively.

GET STARTED

1. **Gather the supplies.** You'll need yarn in various colors and textures, and objects to wrap. These can be anything from household items to natural finds like rocks or branches.

2. **Explore and create.** Yarn wrapping is a straightforward technique of securing the end of the yarn and wrapping it tightly and evenly around an object. You can be adventurous by experimenting with different patterns, color combinations, and layering. You can also add embellishments like beads or fabric for added texture.

---

* Tan Ming Chuan, "Tree-Huggers of a Knitted Sort: National Day 'Yarn Bombing' at Jurong Lake Gardens Attracts Curious Onlookers," TODAY, August 9, 2023, https://www .todayonline.com/singapore/yarn-bombing-knitting-crochet-jurong-lake-gardens-national -day-2228851.

Yodeling

"The doctor told me to keep singing and dancing, so I am."*

—DARREL JOHNSON,
Landscape Business Owner

MUSIC   COST: $

Yodeling is a unique form of singing characterized by rapid and repeated changes in pitch between the low-pitch chest register and the high-pitch head register. This creates a distinct echoing sound that is both enchanting and captivating. Traditionally, yodeling involved a form of communication across the mountains and later evolved into a musical style used in folk songs, particularly in the Alpine regions of Europe. Yodeling is a hobby well-suited to those who enjoy singing and are interested in exploring different vocal techniques. It appeals to individuals who appreciate folk music traditions and are drawn to the cultural heritage that yodeling represents. Additionally, yodeling can be a joyful and liberating experience, offering a unique way to express emotions musically.

GET STARTED

1. **Listen and learn.** Immerse yourself in yodeling music. Listen to traditional yodelers to understand the nuances of this singing style. Practice vocal exercises that help you navigate between chest and head voices effortlessly.

2. **Start with simple songs.** Begin by practicing simple yodeling tunes. Many resources are available online, including tutorials and sheet music, to guide beginners.

---

*   Mara Klecker, "Cottage Grove Man Keeps the Fading Art of Yodeling Alive," Star Tribune, August 1, 2018, https://www.startribune.com/cottage-grove-man-keeps-the-fading-art-of-yodeling-alive/489818721/.

Yoga

"As a creative, I needed to stay devoted to a hobby that was just for me. I love that yoga helps clear my mind to make room for all the new ideas."

—NICOLE SILVA,
Bakery Owner

PHYSICAL FITNESS   COST: $

Yoga is an ancient practice that combines physical postures, breathing techniques, and meditation or relaxation. Originating in India over five thousand years ago, it is much more than just physical exercise; it's a holistic discipline that promotes harmony within the mind, body, and spirit. In yoga practice, the body is moved through various poses or *asanas,* which build strength, flexibility, and balance. Yoga encompasses a range from gentle stretches to challenging poses, making it a lifelong practice adaptable to the changing needs of the practitioner.

GET STARTED

1. **Choose a style.** There are various styles of yoga, from the physically demanding Ashtanga to the gentler Hatha. Start with a style that aligns with your fitness level and goals.

2. **Gather the equipment.** All you need to start is a yoga mat, but you may also want to acquire yoga blocks or a strap to support your poses. Wear comfortable clothing that is fitted or stretchable.

3. **Learn the basics.** Familiarize yourself with basic yoga poses and breathing techniques. This can be through online tutorials or books, but enrolling in classes and learning from a certified instructor is often more beneficial.

Yo-Yoing

*"I've been playing for almost three years now. It's a really cool community once you dive into it. I've met a bunch of my good friends through yo-yo, and it just generally makes me happy."** *

—FAYE WEBSTER,
Singer-Songwriter

TOYS   COST: $

The yo-yo is a small, round toy that consists of two equally sized and weighted discs connected by an axle, with a string wound around it. Yo-yoing is the skillful hobby of throwing the yo-yo and performing various tricks as it spins and moves up and down the string. The yo-yo has historical roots dating back to ancient times with early versions found in Greece around 500 BCE. It was popularized as a modern toy in the Philippines during the sixteenth century. The term "yo-yo" is believed to come from the Tagalog language, meaning "come-come" or "return." Pedro Flores, a Filipino American, was instrumental in popularizing it in the United States during the 1920s, leading to its current design and widespread use. Yo-yoing combines physical skill with creativity and develops intricate hand-eye coordination.

GET STARTED

1. **Select a yo-yo.** Choose a beginner-friendly yo-yo, preferably one that is responsive (returns easily with a tug). As you progress, you can move on to unresponsive yo-yos that are better suited for advanced tricks.

2. **Master the basics.** Begin with basic yo-yoing skills. These include properly winding the string, the basic throw, and simple tricks like "sleeping" (letting the yo-yo spin at the end of the string).

---

* *Chelsea Peng, "Faye Webster Wants Her Music to Make You Feel Understood," Refinery29, August 4, 2021, https://www.refinery29.com/en-us/faye-webster-singer-songwriter-interview.*

Zentangle

"I realized that I love drawing organic shapes with no plan in mind. Now, in my late thirties, I've found that it may have been a hidden talent, and other people seem to enjoy my art as much as I do."

—MAUREEN MOTTINGER,
Lead Customer Service Advocate

(ART)   (COST: $)

The Zentangle Method was created by Maria Thomas and Rick Roberts in 2003. Maria, an artist, and Rick, a former monk, combined their experiences in calligraphy and meditation to develop the method as a way for people to focus their attention and find relaxation through drawing. Zentangle involves creating structured designs through a series of repetitive patterns and shapes. Each piece, called a "tile," is a small square of paper filled with black and white patterns made with a pen. Zentangle embodies a structured yet free-form nature, providing an escape into the world of patterns and shapes through artistic expression and stress relief.

GET STARTED

1. **Gather the supplies.** All you need is a piece of paper (preferably good quality), a pen (fine-tipped pens are preferred), and a pencil for shading.

2. **Start small.** Begin with a small piece of paper and create a "string," which is a simple border or curve, to provide a basic structure. Then fill in the sections with different patterns. You can doodle patterns of your own or learn some basic Zentangle patterns, called "tangles." These can be learned through online resources, books, or workshops.

3. **Practice mindfulness.** Dedicate a space where you'll be undisturbed. Focus on each stroke as you draw and enjoy the process without worrying about the final outcome.

Zumba

"It allows me to dance to a variety of music styles without worrying about getting every move right; I simply follow the music and the instructor's guidance. It's a fantastic way to let loose and have a great time while staying fit."

—CHIH-CHEN LEE,
Professor

PHYSICAL FITNESS　　**COST: $**

Zumba is a dynamic fitness program that combines Latin and international music with dance moves. It integrates interval training—alternating fast and slow rhythms—to help improve cardiovascular fitness. Participants follow the music with repeated steps, often led by an instructor, making it an engaging and fun group activity. Zumba was created in the mid-1990s by Alberto "Beto" Perez, a Colombian dancer and choreographer. The story goes that Perez forgot his regular aerobics music for a class and improvised using his own mix of Latin dance music. The class was a hit, and thus Zumba was born. It quickly spread worldwide, gaining popularity for its infectious music, easy-to-follow moves, and effective fitness results. Unlike traditional exercise, Zumba is more like a dance party than a workout session. It's perfect for those who enjoy music and dance and are looking for an enjoyable way to stay active.

GET STARTED

1. **Find a class.** Look for a Zumba class at local gyms, community centers, or dance studios. Many places offer Zumba classes for different skill levels.

2. **Practice patience and have fun.** The key to Zumba is to enjoy the music and the movement. Don't worry about getting every step right; it's more about the overall experience and enjoying the workout.

Hobbies List

3D Printing 1

A

Acrylic Painting 2
Acrylic Pouring 3
Antiquing 4
Aquascaping 5
Arborsculpting 6
Archery 7
Argentine Tango 8
ASMR Recording 9
Astrology 10
Astronomy 11
Axe Throwing 12

B

Backpacking 13
Ballet 14
Ballroom Dance 15
Barbecuing 16
Basket Weaving 17
Basketball 18
Baton Twirling 19
Beading 20
Beekeeping 21
Beer Brewing 22
Being a Conversation
    Partner 23
Being a Foodie 24
Being an Extra 25
Belly Dancing 26
Bento Art 27
Billiards 28

Bingo 29
Birding 30
Blacksmithing 31
Blogging 32
Board Games 33
Bocce 34
Book Club 35
Bookbinding 36
Bottled Sand
    Art 37
Bowling 38
Boxing 39
Breadmaking 40
Breakdancing 41
Breeding
    Butterflies 42
Bullet Journaling 43
Burlesque 44
Bushcraft 45
Busking 46
Butter Sculpting 47
Button Making 48

C

Cake Making 49
Camping 50
Candle Making 51
Canning 52
Card Collecting and
    Trading 53
Card Games 54
Card Stacking 55
Cartography 56

Catching Sunrises and
    Sunsets 57
Chain Mail Weaving . . . 58
Cheerleading 59
Cheese Making 60
Chess 61
Chess Boxing 62
Choir Singing 63
Circus and Aerial Arts . . . 64
Clay Shooting 65
Clothes Making 66
Cloud Gazing 67
Cobbling and
    Shoemaking 68
Coding 69
Coffee Roasting 70
Coffee Shops 71
Coin Collecting
    (Numismatics) 72
Collaging 73
Coloring 74
Comics 75
Concertgoing 76
Confectionary Art . . . 77
Cookie Decorating 78
Cooking 79
Cornhole 80
Cosplaying 81
Creating Memes 82
Crocheting 83
CrossFit 84
Cross-Stitching 85
Crossword Puzzles 86

Crystal Growing 87
Cycling 88

D

Darts 89
Decoupage 90
Diamond Painting..... 91
Digital Illustrating..... 92
Disc Golf. 93
DJing 94
Dollhouses 95
Domino Toppling 96
Double Dutch Jump
    Roping 97
Drag 98
Dragon Boating....... 99
Driving 100
Drone Flying 101
Drum Circles........ 102
Dumpster Diving..... 103
Dungeons & Dragons
    (D&D). 104

E

Eastern Calligraphy .. 105
Embroidery 106
Engraving........... 107
Entertaining/Hosting
    Dinner Parties 108
Entertainment
    Memorabilia 109
Entomology 110
Environmental
    Restoration 111
Esports 112
Extreme Ironing 113

F

Fanfiction Writing.... 114
Fansubbing 115

Fantasy Sports 116
Felting............. 117
Fight Choreography .. 118
Fire Spinning 119
Fishing 120
Flag Football 121
Flash Mobbing 122
Flower Arranging/
    Ikebana 123
Flower Pressing 124
Foam Carving 125
Food Rescuing....... 126
Foraging 127
Fossicking 128
Freestyling 129
Fursuiting........... 130

G

Galanthomania 131
Gelatin Art 132
Genealogy
    Mapping.......... 133
Geocaching 134
Ghost Hunting....... 135
Gilding 136
Gingerbread House
    Construction...... 137
Glassblowing........ 138
Go-Karting 139
Golfing 140
Graffiti Art 141
Gymnastics 142

H

Ham Radio.......... 143
Handbell Choir 144
Heels Dance 145
Herbalism........... 146
Hikaru Dorodango ... 147
Hiking 148

Historical
    Reenactment...... 149
Hitting Mung 150
Hobbyhorsing 151
Hockey 152
Home Café. 153
Horseback Riding.... 154
Hula Hooping 155
Hunting............. 156
Hydroponics......... 157

I

Ice Sculpting 158
Ice Skating.......... 159
Improv............. 160
Indoor Gardening.... 161
Indoor Wall
    Climbing 162
Investing............ 163

J

Jewelry Making 164
Jigsaw Puzzles....... 165
Jiu-Jitsu/BJJ 166
Judo 167
Jump Roping 168

K

Karaoke 169
Karate 170
Kayaking............ 171
Kek Lapis
    Sarawak.......... 172
Kendo 173
Kite Flying 174
Knitting............. 175
Knotting 176
Kombucha Brewing... 177
K-Pop Dancing 178

L

Lampworking 179
Lapidary Arts 180
LARPing 181
Latte Art 182
Lawn Mower Racing . . . 183
Learning a
    Language 184
Learning an
    Instrument 185
Leatherworking 186
LEGO Building 187
Letter Writing 188
Line Dancing 189
Linocut 190
Live Model Drawing . . . 191
Lock Picking 192

M

Machine Learning . . . 193
Macramé 194
Magic 195
Magic: The
    Gathering 196
Mahjong 197
Makeup Artistry 198
Making Cosmetics . . . 199
Making
    Spreadsheets 200
Making YouTube
    Videos 201
Meringue Art 202
Metal Detecting 203
Meteorology 204
Miniature
    Cooking 205
Miniature Pottery 206
Miniature Tree
    Cultivating 207
Mixology 208

Mixed Martial Arts
    (MMA) 209
Model Figurine
    Building 210
Model Trains 211
Molecular
    Gastronomy 212
Mooing 213
Mosaic 214
Mural Painting 215
Museums 216
Musical Looping 217
Musical Theater 218
Mycology 219

N

Nail Art 220
Noodling 221
Nude Modeling for
    Live Drawings 222

O

Obstacle Course
    Racing (OCR) 223
Oenology 224
Off-Roading 225
Oil Painting 226
Origami 227
Outdoor Gardening . . . 228
Outdoor Rock
    Climbing 229
Outdoor Sketching . . . 230

P

Paintball 231
Palm Reading 232
Paper Quilling 233
Papercutting 234
Papermaking 235
Paragliding 236

Parkour 237
Pet Sports 238
Pet Therapy 239
Phillumeny 240
Photography 241
Pickleball 242
Pickling 243
Pigeon Racing 244
Pilates 245
Piloting 246
Pinball Gaming 247
Plogging 248
Podcasting 249
Poetry 250
Pokémon GO 251
Pole Dancing 252
Polymer Clay 253
Pony Sweat 254
Pop-Up Art 255
Pottery 256
Puppetry 257
Pyrography 258
Pysanky 259

Q

Quidditch 260
Quilting 261

R

Rafting 262
Raising Chickens 263
RC Driving 264
Reading 265
Refurbishing and
    Restoring
    Furniture 266
Resin Casting 267
Retro Gaming 268
Rice Toss Art 269
Robotics 270

Rock Balancing...... 271
Rockhounding....... 272
Rock Painting 273
Roller Coaster
    Riding............ 274
Roller Derby......... 275
Roller Skating 276
Rollerblading........ 277
Rowing 278
Rube Goldberg
    Machines......... 279
Running 280

S

Sailing.............. 281
Salsa Dancing....... 282
Samba.............. 283
Sandcastle
    Building.......... 284
Scrapbooking 285
Screen Printing...... 286
Scuba Diving........ 287
Sepak Takraw 288
Skateboarding....... 289
Skiing 290
Skydiving 291
Slacklining.......... 292
Sleuthing 293
Snorkeling 294
Soap Carving........ 295
Soapmaking......... 296
Soccer (Fútbol) 297
Speedcubing 298
Spelunking.......... 299
Spirographing....... 300
Spoken Word........ 301
Squash 302
Squeegee Painting... 303
Stained Glass Art 304
Stair Climbing....... 305

Stamp Collecting 306
Stamping 307
Stand-Up
    Paddleboarding... 308
Stickers............. 309
Stone Skipping...... 310
Stop Motion
    Animation 311
Story Time at the
    Library........... 312
Sudoku 313
Surfing 314
Swimming 315
Swing Dancing 316

T

Table Tennis
    (Ping-Pong)....... 317
Tae Kwon Do........ 318
Tai Chi............. 319
Taiko 320
Tap Dancing........ 321
Taphophilia 322
Tarot 323
Taxidermy.......... 324
Tea Ceremony 325
Tennis 326
Terrarium Building... 327
Terrazzo 328
Theater............ 329
Thrifting 330
Tie-Dyeing 331
Tintype Photography ..332
Toastmasters........ 333
Trainspotting 334
Trampolining 335
Traveling........... 336
Trivia 337
Tufting............. 338
Tutoring 339

U

Ultimate Frisbee..... 340
Unicycling.......... 341
Upcycling 342

V

Vegetable Carving.... 343
Vexillology 344
Video Gaming 345
Vintage Car
    Restoration 346
Vinyl Records........ 347
Virtual Reality
    (VR) 348
Volunteering as a
    Docent 349

W

Watching Movies 350
Watercolor
    Painting.......... 351
Weightlifting......... 352
Western
    Calligraphy 353
Whittling............ 354
Wikipedia Editing.... 355
Wood Sculpting...... 356
Worm Charming..... 357
Wreath Making...... 358
Wushu.............. 359

Y

Yarn Wrapping....... 360
Yodeling 361
Yoga............... 362
Yo-Yoing............ 363

Z

Zentangle........... 364
Zumba.............. 365

Hobbies by Category

Art

Acrylic Painting 2
Acrylic Pouring 3
Basket Weaving 17
Beading 20
Blacksmithing 31
Bookbinding 36
Bottled Sand Art 37
Bullet Journaling 43
Butter Sculpting 47
Button Making 48
Candle Making 51
Cartography 56
Chain Mail Weaving . . . 58
Collaging 73
Coloring 74
Decoupage 90
Diamond Painting 91
Digital Illustrating 92
Dollhouses 95
Eastern
    Calligraphy 105
Engraving 107
Fan Fiction
    Writing 114
Flower Arranging/
    Ikebana 123
Foam Carving 125
Gilding 136
Glassblowing 138
Graffiti Art 141
Hikaru Dorodango . . . 147
Ice Sculpting 158

Jewelry Making 164
Lampworking 179
Lapidary Arts 180
Leather Working 186
Linocut 190
Live Model
    Drawing 191
Macrame 194
Miniature Cooking . . . 205
Miniature Pottery 206
Mosaic 214
Mural Painting 215
Nail Art 220
Nude Modeling for Live
    Drawings 222
Oil Painting 226
Origami 227
Outdoor Sketching . . . 230
Paper Quilling 233
Papercutting 234
Papermaking 235
Photography 241
Poetry 250
Polymer Clay 253
Pop-Up Art 255
Pottery 256
Puppetry 257
Pyrography 258
Pysanky 259
Resin Casting 267
Rice Toss Art 269
Rock Painting 273
Scrapbooking 285

Screen Printing 286
Soap Carving 295
Spirographing 300
Spoken Word 301
Squeegee Painting . . . 303
Stained Glass Art 304
Stamping 307
Taxidermy 324
Terrazzo 328
Tie-Dyeing 331
Tintype Photography . . 332
Watercolor Painting . . 351
Western Calligraphy . . 353
Whittling 354
Wood Sculpting 356
Wreath Making 358
Yarn Wrapping 360
Zentangle 364

Collecting

Antiquing · · · · · · · · · · · · ·4
Card Collecting and
    Trading · · · · · · · · · ·· 53
Coin Collecting
    (Numismatics) · · · · · 72
Comics · · · · · · · · · · · · · 75
Entertainment
    Memorabilia 109
Entomology 110
Phillumeny 240
Stamp Collecting 306
Stickers 309
Vinyl Records 347

Competitive

Card Stacking 55
Go-Karting 139
Mooing 213
Pet Sports 238
Pigeon Racing 244
Pinball Gaming 247
Speedcubing 298

Dance

Argentine Tango 8
Ballet 14
Ballroom Dance 15
Belly Dancing 26
Breakdancing 41
Burlesque 44
K-Pop Dancing 178
Line Dancing 189
Salsa Dancing 282
Samba 283
Swing Dancing 316
Tap Dancing 321

Educational

Astrology 10
Crossword Puzzles . . . 86
Crystal Growing 87
Herbalism 146
Investing 163
Learning a
    Language 184
Lock Picking 192
Making
    Spreadsheets 200
Meteorology 204
Palm Reading 232
Piloting 246
Reading 265
Rube Goldberg
    Machines 279

Sleuthing 293
Vexillology 344

Fashion/Beauty

Clothes Making 66
Cobbling/
    Shoemaking 68
Cosplaying 81
Drag 98
Makeup Artistry 198
Making Cosmetics . . . 199
Soapmaking 296
Thrifting 330

Fiber Arts

Crocheting 83
Cross-Stitching 85
Embroidery 106
Felting 117
Knitting 175
Quilting 261

Food

Barbecuing 16
Beer Brewing 22
Being a Foodie 24
Bento Art 27
Breadmaking 40
Cake Making 49
Canning 52
Cheese Making 60
Coffee Roasting 70
Confectionary Art 77
Cookie Decorating . . . 78
Cooking 79
Gelatin Art 132
Gingerbread House
    Construction 137
Home Café 153
Kek Lapis Sarawak . . . 172

Kombucha
    Brewing 177
Latte Art 182
Meringue Art 202
Mixology 208
Molecular
    Gastronomy 212
Oenology 224
Pickling 243
Vegetable Carving 343

Games/Social

Being an Extra 25
Billiards 28
Bingo 29
Board Games 33
Bocce 34
Book Club 35
Bowling 38
Busking 46
Card Games 54
Chess 61
Concertgoing 76
Corn Hole 80
Darts 89
Disc Golf 93
Double Dutch Jump
    Roping 97
Dragon Boating 99
Dungeons & Dragons
    (D&D) 104
Fantasy Sports 116
Flash Mobbing 122
Freestyling 129
Fursuiting 130
Ghost Hunting 135
Historical
    Reenactment 149
Hobby Horsing 151

Improv............160
Karaoke 169
LARPing............181
Lawn Mower
    Racing 183
Letter Writing 188
Magic 196
Magic the
    Gathering 196
Mahjong 197
Paintball 231
Quidditch 260
Roller Derby.........275
Sepak Takraw ······288
Table Tennis
    (Ping-Pong).......317
Taiko 320
Theater.............329
Toastmasters 333
Trivia 337
Ultimate Frisbee.....340
Watching Movies 350

Home

Dumpster Diving.....103
Entertaining.........108
Refurbishing and
    Restoring
    Furniture 266
Tufting.............338
Upcycling 342

Introspective

Genealogy
    Mapping..........133
Hitting Mung 150
Jigsaw Puzzles.......165
Knotting 176
Sudoku.............313
Taphophilia 322

Tarot 323
Tea Ceremony 325

Music

Choir Singing 63
DJing................94
Drum Circles........102
Handbell Choir 145
Learning an
    Instrument........185
Musical Theater 218
Yodeling 361

Nature/Outdoor

Aquascaping 5
Arborsculpting.........6
Astronomy 11
Backpacking 13
Beekeeping 21
Birding 30
Breeding Butterflies...42
Bushcraft 45
Camping............50
Catching Sunrises and
    Sunsets 57
Cloud Gazing.........67
Coffee Shops........71
Driving 100
Extreme Ironing 113
Fishing 120
Flower Pressing 124
Foraging...........127
Fossicking 128
Galanthomania 131
Geocaching 134
Horseback Riding....154
Hunting.............156
Hydroponics........157
Indoor Gardening....161
Kite Flying 174

Metal Detecting......203
Miniature Tree
    Cultivating........207
Museums 216
Mycology...........219
Noodling............221
Off-Roading 221
Outdoor
    Gardening........228
Outdoor Rock
    Climbing 229
Paragliding..........236
Parkour.............237
Plogging............248
Rafting 262
Raising Chickens 263
Rock Balancing......271
Rockhounding.......272
Roller Coaster
    Riding............274
Sailing..............281
Sandcastle Building
Skiing 290
Skydiving 291
Snorkeling 294
Spelunking..........299
Stand-Up
    Paddleboarding ...308
Stone Skipping......310
Terrarium Building...327
Trainspotting 334
Traveling...........336
Vintage Car
    Restoration 346
Worm Charming.....357

Physical Fitness

Archery..............7
Axe Throwing 12

Basketball............ 18

Baton Twirling........ 19

Boxing............... 39

Cheerleading......... 59

Chess Boxing 62

Circus and Aerial
   Arts............... 64

Clay Shooting 65

CrossFit 84

Cycling 88

Fight
   Choreography..... 118

Fire Spinning 119

Flag Football 121

Golfing 140

Gymnastics 142

Heels Dance 145

Hiking.............. 148

Hockey 152

Hula Hooping 155

Ice Skating.......... 159

Indoor Wall
   Climbing 162

Jiu-Jitsu/BJJ.......... 166

Judo 167

Jump Roping 168

Karate.............. 170

Kayaking............ 171

Kendo 173

Mixed Martial
   Arts (MMA)........ 209

Obstacle Course Racing
   (OCR)............ 223

Pickleball 242

Pilates.............. 245

Pole Dancing........ 252

Pony Sweat 254

Roller Skating 276

Rollerblading 277

Rowing 278

Running 280

Scuba Diving........ 287

Skateboarding....... 289

Slacklining.......... 292

Soccer (Fútbol) 297

Squash 302

Stair Climbing....... 305

Surfing 314

Swimming 315

Tae Kwon Do........ 318

Tai Chi.............. 319

Tennis 326

Trampolining 335

Unicycling.......... 341

Weightlifting........ 352

Wushu.............. 359

Yoga................ 362

Zumba.............. 365

Tech

3D Printing 1

ASMR Recording...... 9

Blogging............. 32

Coding.............. 69

Creating Memes...... 82

Drone Flying 101

Esports 112

Fansubbing 115

Ham Radio.......... 143

Machine Learning ... 193

Making YouTube
   Videos 201

Musical Looping..... 217

Podcasting.......... 249

Pokémon GO........ 251

RC Driving.......... 264

Retro Gaming 268

Robotics 270

Stop Motion
   Animation 311

Video Gaming 345

Virtual Reality
   (VR) 348

Toys

Domino Toppling ····· 96

LEGO Building...... 187

Model Figurine
   Building 210

Model Trains 211

Yo-Yoing............ 363

Volunteering

Being a Conversation
   Partner........... 23

Environmental
   Restoration ······· 111

Food Rescuing...... 126

Pet Therapy........ 239

Story Time at the
   Library........... 312

Tutoring 339

Volunteering as a
   Docent........... 349

Wikipedia Editing.... 355

About the Author

Jasmine M. Cho (Art Therapy and Creativity Development, MPS) is a Pittsburgh-based author and artist whose passions for baking, social justice, and mental health and wellness led her to becoming internationally known as a cookie activist and bake therapy pioneer. A TEDx speaker, Food Network Baking Champion, and Third Degree Black Belt in Tae Kwon Do, Jasmine stays joyfully grounded by practicing a wide array of hobbies, from martial arts to building LEGO.